D1617328

The Irish Revival Reappraised

The first two volumes in this series are published by Irish Academic Press.

The Irish Revival Reappraised

EDITED BY

Betsey Taylor FitzSimon and James H. Murphy

FOUR COURTS PRESS

Set in 10.5 on 12 point Bembo for
FOUR COURTS PRESS
7 Malpas Street, Dublin 8, Ireland
e-mail: info@four-courts-press.ie
http://www.four-courts-press.ie
and in North America by
FOUR COURTS PRESS
c/o ISBS, 920 N.E. 58th Street, Suite 300, Portland, OR 97213.

A catalogue record for this title
is available from the British Library.

ISBN 1–85182–757–9

Printed in Great Britain
by Antony Rowe Ltd, Chippenham, Wilts.

Contents

For Todd Wesley Taylor

Contributors

MARY BURKE is a doctoral student at Queen's University, Belfast and is the author of '"Phoenician Tinsmiths" and "degenerated Tuatha De Danaan": the origins and implications of the orientalisation of Irish Travellers', *Australian Journal of Irish Studies*, 2 (2002).

ELIZABETH CROOKE is affiliated with the Academy for Irish Cultural Heritages, University of Ulster, and is the author of *Politics, archaeology, and the creation of a national museum of Ireland: an expression of national life* (Dublin, 2000).

ALEX DAVIS lectures in English at University College, Cork. *a broken line: Denis Devlin and Irish poetic modernism* (Dublin, 2000) is his most recent book.

BETSEY TAYLOR FITZSIMON lectures in English at All Hallows College, Dublin. She is a contributor to the forthcoming volume, *Converts and conversions in eighteenth-century Ireland* (Four Courts Press) and is working on an annotated edition of the letters of Katherine Lady Ranelagh.

BRIAN GRIFFIN is a lecturer in History and Irish Studies at Bath Spa University College and author of *The Bulkies: police and crime in Belfast, 1800–1865* (Dublin, 1997).

SELINA GUINNESS is lecturer in Irish Writing in the Department of Humanities, Dun Laoghaire Institute of Art, Design and Technology. She currently holds a Government of Ireland Senior Research Scholarship, awarded by the Irish Research Council for the Humanities and Social Sciences. A companion article to the one in this volume appears in *Irish University Review*, 33.1 (Spring/Summer 2003), entitled, '"Protestant magic" reappraised: theosophy, evangelicalism and dissent'.

MARNIE HAY is researching a PhD thesis on Bulmer Hobson (1883–1969), an Irish nationalist and Ulster Quaker, in the Combined Departments of History at University College Dublin.

JANICE HELLAND is Professor of Art History and Women's Studies and Queen's National Scholar at Queen's University, Kingston, Canada. She is the author of *The studios of Frances and Margaret Macdonald* (Manchester, 1996) and *Professional women painters in nineteenth-century Scotland: commitment, friendship, pleasure* (London,

2000), and co-editor of *Women artists and the decorative arts, 1880–1935: the gender of ornament* (London, forthcoming) and *Studio, space and sociality: new narratives of nineteenth-century women artists* (London, forthcoming). Her new research project on British and Irish Home Arts and Industries is funded by the Social Science and Humanities Research Council of Canada.

LEEANN LANE lectures in Irish Studies at Mater Dei Institute of Education, Dublin. A contributor to the spring/summer 2003 special issue of *Irish University Review*, she is currently working on a biography of Rosamond Jacob.

PATRICK LONERGAN is a doctoral student at NUI Galway and the book reviews editor for the *Irish Theatre Magazine*.

MICHAEL MC ATEER lectures in English at Queen's University, Belfast and edited *Standish O'Grady, Yeats and Æ* (Dublin, 2002).

LUCY MC DIARMID is Professor of English at Villanova University and former president of the American Conference for Irish Studies. She is author of *Saving civilization: Yeats, Eliot and Auden between the wars* (Cambridge, 1984) and Auden's *Apologies for poetry* (Princeton, 1990). She edited *Irish secular relics* for the Irish Studies issue of *Textual Practice* (Summer, 2002) and co-edited *Lady Gregory: selected writings* (London, 1995) and *High and low moderns: literature & culture, 1889–1939* (Oxford, 1996). Her book, *The Irish art of controversy*, is forthcoming.

LIAM MAC MATHUNA is registrar of St Patrick's College, Drumcondra. His most recent books are *Ar thóir an fhocail chruinn: iriseoirí, téarmeolaithe agus fadhbanna an aistriúchán* (Dublin, 1997) and *Teanga, pobal agus réigiún: aistí ar chultúr na Gaelachta inniu* (Dublin, 2000).

JAMES H. MURPHY teaches English at DePaul University, Chicago. His most recent book is *Ireland, a social, cultural and literary history* (Dublin, 2003).

UNA NI BHROIMEIL lectures in history at Mary Immaculate College, University of Limerick. Her recent publications include 'The creation of an Irish culture in the United States: the Gaelic movement, 1870–1915', in *New Hibernia Review*, 5:4 (Autumn, 2001) and *Building Irish identity in America, 1870–1915: the Gaelic Revival* (Dublin, 2003).

MARIA O'BRIEN is a DPhil student at Magee Campus, University of Ulster, Derry, and is the author of 'T. W. Rolleston, W.B. Yeats and the new Library of Ireland controversy', in *History Review*, 13 (2002).

ELAINE CHEASLEY PATERSON is a PhD candidate and Social Sciences and Humanities Research Council of Canada fellow in the Department of Art, Queen's University, Canada. She has several articles forthcoming from her doctoral research on late nineteenth-century British and Irish home arts and industries. Her research examines Mary Seton Watts' Compton Potters' Art Guild and the Dun Emer Guild established by Evelyn Gleeson with Lily and Elizabeth Yeats.

G.K. PEATLING is a postdoctoral fellow in the Department of History, Guelph University, Ontario, Canada, and is the author of *British opinion and Irish self-government, 1865–1925: From unionism to liberal Commonwealth* (Dublin, 2001).

MARY STAKELUM is a lecturer in music education at Mary Immaculate College, University of Limerick. She is currently involved in research on the construction of musical knowledge from a socio-cultural and historical perspective.

Introduction

BETSEY TAYLOR FITZSIMON & JAMES H. MURPHY

The phrase, Irish Revival, is like a net that has been cast over a whole series of movements that swept across the cultural landscape of Ireland at the end of the nineteenth and the beginning of the twentieth century. These include: the Irish language revival spearheaded by Douglas Hyde's Gaelic League; the Co-operative movement with which Horace Plunkett and Æ were associated; the Anglo-Irish literary revival of Yeats, Gregory, and Synge; D.P. Moran's trenchant Irish Ireland; and new political movements such as Arthur Griffith's Sinn Féin.

Two aspects of the Irish Revival explain the scholarly interest in it. Firstly, its movements flourished during that crucial period of political and social transformation that produced the Ireland of today. Struggle and controversy marked the Revival decades. Voices contested national and linguistic identities, the roles of religion and culture, and the economic and political shape of the future. Such struggles led to the island's partition into the six northern counties still linked with Britain and twenty-six counties of the Irish Free State, later the Republic of Ireland. Secondly, the period produced a number of writers who remain prominent in the international canon of literature in English. Most notable of these are Yeats and Joyce who still continue as subjects for outstanding scholarship such as Marjorie Howes' *Yeats's Nations: Gender, Class and Irishness* (1996) and John McCourt's *The Years of Bloom: James Joyce in Trieste, 1904–1920* (2000).

Clearly, a thoroughgoing reappraisal of the Irish Revival is a tall order. A collection of seventeen essays such as this cannot fully achieve such an objective, but it can begin the process. As a product of the tenth international conference of the Society for the Study of Nineteenth-Century Ireland, held at All Hallows College, Dublin, 28–30 June 2000, the volume offers a reappraisal of the Revival that advocates a widening of the lens. That is, it is a call to include more, to expand the number of individuals, movements and viewpoints within the panorama of what constitutes the Revival. Such a reappraisal provides openings to the highly complex cultural environments in which the Revival movements flourished.

The naming above of movements and individuals conventionally associated with the Irish Revival was deliberately done. Several essays scrutinize some of the figures associated with the Irish Revival, such as Æ, Yeats, Synge and O'Casey; however, attention, is also paid to other figures who have hitherto been thought of as marginal or have never been featured before. Among them are Charles Johnston, Seosamh Laoide, Alice Hart, Evelyn Gleeson, Robert Lynd, Joseph Campbell, Thomas William Rolleston and Katherine Frances Purdon. Another such figure is Ishbel Aberdeen, whose advocacy of Irish industry and design is reflected in several essays. Her presence attests to the challenge that these essays make to traditional notions of the Irish Revival, not because she was the wife of the British viceroy but because of her interests in neglected dimensions of the period.

The Revival occurred during a period of significant transition and transformation in Irish society, a period that was marked by negotiations on all cultural fronts for personal and national identities. Stimulated by this transitional context, the approaches in these essays reflect an exploration of historical and critical intersections concerning revival movements. In part, the shared agendas of the contributing writers arise from evolving responses to cultural similarity and difference, responses that reappraise the cultural contexts of the Revival which includes both the cosmopolitan and provincial. As will emerge from many of the essays, the intersection between the cosmopolitan and the provincial was a prime cause of tension within a number of revival movements.

The first section, 'Idealism and Activism', explores some of the communities and institutions traditionally associated with the Irish Revival as vehicles of negotiation between individual commitment, collective political agendas, and ideologies of Irishness, both cosmopolitan and provincial. Selina Guinness explores the popularity of theosophy from the perspectives of both the metropolitan centre of empire and the empire's margins. In British India, it contributed to the deconstruction of the imperial mindset. In the Dublin context, it allowed some individuals to escape from the fixed narratives of identity then available to Irish Protestants. She thus reads Charles Johnston's commitment to theosophy as enabling him to effect a transition between unionism and separatist nationalism.

On the other hand, Leeann Lane argues that the idealization of the Irish peasant by Æ and his own theosophical pursuits resonated with his desire for perpetuating an Anglo-Irish leadership, a perpetuation of political power which was seen as a bulwark against a perceived philistine Catholic middle class. In the end, Lane finds Æ's depiction of the Irish peasant as patronizing and plainly ignorant of the harsher realities of rural Irish life.

Úna Ní Bhroiméil and Liam MacMathúna address the revival of the Irish language. In her essay, Ní Bhroiméil examines the trans-Atlantic relationships between the Gaelic League and Irish-Americans. Asserting that Irish-American interest in the Irish language was one of the means to retain their Irish identity within the United States, Ní Bhroiméil concludes that Irish-Americans were ultimately more interested in the identity-centred aspect in preserving the Irish language abroad rather than attending to cultural developments back in Ireland. MacMathúna addresses issues of literacy in Irish and evaluates the successes and failures of the Gaelic League's ideological programmes, programmes that affected both public and private sectors of Irish life. For example, the League was remarkably successful in highly visible, ideological campaigns against official hostility to Irish. Battles to have Dublin street names in Irish, to be able to address letters and parcels in Irish and to have names on handcarts in Irish garnered remarkable support. The League's efforts to make Irish texts available to the public through the publication of journals and books, however, ultimately met with commercial disinterest.

The final essay in Section One is by Mary Stakelum who examines the role of music in national school education and the negotiations between European and Irish musical traditions in the evolving curriculum throughout the Revival period. Her essay comes at the end of the 'Idealism and Activism' section, but its move away from the spoken or written word also heralds a transition to the next section on 'Material Culture'.

In the world of Irish archaeology and museums and that of embroidery and home arts and industries, other trajectories for the term Irish Revival begin to open up. Elizabeth Cooke's essay maps the development of the National Museum of Ireland as a site of assertive cultural nationalism and of struggle with competing institutions in Britain. The controversy over the Broighter Hoard, a trove of golden Irish artefacts, which had found its way into the collection of the British Museum, echoes those of the Gaelic League and foreshadows those of the period which Lucy McDiarmid deals with later on. In an ironic triumph for Irish cultural nationalism, the Hoard was returned to Ireland because it was treasure trove and belonged to the British crown.

A similar irony exists in the role of Ishbel Aberdeen, the once and future vicereine, in Janice Helland's essay on design, embroidery and dressmaking. Aberdeen, a supporter of home rule, fused aristocratic pleasure with Celtic revival. She promoted, through the dresses she had made for herself, the embroidery of Alice Hart's Donegal Industrial Fund with its use of designs from the Book of Kells. The two women, however, fell out and mounted rival Irish villages with competing castles at the 1893 Chicago World's Fair.

Complementing Helland's work is the essay by Elaine Cheasley Patterson, who examines the Dun Emer Guild. Dun Emer was principally the work of Evelyn Gleeson who was assisted by Lily and Elizabeth Yeats. Concentrating on weaving, embroidery, and hand-press printing, they hoped to encourage women in creating art objects from Irish materials. Paterson sees their work as a form of a cultural nationalism that attempted to elide class differences between the middle-class directors and the lower-class beneficiaries of the enterprise.

'In the Context of the City' views the Irish Revival from the vantage points of Belfast, Dublin and London. Marnie Hay looks at *Uladh*, the journal of literature and criticism which flourished briefly between 1904 and 1905, and sees it as more than simply an offshoot of the Ulster Literary Theatre. It was the work largely of Belfast Presbyterian intellectuals who were either cultural or political nationalists or both and who helped to develop a sense of Ulster regional identity. The relative largeness of the city of Belfast, most of whose population would not have been sympathetic to the enterprise, nonetheless enabled some contributors to remain shrouded in a protective cloak of anonymity. Thus Robert Lynd, who is also the subject of a latter essay in this collection, wrote under the name Ríobárd Ua Fhloinn.

Cities can provide the space for new and dissident points of view. However, when dissent becomes a matter of public interest beyond that of sympathetic constituencies, it can become subject to the pressure of pubic controversy. In her essay, Lucy McDiarmid charts the progress of several key public controversies during the period of the Irish Revival, touching on the role of the Irish language, of art, and of religion in Irish society. The dismissal of Michael O'Hickey from the chair of Irish at Maynooth College for his vehement criticism of clerical opposition to having Irish as a compulsory matriculation subject in the new National University was a national controversy. That between some Catholics and the socialists who wanted to remove a number of destitute Dublin children to England during the 1913 Dublin lockout was, in some ways, an international clash of worldviews. In contrast, the controversy over Hugh Lane's insistence that his generous gift of paintings to Dublin be housed in a gallery which he considered appropriate seemed at first sight a more municipal affair.

One of the themes which emerges from this collection is that of linkages between the Irish Revival and political and cultural movements in Britain and elsewhere. Alex Davis shows how the process of influence went both ways. He places the literary revival in the context of movements associated with the cosmopolitan, namely Imagism, Vorticism, and Futurism, by focusing on the experiences of the Irish nationalist poet, Joseph Campbell, and his admirer, Thomas MacDonagh. Davis pursues MacDonagh's view that Irish writers such as Campbell who, by rejecting traditional literary models, were actually forerunners of the London avant-garde. Such a view subverts the perceived literary dependence of the provincial on the cosmopolitan centre.

The final two sections of *The Irish Revival Reappraised* complement each other. 'History and the Text' presents plays by three canonically central figures, Yeats, Synge and O'Casey, in an historicizing perspective. 'Other Paths', however, provides introductions to the lives and careers of three individuals who, if known at all, are regarded as being on the periphery of the Irish Revival. The critic Thomas William Rolleston, of whom Maria O'Brien writes, spent twenty-five years involved in various facets of the Irish Revival, before going to London and becoming a literary reviewer for the *Times Literary Supplement*. He was a central figure in the *Dublin University Review* and the Irish Literary Society of London, getting caught up in the latter in the power-struggle between Charles Gavan Duffy and the young, and as yet politically unsophisticated, Yeats. He was an enthusiastic but skeptical supporter of the Gaelic League and fought hard against what he saw as the spread of sectarianism within the movement. He was also an advocate for the Co-operative movement, though this was not initially with Horace Plunkett but with Ishbel Aberdeen's Irish Industries Association.

G.K. Peatling takes up the later career of Robert Lynd, last seen as a contributor to *Uladh*. Lynd carved out a long and successful career for himself in journalism in England. Peatling is interested in the extent to which Lynd 'acted-out' rather than 'worked-through' the debilitating stereotypes of Irishness then prevalent in England. Brian Giffin's essay on Katherine Frances Purdon raises questions about the privileged geography of certain strands of the Irish Revival. Purdon came from an Ascendancy background in County Meath and wrote fairy stories and rural tales of her home area. Her vision of a homely, rural Ireland contrasts with the more untamed depictions of rural life found in those Revivalist writers who focused on the west of Ireland. Concurrently, such a vision elided the tensions existing among the diverse rural social classes.

In his essay on Yeats's *The Countess Cathleen,* Michael McAteer calls for a fresh critical approach that avoids the more traditional interpretations of the play. Rather than seeing the play as a personal reflection of Yeats's relationship with Maude Gonne or as dramatizing the conflict between materialism and spirituality, McAteer argues that it reflects a colder view. The countess's selling of her soul to the devil in fact signals that everything has its price and heralds the victory of materialism over nobility and civility.

Mary Burke's reading of Synge's *The Tinker's Wedding* has a similar purpose to that of McAteer's reading of *The Countess Cathleen*, inasmuch as both are intent on debunking naïve, humanistic readings of their chosen texts. In the case of *The Tinker's Wedding*, Burke challenges interpretations of the play that celebrate the tinker's unwillingness to conform to social norms for sexual relationships. She traces the creation of the heathen gypsy to eighteenth-century scholarship and the orientalization of the Irish tinker to the late nineteenth century. The tinker's pagan amorality is thus just as much a social construct as the Christianity which the play presents as its antithesis.

Patrick Lonergan's essay on O'Casey concludes *The Irish Revival Reappraised*. It is a piece which, ironically but most appropriately for this collection of essays, reads the work of one of the most important dramatists of the period as itself offering an early, and often sharp, reappraisal of the Anglo-Irish literary revival. O'Casey, Lonergan argues, was critical of the Literary Revival on the grounds of its narrow exclusion of popular culture and made sure that his own practice as a dramatist challenged that exclusion. O'Casey's criticism reached its climax in his 1940 play, *Purple Dust*, but Lonergan uses that play to detect signs of a similar critique of the literary revival in earlier works, such as *Juno and the Paycock*. O'Casey's belief that the literary revival needed a broader perspective on Irish life is surely an apt point at which to conclude the introduction to a volume of essays whose aim is to foster a broader perspective on the Irish Revival that will penetrate the complex cultural environment in which its movements, authors and advocates flourished.

Ireland through the stereoscope: reading the cultural politics of theosophy in the Irish Literary Revival

SELINA GUINNESS

In 1907, Charles Johnston, W.B. Yeats's one-time school-friend, member of the first Dublin Hermetic Society and now better acquainted with the poet's father in New York, published an intriguing guidebook for the emigrant market called *Ireland through the Stereoscope*.[1] Sir Charles Wheatstone had invented the stereoscope in 1838, a year before Daguerre unveiled his early photographic discoveries in Paris. It consisted of a double lens and a sliding rack into which one placed a stereograph (a double image of the same scene taken from slightly different angles). When viewed through the lens, this double image was resolved into a single three-dimensional photograph. Twenty years after its invention, the American essayist, Oliver Wendell Holmes, took out a patent on his own design for the mass market and described the stereoscope's enduring appeal:

> All pictures, in which perspective and light and shade are properly managed, have more or less of the effect of solidity; but by this instrument that effect is so heightened as to produce an appearance of reality, which cheats the senses with its seeming truth.[2]

Johnston echoes these large claims in his prefatory instructions for using the apparatus:

> 3. Hold the stereoscope with the hood close against the forehead and temples, shutting off entirely all immediate surroundings. The less you are conscious of things close about you, the more strong will be your feeling of actual presence in the scenes you are studying.

> 4. Think definitely, while you have your face in the hood just where your position is, as learned from the maps and explanatory text. Recall your surroundings to mind, i.e., think what is behind you; what lies off at the

1 Charles Johnston, *Ireland through the stereoscope* (New York and London: Underwood and Underwood, 1907). **2** Oliver Wendell Holmes, 'The stereoscope and the stereograph,' *Atlantic Monthly* 3 (June 1859), pp 738–48. For more details about the stereoscope and stereographs, see the website of the National Stereoscopic Association at www.stereoview.org.

right; at the left. You will find yourself richly repaid for the effort by your fuller sense of presence in Ireland.

Note that the general map of Ireland, though referred to from the beginning, is numbered 7 and inserted last; this is in order that it may conveniently be kept unfolded during the reading of the book ready for comparison with any one of the other sectional maps as may be desired.

5. Do not hurry. Take plenty of time to see what is before you. Notice all the little details, or rather, notice as many as you can each time; you will be surprised to find, the next time you look at the same place, how many things you had failed to notice at first. By taking time to notice some of these numberless details, and by thinking definitely of your surroundings, you are helped especially to feel you are in Ireland – which should be your constant purpose.

In effect, Johnston suggests that once 'the immediate surroundings' of the city's brownstones are shut out by darkness, the stereoscope will transport the viewer to Queenstown or Upper Lough Leane with his or her position to be verified against the co-ordinates on the accompanying maps: pictorial record gives way to the sense of real presence for the user.

Johnston's access to the Ireland of the emigrant imagination, then, is mediated by a device that replicates the conditions of the séance room with its cloth-covered darkness, meditation, and the awareness of a supernatural presence in the visualized phenomenon. The spiritist resonances of these instructions may be more than incidental, by hinting as they do at the author's own familiarity with such pursuits. Charles Johnston's early enthusiasm for theosophy, sparked by Mohini Chatterjee's visit to Yeats's Hermetic Society in 1884, was further strengthened by his scandalous marriage some five years later to Vera Zhelikovskaya, the niece of Madame Blavatsky, founder of the international Society. Mediumship, while officially disapproved of by the founder, fascinated many members. More generally, the resemblance between the stereoscope which 'cheats the senses with its seeming truth' and Madame Blavatsky's nightly dictations from her two Tibetan spirit masters may have a broader cultural resonance, for esoteric science often anticipated the patent claims made for new technology in the nineteenth century. Lisa Gitelman has described in her book, *Scripts, Grooves, and Writing Machines*, how shorthand and the first typewriters were indebted to new constructions of agency experienced in automatic writing. Gitelman also notes that Thomas Edison joined the Theosophical Society soon after its establishment in 1877.[3]

---

3 Lisa Gitelman, *Scripts, grooves, and writing machines: representing technology in the Edison era* (Stanford, Cal: Stanford UP, 1998), pp 184–218, p. 193.

In this essay I want to reverse the stereoscope and use it to reveal how the author of this guidebook or manual recognized in theosophy a way of negotiating Ireland's double status as both sister kingdom in the British empire and internal colony. The second son of the Orange MP for South Belfast, Charles Johnston had been introduced to theosophy by his classmate at the Erasmus Smith High School, W.B.Yeats, who lent him a copy of A.P. Sinnett's *Esoteric Buddhism* (1881), a founding text of the movement. Yeats had first heard the book discussed at a soirée held by Edward Dowden, whose high Victorian respectability did not prevent his daughter, Hester, becoming one of London's most successful mediums.[4] As is now a matter of record, Johnston and Yeats linked up with two other High School *alumni*, Claude Falls Wright and Charles Weekes, to form the first Dublin Hermetic Society, which held its inaugural meeting on 16 June 1884.[5] This auspicious date might explain the prevalent musings about theosophy that pass through the pages of *Ulysses*.[6]

Yeats's later recollection of this group as meeting in a York street attic is deceptive, perhaps designed to associate it with the Young Ireland Society which did meet there under O'Leary's auspices.[7] Instead, the group met in Trinity College Dublin, where its founding coincided with the emergence of the Irish Protestant Home Rule Association and the magazine that broadly served as its organ, the *Dublin University Review*. Although Yeats later maintained that the society he chaired was 'not Theosophical at the start', his interest in a more aesthetic and self-serving mysticism was very much the minority view.[8] Johnston's inaugural paper, titled 'Esoteric Buddhism' in homage to Sinnett, makes clear the younger Hermeticists' keen alignment with the international Society, as confirmed in the *Dublin University Review*'s brief report on their first meeting which begins: 'A society has been started in Dublin to promote the study of Oriental Religions and theosophy generally.'[9] The physicist, and a founding member of the Society for Psychical Research, Professor William Barrett (FRS), also took the chair on occasion. By April 1886, when Charles Johnston and Claude Falls Wright obtained the charter for the first Dublin lodge of the Theosophical Society from Sinnett, now in London, the Society had issued 121 charters for lodges, with 106 of these in India, Burma and Ceylon.[10] Within a decade of its founding,

4 See Ann Saddlemyer, *Becoming George: the life of Mrs W.B.Yeats* (Oxford and NewYork: Oxford UP, 2002), pp 353. **5** See R.F. Foster, *W.B.Yeats: a life, the apprentice mage*, vol. 1 (Oxford and New York: Oxford UP, 1997), pp 46–7. **6** J.J. O'Molloy's question to Stephen about theosophy's cultural significance still poses a genuine conundrum for the Revival: 'What do you think really of that hermetic crowd, the opal hush poets: Æ – the master mystic? That Blavatsky woman started it. She was a nice old bag of tricks', in Hans Walter Gabler (ed.), *James Joyce: Ulysses, the corrected text* (London: Bodley Head, 1986), p. 115. **7** W.B.Yeats, *Autobiographies* (London: Papermac, 1992), p. 90. **8** Allan Wade (ed.), *The letters of W.B.Yeats* (London: Rupert Hart-Davis, 1954), pp 591–2. **9** *Dublin University Review*, July 1885, p. 155. **10** Peter Washington, *Madame Blavatsky's baboon: theosophy and the emergence of the western guru* (London: Secker & Warburg, 1993), p. 68.

membership was numbered in the thousands.[11] Theosophy had gone from being a metropolitan exoticism to a complex colonial endeavour.

It may at first seem remarkable that Johnston and his early associates from the Hermetic Society should have joined the Society at a time when Blavatsky was being investigated for producing fraudulent phenomena by the Society for Psychical Research. When the damning report was eventually published in December 1885, its contents do not seem to have deterred W.B.Yeats, Johnston, Wright or Æ from pursuing the syncretic philosophy she had founded.[12] Yeats was typical of the group in finding arguments to rebuff the scientism of the SPR as inappropriate to the investigation of a medium, who might employ a certain level of trickery to heighten and dramatize real revelations from the spirit world.[13] Yet the attraction of theosophy was that it promised more than the phenomena of the séance room. The Society had a broadly utopian appeal. In Britain, theosophy enjoyed a core support among social reformers, epitomized by Anna Kingsford, anti-vivisectionist and dress reformer, and Annie Besant, labour activist, freethinker and birth control campaigner.[14] They responded to the idealism of the Society's aspirations, as described self-deprecatingly by its president, Colonel Henry Steele Olcott:

John Kelly suggests Yeats was a close associate, but not a member, of the Dublin Lodge. See John Kelly and Eric Domville (eds), *The collected letters of W.B.Yeats, vol. 1, 1865–1895* (Oxford: Clarendon, 1986), p. 514 (hereafter *CL,* 1). However R.F. Foster includes his name among the charter members, listed as L.A.M. Johnston, W.B.Yeats, F.T. Gregg, H.M. Magee, E.A. Seale, W.F. Smeeth, R.A. Potterton and Charles Johnston. See Foster, *The apprentice mage*, pp 45–52; p. 552n. Yeats certainly joined the Esoteric Section of the Blavatsky Lodge in London in Dec. 1888. Ibid. p. 102.   **11** Ibid., p. 68.   **12** Cf. R. Hodgson, 'Report of committee appointed to investigate phenomena in connection with the Theosophical Society', Society for Psychical Research, Dec. 1885. **13** In trying to fathom his own arguments about the spiritual existence of Madame Blavatsky's teachers, Yeats propounded four hypotheses: 'I as yet refuse to decide between the following alternatives, having too few facts to go on, (1) They are probably living occultists, as HPB says, (2) They are possibly unconscious dramatizations of HPB's own trance nature, (3) They are also possibly but not likely, as the mediums assert, spirits (4) They may be the trance principle of nature expressing itself symbolically. The fraud theory in its most pronounced form I have never held for more than a few minutes as it is wholly unable to cover the facts.' See Yeats's 'Occult notes and diary, etc.', Appendix A, in Denis Donoghue (ed.), *Memoirs* (London: Macmillan, 1972), pp 281–2.   **14** Anna Kingsford broke with the London Lodge in Apr. 1884, in protest at the Society's endorsement of A.P. Sinnett's *Esoteric Buddhism*. She established the rival Hermetic Society which sought to correct theosophy's increasingly Asiatic turn by firmly embracing gnostic and neo-Platonist mysticism. Although the shared name might suggest connections between her breakaway society and Yeats's group, this should not be over-stressed as Sinnett remained an important influence on all members of the Dublin circle. Lady Wilde and her two sons attended the inaugural meeting of Kingsford's society and Yeats later met Kingsford's biographer, Edward Maitland, at a dinner held at the Wildes. See Col. Henry Steele Olcott, *Old diary leaves*, vol. 3 (Madras: Theosophical Publishing Society, 1904), pp 90–8; *CL,* 1, p. 118. For a fuller account of Kingsford's life and visions, see E. Maitland, *Anna Kingsford: her life, letters, diary and work*, 2 vols (London: George Redway, 1896).

Fanatics if you please; crazy enthuasiasts; dreamers of impractical dreams; devotees of a hobby; dupes of our imaginations. Yet our dreams were of human perfectability, our yearnings after divine wisdom; our sole hope to help mankind to higher thinking and nobler living.[15]

This sense of social mission meant that theosophy could compete with a career in the imperial services or the church in serving the Protestant middle-class conscience.

These affiliations with the High School and Trinity College might suggest that part of theosophy's appeal for Æ, Johnston, and later James Cousins, lay in the echoes of imperial sentiment fostered in these bastions of Protestant education. Cousins, who taught in the High School, reports in *We Two Together* that its 'special pride' was founded on the numbers of 'old-boy Bishops and members of the Indian Civil Service' among their ex-pupils and, as Yeats noted, Charles Johnston was very much their rising star.[16] When his inaugural paper on 'Esoteric Buddhism' was published in the *Dublin University Review*, it found its proper home in a journal that balanced home rule principles with reminders of Ireland's part in the administration of the wider empire.[17] Two months earlier, an article titled 'The Irish Universities and the Imperial Services' observed that at a ceremony held to award honorary degrees to graduates of Queen's University Belfast in February 1882, out of twenty-six recipients, fourteen were in the British imperial service, with eleven serving in India.[18] Johnston's own Sanskrit studies helped prepare him for his post as assistant magistrate and revenue collector in the district of Murshidabad, which he took up after eloping with Vera (much to her aunt's displeasure) in January 1889; while in 1896, he followed up his textbook, *Useful Sanskrit Nouns and Verbs* (1892), with a selection from the *Upanishads*.[19] In a letter home from Berhampore, he told his father

---

15 Col. Henry Steele Olcott, *Old diary leaves*, vol. 2, p. 25. **16** James H. and Margaret Cousing, *We two together* (Madras: Ganesh, 1950), p. 98; Yeats, *Autobiographies*, p. 90. **17** *Dublin University Review*, 6 (July 1885), pp 144–6. For an extended profile of the *Review*'s political and cultural outlook, see Yug Mohit Chaudhry, *Yeats, the Irish literary revival and the politics of rint* (Cork: Cork UP, 2001). **18** Edward Stanley Robertson, 'The Irish universities and the imperial services', *Dublin University Review*, 4 (May 1885), pp 79–82. **19** Several members of the Irish gentry escaped financial scandal via the imperial civil service. Alvin Jackson reports that Charles' father, William, bankrupted by the collapse in earnings from his estate and the costs of pursuing a parliamentary career in Westminster, 'sought relief from his creditors through a colonial governorship.' See Alvin Jackson, 'Irish unionists and the empire, 1880–1920, classes and masses' in Keith Jeffrey (ed.), *An Irish empire?* (Manchester: Manchester UP, 1996), p. 129. Yeats took notes on the progress of Charles's courtship for Katharine Tynan's amusement: 'Charley Johnston was at Madame Blavatsky's the other day with that air of clever insolence and elaborate efficiency he has ripened to such perfection. The before mentioned penitent frivilous [*sic*] delight in him. If you only saw him talking French and smoking ciggaretts [*sic*] with Madame's neice [*sic*]. He looked a veritable peacock. Such an air too of the world worn

that he was learning 'Hindi, Bengali and Russian, so that with routine work my time is pretty well filled up.'[20]

With the establishment of 'the Household', a commune founded by an engineer Frederick J. Dick at his home address, 3 Upper Ely Place, in April 1891, the Dublin lodge became more rigorous in its pursuit of theosophical study. Monday nights were spent discussing Madame Blavatsky's two-tome exegesis of the dictations she took under spirit direction, *The Secret Doctrine* (1888), while Friday nights were devoted to theosophical texts of a more elementary nature.[21] Sanskrit study groups were held in the Georgian rooms decorated by Æ's murals of ethereal beings and Dick entertained his houseguests on the piano.[22] William Kirkpatrick Magee ('John Eglinton') frequently visited his elder brother, Malcolm, who shared a room there with Æ. Yeats also dropped in for conversation where he was amused by Dick's attempts to restrict debates to members of the lodge only, against Æ's insistence on a more open and heterodox approach to their meetings.[23] Meals could be got from the vegetarian restaurant established by D.N. Dunlop and his future wife, Eleanor Fitzpatrick, where Hindu medical students, impoverished young authors and the Irish theosophists were brought together out of shared dietary necessity.[24] Ada and Georgiana Johnston took up their brother's interest and worked in the restaurant, while Lewis, an elder brother, whose name appears alongside his brother's on the charter, also joined them. Georgie became briefly engaged to Claude Falls Wright, a lifelong Irish theosophist who later rose through the ranks of the American section, and also organized what Katharine Tynan cruelly describes as 'a debating society of an appalling dullness', identified as the Ethical Society by the editors of the Yeats letters, but more likely I think, the Vegetarian Society, in which both Georgie and her mother took a keen interest.[25] Charles, meanwhile, had been invalided out of the Indian Civil Service after eighteen months, and after returning to

man of society about him. As if he also were one of the penitent frivilous instead of a crusading undergraduate': *CL*, 1, p. 99; see also, pp 101, 104, 105, 108. **20** Manuscript letter from Charles Johnston to his father, dated 9 Aug. 1889, and enclosed loose in William Johnston's diary for 1885, PRONI D/880/2/37. **21** Henry Summerfield, *That myriad-minded man: a biography of G.W. Russell – 'Æ', 1867–1935* (Gerards Cross, Bucks.: Colin Smythe, 1975), p. 35. **22** Ibid., p. 36. **23** W.B. Yeats, *Autobiographies*, pp 239–40. **24** T.H. Meyer, *D.N. Dunlop: a man of our time*, trans. Ian Bass (London: Temple Lodge, 1992), pp 33–8. The 'pretty' Sunshine Vegetarian Dining Rooms was located at 48 Grafton street; entry for 23 Mar. 1891, William Johnston's diary, PRONI D/880/2/43. **25** For a biographical note on Ada Johnston, see *CL*, 1, p. 212 n; for Georgiana Johnston, see *CL*, 1, p. 73. Jan. 1889 must have been a bad month for William Johnston the *paterfamilias* who attended church twice on Sundays and was grand master of the Black Preceptory as two of his children became engaged to Irish theosophists. His diary entry of 29 Jan. 1889 reads: 'Georgie astonished me by announcing she intended immediate marriage to Claude Wright. I wish the dear child had been better guided.' William Johnston's diary for 1889, PRONI D/880/2/41. There are several entries recording Georgie and Ina's attendance at 'vegetarian lectures' between 1890 and 1891. Ibid.

Ballykilbeg for a time, where W.B. Yeats visited him in the summer of 1891, he left Ireland, first for London and then for New York.[26] Five years later, John Butler Yeats reported to his son that Charles had 'become a fervent Celt', and by 1909, a committed Sinn Féin supporter.[27]

Such activities must have stretched the patience of their devoted father, William, Grand Master of the Black Preceptory, Unionist MP for South Belfast, and author of several marching ballads including 'The Orange Standard.' Some indication of his attitude to his children's beliefs is provided by what seems to be a draft copy of a letter dated 6 July 1889, simply addressed 'Sir', and tucked into his diary for the same year. Its substance is a strenuous objection to being misidentified as a vegetarian in a brief notice for 'a fruit and cake conference,' held in Farringdon street Memorial Hall, in the Vegetarian Society's eponymously titled journal.[28]

> I have lately looked at the *Vegetarian* with a desire to see reasons in favour of the diet recommended; and I have seen its columns advocate Socialism and Theosophy. I see a tendency, also, to disparage the Great Sacrifice ... while this is so, I cannot embrace Vegetarianism. Rather I would shun it as Anti-Christian. I believe in Christ; and sooner than give up this faith, which is so made incompatible with the teaching of this new creed, I will antagonise, and not advocate, the strange mixture of diet and diabolism.[29]

Taking Charles Johnston's colourful trajectory from Orange to Sinn Féin green as an extreme example for this group of Protestant mystics, how are we to explain the dominant narrative of political conversion from unionism to a form of mystic nationalism? What part does theosophy play? More generally, how are we to fit this group of Protestant mystics into our histories of the early Revival? I believe that the answers lie within the cultural history of the Society itself, and its awkward engagement with issues of self-determination and empire as it stretched to appeal to all classes and religions across the metropolitan and colonial societies of England, America, Ireland, India and Ceylon. My more general argument is that

26 See W.B. Yeats, *Memoirs*, ed. Denis Donoghue (London: Papermac, 1988), pp 43–4. Johnston's transition from Orange 'show-boy' to theosophical dandy greatly amused Yeats. 'Johnston was in the running for Mahatmaship and now how are the mighty fallen ... If you only heard Madame Blavatsky trying to pronounce Ballykilbeg.' *CL*, I, p. 101. **27** Richard J. Finneran, George Mills Harper and William Martin Murphy (eds), *Letters to W.B. Yeats*, 2 vols (London and New York: Macmillan, and Columbia UP, 1977), vol. I, pp 27, 213. **28** According to an entry in his diary, William Johnston did attend the 'Fruit and Cake conference of the Vegetarian Society' on 27 June 1889, perhaps accompanying C.V. Coates, a friend of Charles and Lewis's, whose brothers John and Robert Coates were prominent members of the Dublin lodge. PRONI, D/880/2/41. **29** Manuscript letter on headed notepaper, Ballykilbeg, Co. Down, dated 6 July 1899, enclosed loose in William Johnston's diary for 1889, PRONI, D/880/2/41.

the Dublin lodge, in its own knotted engagement with the dilemmas of individual responsibility within a newly secular democracy, acted as a forum which made possible a liberal dissent from the increasingly narrow, and increasingly sectarian, narratives of identity available in Irish Protestantism, particularly among Dissenting congregations in Ulster. By fuelling this dissent with prophecies of spiritual and racial revival, upheld by the principle of non-sectarianism embodied in international fellowship, and discursively structured by a syncretic approach to world religions, it facilitated the transition to a new Protestant home rule identity through the structures of cultural revival. In this essay, however, I wish to address an argument made by Edward Hagan that theosophy's Aryanism allowed an existing elite to find a substitute belief system for their conservative, anti-Catholic ideologies.[30] In answer, I would suggest that theosophy's political inflections are much more varied, complex, and open than are often allowed.

The Society's three aims inscribed on the charter of every lodge were:

> The formation of a universal brotherhood, without distinction of race, creed, sex, caste or colour.
>
> The encouragement of studies in comparative religion, philosophy and science.
>
> The investigation of unexplained laws of nature and the powers latent in man.[31]

In the *Irish Theosophist*, Æ explains that the first two aims should be taken together for the old philosophies of the East are an inspiration to 'brotherly action', because their wisdom is to declare the final unity of spirit and matter – a perception broken by the Darwinian competitions of the materialist West.[32] This line of thinking is advocated as an applied metaphysics. Æ's desire is to replace the polarities of identity, the 'race, creed, sex, caste and colour' of the first aim, with a holistic humanitarianism that will stress the interdependence of all life. The third aim, he described, as 'pursued only by a portion of members' of the Dublin lodge. The members he had in mind were probably Dunlop, and his

30 Edward A. Hagan, 'The Aryan myth: a nineteenth-century Anglo-Irish will to power,' in Tadhg Foley and Seán Ryder (eds), *Ideology and Ireland in the nineteenth century* (Dublin: Four Courts Press, 1998), pp 197–205. 31 This is the final formulation of the Society's aims as formally adopted in 1896, quoted in Washington, *Madame Blavatsky's baboon*, p. 69. An earlier version is given by Olcott in a letter to the government of Madras in 1883: '(a) To promote the feeling of mutual tolerance and kindness between people of different races and religions; (b) To encourage the study of the philosophies, religions and science of the ancients, particularly of the Aryans; (c) To aid scientific research into the higher nature and powers of man.' Olcott, *Old diary leaves*, vol. 3, p. 4. 32 Æ, 'A word upon the objects of the Theosophical Society,' *Irish Theosophist*, 1:2 (Nov. 1892), p. 10.

occasional collaborator Yeats, who belonged not to the Dublin branch but to the Esoteric Section of Blavatksy's lodge in London.[33]

The Secret Doctrine (the 'Bible' of the Dublin lodge) offered receptive Irish readers an idiosyncratic application of Darwinian theory to the spirit world. In essence, Blavatsky promised to reconcile evolution with a version of reincarnation linking the spiritual progress of the individual with that of his or her race. Her two volumes put forward a complex account of man's spiritual evolution through a cycle of seven mythical root races that are further subdivided to explain the differing rates of civilization among present-day peoples. While this system might lend weight to the charge of a fixed hierarchy operating at the centre of Blavatsky's system, her engagement with contemporary race thinking was profound, bizarre and complex, and often, I believe, designed to expose prejudice within an academy from which she felt excluded.[34]

In 1888, the date of publication, the current era was that of the Fifth Root race, the Aryans, which the Irish theosophists believed began with the death of Krishna in 3102 BC. The choice of Krishna over Christ as avatar of the era dubbed the *Kali Yuga* demonstrates the extent to which theosophy now followed brahmanical orthodoxy in believing that the present age marked the nadir of human development, and that the restoration of spiritual order would only be achieved by returning to Vedic principles.[35] The modern-day Celts could welcome this Vedic turn under the framework of a shared, if unequal, Aryan identity. Charles Johnston carefully explained in his opening address that 'the Asiatic Aryans belong to the first branch race, while we, the European Aryans, belong to the seventh branch race of the fifth great race'.[36] Under theosophy's special terms of evolution this meant that Europeans were marginally closer to attaining the spiritual purity promised in the Sixth Race. After Blavatsky's death, her successor in the London lodge, Annie Besant, would draw tighter parallels between these two book-ends of the Indo-European family, and her assertion that 'Ireland is to the West what India is to the East' sounds a constant refrain through the Revival.[37]

---

33 Ibid., p. 10. **34** Gauri Viswanathan's stimulating analysis of the ways in which theosophical ideas of race revival informed Annie Besant's home rule politics provides the most considered and engaged response to theosophy's complex politics. However, I would suggest that Blavatsky's ideas are leavened with a sharp sense of burlesque directed at the academy (and ignored by her successor) which needs to be taken into account when considering theosophy's cultural politics as a whole. See Gauri Viswanathan, *Outside the fold: conversion, modernity and belief* (Princeton, NJ: Princeton UP, 1998), pp 177–207. **35** Æ explained, 'We are in what Hindus call the *Kali Yuga* or Dark Age … Humanity is passing through a cycle of evolution during which the brain-intellect is developing at the expense (temporarily) of the direct spiritual intuition of early man.' *Irish Theosophist* 1:4 (Jan. 1893), p. 31. Also see: Tony Ballantyne, *Orientalism and race: Aryanism in the British empire* (Basingstoke and New York: Palgrave, 2002), pp 174–5. I would like to thank Tadhg Foley for lending me a copy of the latter. **36** Johnston, Charles, 'Esoteric Buddhism', *Dublin University Review*, 6 (July 1885), p. 144. **37** Unpublished lecture, quoted in Leslie Pielou, *The growth of the Theosophical Society in*

This kind of thinking left theosophy with one core dilemma – how to fit Blavatsky's unique mythology of successive racial and spiritual elites to its stated commitment to universal brotherhood. One could reasonably argue along with Hagan and Gauri Viswanathan that a cultural revival stimulated by ethnological arguments which identify the native population with the founding race of Europe writes an elitist narrative into the vanguard of a newly racialized, and implicitly anti-modern, nationalism, both in Ireland and India.[38] Aryanism explicitly validated Northern India as the *Aryavarta*, or Aryan homeland, with a concomitant disparaging of the Dravidian South. It identified Indian nationality with Hinduism, particularly animating the brahminical reform movement founded by Dayananda Sarasvati in 1875, the Arya Samaj, which aimed to regenerate contemporary Indian society by rejecting Christian influences and returning Hinduism to its Vedic origins. However, Aryanism was a more contested ideology than these bluntly stated alignments might suggest. Tony Ballantyne cites Aurobindo Ghose and Lala Lajpat Rai as two scholars who attempted to use Aryanism to argue for a more inclusive vision of Indian nationality, while admitting that these attempts were 'largely unsuccessful'.[39] Bal Ghanghadar Tilak, co-founder of the Indian Home Rule League with Annie Besant, and an early proponent of separatism, was another who found in his own interpretations of the *Rig Veda* a vision of a more inclusive national unity.[40] In the 1870s and 1880s, the political consequences of the Aryan myth were still a topic for debate. The problems faced by theosophy in reconciling its core beliefs mirrored those facing the task of cultural nationalism in India and Ireland.

At the 1996 conference of the Society for the Study of Nineteenth-Century Ireland, Hagan argued that theosophy's development of the Aryan hypothesis chimed with an Ascendancy who were receptive to its allegedly anti-Catholic undertones, and who found in the myth 'a new Anglo-Irish "will to power"'.[41] Yet Aryanism in Ireland was not axiomatically anti-Catholic; indeed, it forms one of the chief philological planks on which the case for the Irish language was built by the Very Revd Ulick J. Bourke of the Society for the Preservation of the Irish Language. His book, *The Aryan Origin of the Gaelic Race and Language* was dedicated to Archbishop MacHale of Tuam (further monikered 'the shield of the poor and the persecuted, the defender of a neglected race') on the fiftieth anniversary of his consecration in 1875.[42] Bourke's explicit aim was to serve

Ireland (Dublin: privately printed, 1927), p. 7. **38** See note 31 above. **39** Ballantyne, *Orientalism and race*, p. 183. **40** Ibid., pp 179–81. **41** Hagan, 'The Aryan myth', pp 197–205. The allegation of anti-Catholic bias is based on a lecture by John Rhys, but Aryanism was more commonly used as an Indo-European stick with which to beat the continent's Semitic heritage. **42** Ulick J. Bourke, *The Aryan origin of the Gaelic race and language: showing the present and past literary position of the Irish Gaelic; its phonesis, the fountain of classical pronunciation; its laws accord with Grimm's laws, its bardic beauties the source of rhyme; the civilization of pagan Ireland; early knowledge of letters; the art of illuminating, ancient architecture, etc.* (London: Longmans, Green, 1875).

the preservation of the Irish language from linguistic colonization by proving its superiority to other Gaelics due to the deeper 'impress of its Aryan mother tongue'; and 'to reconcile the Anglo-Saxon with the Gael, by pointing out the identity of their Aryan origin, and thus helping to break down the wall of separation between the two races, which had been built up by ignorance, prejudice and religious hate'.[43] This may seem like an implicitly pro-union argument, but for Bourke reconciliation between the races and restoration of Ireland's Aryan heritage would be greatly aided by home rule.[44] Bourke's example suggests that the type of politics into which a newly confident Aryan-Irish spirit of nationality might incarnate is less proscriptive and more complex than Hagan's argument allows. Theosophy, too, needs to be understood as more than just 'a compensation of power, purpose and ideology' for a ruling elite; the paradoxical marriage of social egalitarianism and spiritual and racial hierarchies served a variety of ideological interests, inflected differently across class, religious and gender lines in metropolitan and colonial cultures.[45]

While Blavatsky's writings share features with Orientalism, she persistently mined for paratextual evidence to bolster her claims for the Masters. By the time she came to write *The Secret Doctrine*, she had been made alive to the imperial imprecations of the late Victorian academy by her own experiences in India. Arriving in Bombay from New York in 1879, full of Orientalist desire to see the famed Aryavarta, Olcott and Blavatsky were appalled at the ranks of 'sumptuous bungalows' that blocked out their view of the temple complex of Elephanta.[46] Harishchandra Chintamani of the Bombay Arja Samaj put them up. The de-anglicization of India was a common objective for guests and hosts alike; however, the latter group pursued an aggressive policy of brahminical puritanism that could not sit easily with theosophy's stated policy of caste reform and non-sectarianism. Within a year, theosophy and the Samaj had parted company amid recriminations over unpaid bills.

As Olcott travelled, his disappointment at the rupture between Orientalist phantasm and the reality of colonized India grew. It reverberates in his memoirs as a hurt that must be addressed by constant committee work and campaigns on behalf of different religious communities, most significantly, Ceylon's Buddhists who were granted equal educational rights partly in response to Olcott's petitions to London.[47] His many representations to Government House asking the police authorities to lift their surveillance of members is evidence of just how unwelcome this interference in India's internal affairs was to imperial administrators.[48] Two years after their arrival in India, he advised Blavatsky to 'reconstruct

43 Ibid., pp 193, 7. 44 Ibid., p. 62. 45 Hagan, 'The Aryan myth', p. 204. 46 Olcott, *Old diary leaves*, vol. 2, p. 14. 47 Olcott published his memoirs in six volumes as *Old diary leaves*, republished in Madras by the Theosophical Publishing Society between 1972 and 1975. An account of his campaign on behalf of the Singhalese Buddhists is given in *Old diary leaves*, vol. 3, pp 112–38. 48 Ibid., vol. 2, p. 246; vol. 3, p. 8.

the Theosophical Society on a different basis, putting the Brotherhood idea forward more prominently, and keeping the occultism more in the background …'[49] This shift in emphasis, from private metaphysical experience to social mission, is vital in setting theosophy apart from spiritualism and gives it an explicitly political character, which was recognized by contemporary observers. A.O. Hume, founder of the Indian National Congress, and later, Annie Besant, president of the Congress in 1919, were two Irish theosophists who would take the brotherhood ideal along rather differing paths towards home rule.[50]

In 1889, Olcott lectured twice in Dublin's Antient Concert Rooms, capitalizing on the success of Mohini Chatterjee's tour five years earlier. In the 1890s and early 1900s, Annie Besant, herself of Irish parentage, was a regular visitor, lecturing on Ireland's destiny as the spiritual leader of Europe.[51] W.Q. Judge, president of the American Section of the Society, and G.R.S. Mead of the Esoteric Section, were two other frequent visitors in the early 1890s who endorsed this message.[52] If theosophy did in part attract its Ulster Protestant members because of its imperial connections, its place by the mid-1880s lay as much in subverting imperial prejudice because of its early anticipation of, and later participation in, the movement towards home rule. Although it seems that Charles Johnston's return to Europe via Russia was motivated by concerns for his wife's health in a typical display of colonial chivalry, there are sufficient reports in the *Irish Theosophist* on the anti-colonial impetus of Indian theosophy to speculate whether these interests and his wife's contacts led him into the closer engagement with Indian nationalism, as D.K. Chatterjee has done.[53] A series titled 'Light from the East', providing quotations from the *Upanishads* and the *Bhagavad Gita* in the style of Edwin Arnold, ran through volume two, while in early 1894, Dunlop rapturously recorded the testimony of Professor Charkravarti from the World Parliament of Religions in Chicago that he owed to Madame Blavatsky the ability to see 'the withered and gaunt hands of the spirit of my motherland, … stretching out across oceans and continents, shedding its blessings of peace and love'.[54] When Annie Besant, Blavatsky's successor at the London Lodge, went on her first tour of India in 1893–4, the journal recorded with approval the surprise of the Indian crowd at 'her knowledge of their own scriptures'.[55] In his report of the tour, Dunlop himself quoted from

49 Ibid., vol. 2, p. 294. **50** See Viswanathan, *Outside the fold*, pp 177–207. **51** Olcott's first lecture was on 'Theosophy' and the second on 'Irish fairies'; both were attended by Douglas Hyde to whom Yeats wrote requesting a précis. *CL*, 1, p. 194n. **52** Pielou, *The growth of the Theosophical Society in Ireland*, p. 2. **53** The editors of the Yeats letters cite haemoptysis as the official reason for Johnston's home leave. He left the service permanently in Apr. 1892. *CL*, 1, p. 238n. In the letter, dated 9 Aug. 1889, cited above, the prospect of 'a permanent breakdown in health' leads him to ask his father to look out for a post in England or Ireland 'during the next year.' See note 18 above. Dilip Kumar Chatterjee, *James Henry Cousins: a study of his works in the light of the theosophical movement in India and the west* (Delhi: Sharada, 1994), p. 153. **54** *Irish Theosophist*, 2:4 (Jan. 1894), p. 43. **55** *Irish Theosophist*, 2:5 (Feb. 1894), p. 59.

missionary descriptions of Hinduism, angrily dismissing them as 'sectarian jargon.'[56]

What becomes clear from reading the *Irish Theosophist* alongside Olcott's memoirs, is that this undoubtedly Orientalist interest in Hinduism as a repository of Aryan wisdom went hand in hand with speculations about the demise of empire. In an interview with D.N. Dunlop, Yeats recollected one Blavatsky prophecy, allegedly obtained direct from 'the Masters', that 'the power of England would not outlive the century'.[57] In March 1897, 'The Outlook', probably penned by Æ, envisaged the imminent end of the 'dark age'. In explicitly anti-colonial terms, it comparing Ireland and India as 'little' nations who had the wherewithal to upset the great; the latter, like Ireland, suffering famine as 'shillings are being collected on every hand to celebrate the long reign of India's empress'.[58]

> In Ireland the excitement over financial grievances has considerably subsided. The people seem to be awaiting the blast of a trumpet which will sound a note more directed to their real needs. When the hour is ripe the hero shall appear full armed. In a quiet mood one can catch the stain of the battle song reverberating through the hills and sleepy hollows.'[59]

Æ made a more explicit attack on imperialism in an article called 'On the March' for the *Internationalist*, the successor to the *Irish Theosophist*. Occasioned by the French attack on Madagascar and the continuing 'scramble for Africa', he declared his solidarity with native populations in unambiguous terms: 'our own life is wounded by every blow that is struck at them'.[60] For James Cousins, who came late to theosophy (in 1908) and served briefly as editor of the *New India* at Annie Besant's invitation (in 1916), theosophy's history in India (as in Ireland) was explicitly part of the process of cultural decolonization:

> When life brought Annie Besant to India, and she found that a spurious alien-imposed education had left the school-and-college-going members of the Hindu section of the people a prey to the poison of religious inferiority injected by foreign proselytising agencies, she inspired and led a movement for the restoration of understanding of their ancient faith, and respect for its observances and its vision of human origins and destiny and the technique of individual and social life; and she pioneered the Indianisation of education for Indians in India.[61]

These articles and editorials suggest that the Dublin Irish theosophists were aware of, and actively discussing, the intersections between cultural revival and anti-colonial politics.

---

56 Ibid. **57** *Irish Theosophist*, 2:1 (Oct. 1893), p. 148. **58** *Irish Theosophist*, 5:6 (Mar. 1897), p. 117. **59** Ibid., p. 118. **60** *Internationalist*, 1:2 (15 Nov. 1897), pp 35–8, 35. **61** Cousins, *We two together*, p. 274.

To conclude I want to take one last look through the stereoscope. Unknown to the user of his guide, Johnston's tour in fact describes a reverse narrative of his own conversion, from the archetypal Irish emigrant on the Queenstown quayside, to Killarney, a sacred place for the American Section of the Theosophical Lodge which took the foundation stone for its utopian community at Point Loma, California, from the hills above Lough Leane.[62] That Johnston should choose this spot to reveal the 'power and the fascination of this Isle of Destiny', I suppose, maybe fancifully, is more than tourist convention, indicating the place theosophy holds in his own mind as the keeper of a Celtic spirituality.[63] The exile's nostalgia blends indelibly in this text with a theosophical belief in the reality of Ireland's supernatural folk:

> Under the brown wings of the dark, the night throbs with mystic presences; the hills glimmer with an inward life; whispering voices hurry through the air. Another and magical land awakens in the dark, full of living restlessness, sleepless as the ever-moving sea … There is no sense of loneliness anywhere but rather a host of teeming lives on every hand, palpable though hidden, remote from us though touching our lives, calling to us through the gloom with wordless voices, inviting us to enter and share with them the mystical life of this miraculous earth, great mother of us all. The dark is full of watching eyes.[64]

Through the stereoscope, this supernatural population may act as metaphor with a double referent: firstly, to the Irish-American reader who, looking at the unpeopled scenes of the landscape through the viewfinder, may wish to see shadows of his/her own family inviting the spectator to return to his/her ancestral land. Yet, perhaps there are also traces of India in the surveillance of the closing sentence, combined with the unnamed appeal of the 'teeming lives', remote from, yet touching, the traveller, that betray a memory of the author's brief stint in Murshidabad, Bengal, as collector of taxes. The stereoscope, like theosophy, through its double viewfinder allows this colonial discourse to be interpolated by the appeal of a colonized population, which it must answer. In its doubleness, colonially structured but eagerly anticipating the demise of empire with the arrival of the avatar of the next race, I wish to suggest that theosophy's complex, insinuating presence is the ghost discourse of the Revival.

---

62 See Washington, *Madame Blavatsky's baboon*, p. 111. The president of the American section till 1895; William Quan Judge thought that Irish folklore was 'almost undiluted Theosophy in essence', and descibed Killarney as 'one of the world's sacred places, covered with the invisible records of an ancient and noble civilisation': W.Q. Judge, *International Theosophical Chronicle*, 1:1 (Jan. 1905), p. 12.   63 Johnston, *Ireland through the stereoscope*, p. 227.1:1 (Jan. 1905), p. 12.   64 Ibid., p. 17.

'There are compensations in the congested districts for their poverty': Æ and the idealized peasant of the agricultural co-operative movement

LEEANN LANE

The mentality of the Anglo-Irish involved in the cultural revival at the turn of the century has, for the most part, been culled from an analysis of the literary works produced. This essay proposes to widen the context by examining aspects of the mentality of Æ in the *Irish Homestead*, the organ of the Irish Agricultural Organisation Society, which he edited from 1905 to 1923 and from 1923 to 1930, when it was subsumed into the *Irish Statesman*.

The *Irish Homestead* is very much a paper of the cultural revival. All the major concerns of the revival, notably the antagonism between Irish spirituality and English materialism, the use of ancient Ireland as a cultural tool, and the creation of a peasantry, are present in its volumes. The Anglo-Irish concern to regain leadership in a changing social, economic and political environment is also evident as a continuous sub-text of the paper. An analysis of the *Irish Homestead* as a cultural revival text, a context hitherto ignored, is vital. Such an analysis provides insight into the links between the revival and the journalism produced during the period and the connections between the revival and contemporary social and economic movements such as that of agricultural co-operation. This essay will focus on the idealized nature of the peasantry to be found in the writings of Æ in the *Irish Homestead*. A close reading of these writings reveals that Æ 'created' a peasantry that favoured the small farmer whom he saw as more amenable to leadership from a newly regenerated Anglo-Irish 'aristocracy' of intellect and character.[1] Æ's idealization of the lifestyle of the small farmer in his co-operative writings placed him firmly within the context of the cultural revival and indicates that the historian of the revival must look further than the purely literary texts if the movement is to be understood in all its facets.

The contrast between the depictions of the Irish peasantry in the works of George Moore and J.M. Synge offers a reminder that there was not one image

---

1 See 'Thinking in a vacuum', *Irish Homestead*, 21 Apr. 1917, p. 286, where Æ defined that section of rural society which the IAOS was most concerned to aid: 'we mean that most numerous class whose holdings are twenty acres or thereabouts, going as low as five or seven acres, or rising to thirty or thirty-five acres ...'

of the peasant created by the revival. There were several; however, each of these
images reflects different social and political concerns of the creator rather than
any reality. F.S.L. Lyons claims that Synge did not idealize the Irish peasant but
rather, 'they were earthy men and women, differing from their kind elsewhere
only in the beauty of the language Synge put into their mouths'.[2] Many of Synge's
descriptions of the Irish peasantry, however, did attribute a dignity to their lifestyle.
In the words of Seamus Deane, it is a peasantry 'blessed by refinement', which
was a characteristic feature of romantic Anglo-Irish writing since Samuel
Ferguson.[3] According to Declan Kiberd, in *The Aran Islands*, Synge locates among
the poor the values and attributes of a lost Gaelic aristocracy.[4] One can, however, contrast Synge's dignified description of the Irish peasantry with depictions
of the peasantry in the work of George Moore. As a Catholic landlord, Moore's
concern was to maintain a barrier between himself and the Catholic peasant by
stressing what divided them, that is, the peasant's poverty, lack of education, back-
wardness, and inhumanity. This is exemplified in Moore's *The Untilled Field*:

> And when he caught sight of the priest he stuck his spade in the ground
> and came to meet him, almost as naked as an animal, bare feet protrud-
> ing from ragged trousers; there was a shirt, but it was buttonless, and the
> breast-hair trembled in the wind – a likely creature to come out of the
> hovel behind him.[5]

This essay will add Æ's 'created' peasant to the revival list. What is interesting about
Æ in this context is that his peasant was 'created' in the context of journalistic as
much as in fictional writing. An analysis of Æ's 'created' peasant in the *Irish
Homestead* necessitates in turn a reassessment of the canon of cultural revival texts.

The *Irish Homestead* was a paper that went out weekly for over twenty years
to the farming community throughout Ireland. As such, it had a wider audience
for its revival ideologies than the fictional work of other revivalists, such as Synge
or Yeats. Furthermore, Æ's attempts to disperse the dogmas of the revival in a
self-help paper for farmers was a much more subversive project than the literary designs of Yeats and the other revival leaders. Poetry and drama inhabited

---

2 F.S.L. Lyons, *Ireland since the famine* (London: Weidenfeld and Nicolson, 1971), p. 238. 3
Seamus Deane, *Celtic revivals: essays in modern Irish literature, 1880–1980* (London: Faber and
Faber, 1987), pp 56–7. 4 Declan Kiberd, *Irish classics* (London: Granta, 2000), p. 421. 5 George
Moore, 'A letter to Rome,' in his *The untilled field* (Dublin: Gill and Macmillan, 1987), p. 90.
For Moore's treatment of the Irish peasant see Leeann Lane, 'The Moores of Moore Hall:
political and literary responses to the dilemma of the Irish Catholic landlord,' unpublished
MA thesis, University College, Cork, 1992. James Murphy, by contrast, sees *The untilled field*
as a 'manifesto for an alliance against Catholic Ireland between the peasantry and the Catholic
intelligensia or, at least, for the intelligentsia to be seen as agitating on behalf of the whole
nation'. James H. Murphy, *Catholic fiction and social reality in Ireland, 1873–1922* (Westport:
Greenwood, 1997), p. 129.

the realm of fiction after all and could be dismissed by those who desired to repudiate the revival leaders. From this perspective, the *Irish Homestead* was a much more subversive revival text and needs to be recognised as such.

The *Irish Homestead* did include literary contributions, such as Joyce's first short story, 'The Sisters', which was published in 1904; however, this sort of contribution was usually included in the end sections. A cursory reading may indicate that the paper expressed a disinterested concern to extricate the farmer from unscrupulous moneylenders and to guide the rural small holder towards better business and marketing methods. That the journal was perceived as a farmer's journal is reflected in the fact that Joyce employed the name 'Stephen Daedalus' to cope with his shame at appearing in the 'pig's paper'.[6]

A closer reading the *Irish Homestead*, however, shows an implicit connection between the programme of the Irish cultural revival and the sentiments expressed, often as a subtext. Although precise circulation figures for the paper are irretrievable, the subscriptions taken by the co-operative societies throughout the country indicates a wide scale circulation of Æ's views and among an audience who arguably might not have been immediately attracted to the literary productions of the revival. The impression of the paper as one concerned with explaining the merits of agricultural co-operation allowed Æ to transmit values of the cultural revival to an audience who might not have engaged otherwise in the cultural debates of an urban intellectual minority. The *Irish Homestead* thus had a potentially diverse appeal. For example, it appealed both to those who were interested in co-operative farming and who embraced the ethos of the cultural revival. Concurrently, it also appealed to whose who were attracted to the political and economic philosophies advocated by individuals such as Æ and Horace Plunkett who sought to transcend what they viewed as the narrow commitment to parliamentary-style politics.

The opinions Æ enunciated and the attitudes he expressed in his role of editor of the *Irish Homestead* have to be viewed in the context of social, economic and political change in Ireland at the time. By the closing decades of the nineteenth century, a new rural elite had emerged in Irish society. Made up of large farmers, shopkeepers, merchants, and professional men, this elite was the result of the post-Famine social, economic and political transformation of Ireland.[7] Despite Æ's theosophical concern to promote the brotherhood of man, he was primarily concerned to better the life of the small farmer. An examination of his editorials and weekly notes in the *Irish Homestead* shows him to be opposed to the larger farmer whom he viewed negatively as a member of the rising middle-class in early twentieth-century Ireland.[8] Throughout the pages

6 Declan Kiberd, 'Irish literature and Irish history,' in Roy Foster (ed.), *The Oxford illustrated history of Ireland* (Oxford: Oxford UP, 1989), p. 322. **7** Donald E. Jordan, *Land and popular politics in Ireland: County Mayo from the plantation to the Land War* (Cambridge: Cambridge UP, 1994), p. 7. **8** Æ attended meetings of the Dublin lodge of the Theosophical Society from

of the *Irish Homestead,* the large farmer was described negatively and abusively.[9] Along with the gombeenman, he was presented as the source of ill in the Irish countryside.[10] Æ's focus on the small farmer, his obvious dislike of the large farmer, and his furious and sustained attacks on the gombeenman indicated his discomfort with, and dislike of, the new configuration of social, economic and political power in early twentieth-century Ireland. Throughout his writings, Æ stressed the uncultured aspects of the Irish middle-class, often contrasting their lack of cultural achievement with the glory of the Anglo-Irish contribution to Irish literature and the arts in general.[11]

The co-operative values preached by Æ in the *Irish Homestead* were, there-fore, an attempt to grapple with social change. Far from a utilitarian self-aid paper for farmers concerned with tillage farming and pig rearing, the sub-text of the *Irish Homestead* was an idealistic attempt to halt the full effects of mass democ-racy in Irish society and retain a leadership role for the Anglo-Irish. Æ believed that it was possible to diminish the impact of what he saw as the vulgar Catholic bourgeois class in Irish society. From his perspective, it was a class that preferred 'the decorations in a gaudy public house to a poem in stone by Lutyens'.[12] This statement was made in reference to the failure of the Dublin municipality to finance the building of an art gallery to house Hugh Lane's proposed gift of impressionist paintings to the city. Æ desired to create an affiliation between the

early 1888, perhaps joining the society in late 1888 or early 1889. However, as his letters to his childhood friend Carrie Rea indicate he was well verse in the tenets of the Society at least as early as 1887. Although Æ broke formally with the Society in 1898, its tenets were the fundamental beliefs that informed his actions in the IAOS; although the Theosophist had an other-world focus; his commitment to social reform and the improvement of the present life was central to preparation for his next reincarnation.   9 See 'Large and small farmers,' *Irish Homestead,* 29 Dec. 1905; 'Templecrone a record of co-operative activity,' *Irish Homestead,* 11 Nov. 1916; 'The membership of agricultural banks,' *Irish Homestead,* 14 Oct. 1905. In the latter Æ wrote: 'If the Book of Life, out of which they will be judged hereafter, turns out to be the hearts of their neighbours whom they have helped or neglected there will be pretty barren records for some big farmers in Ireland.'   10 For Æ's opposition to the gombeenman, see: 'The case for agricultural co-operation,' *Irish Homestead,* 27 Apr. 1912; G. W. Russell, *Co-operation and nationality: a guide for rural reformers from this to the next generation.* (Dublin: Irish Academic Press, 1982), p. 13. In the latter work, Æ wrote of 'swollen gombeenmen straddling right across whole parishes, sucking up like a sponge all the wealth in the district'.   11 See 'Old traditions and the new era,' *Irish Statesman,* 3 Jan. 1925, pp 522–3, where Æ wrote: 'if the Anglo-Irish tradition is repudiated, Ireland becomes a country populated by nonentities'. Certainly, coming from a middle-class, even lower-middle class family, Æ cannot be fitted into the classic Protestant Ascendancy mould. However, for Æ, as indeed for the middle-class Yeats, 'Anglo-Irish' was a state of mind as much as a description of class. Throughout his life, Æ saw no contradiction between his scathing attacks on middle-class lack of culture, the result, as he saw it, of their commercial and materialistic values, and his own position as a member of that middle-class.   12 'The practical business man in Ireland,' *Irish Homestead,* 6 Sept. 1913 in Henry Summerfield (ed.), *Selections from the contributions to the* Irish Homestead *by G. W. Russell – Æ,* vol. 1 (Gerrards Cross, Bucks.: Smythe, 1978), p. 371.

Anglo-Irish and the smaller farmers. From his point of view, the small farmers would be released by agricultural co-operation from debt bondage to the Irish gombeenman, who represented the rise of the new materialistic middle-class in Irish society.[13] Recreated as an aristocracy of intellect and character, the Anglo-Irish would establish themselves as the leaders of rural Ireland that would be newly reconstructed through agricultural co-operation.

In 1908, Plunkett published 'Noblesse Oblige, an Irish Rendering', which appealed to the landlords of Ireland to use their superior education and character to work for the future social and economic betterment of Irish society and thereby would ensure their place in that future society. In the editorial of the 1 February 1908 issue of the *Irish Homestead*, Æ ringingly endorsed the sentiments expressed in the pamphlet, sentiments he himself expressed and enlarged on repeatedly in his co-operative writings. In the past, Æ argued for Irish farmers to follow whoever helped them in the land struggle. In future, he declared that support would be granted to whoever helped in solving the problems of the small proprietor.[14]

One finds in the *Irish Homestead* a focus on agricultural occupations suited to the small farmer and agricultural labourer, for example, horticultural, bee keeping and poultry societies.[15] In July 1908, Æ waxed eloquently on the 'variety of vegetables that can be got out of a very small plot' and went on to declare that with 'an acre to cultivate, no one should be able to complain of want of proper variety at their meals'.[16] In April 1906, discussing the Munster-Connaught Agricultural Exhibition, which was to take place in July, he focused on the Home Life and Home Industries Section. Here, he declared, 'will be model labourers' cottages, with demonstrations in household management; a small farmer's house, with model furniture and demonstrations of domestic economy in keeping with the small farmer's means'.[17] The 'Household Hints' section of the paper similarly had a bias towards providing information for the less well off members of rural society. The 18 March 1905 edition included a pieced entitled 'Plain Fare Made Palatable' that was intended to help the country housewife or cottager to provide for her family 'a variety of palatable dishes composed from the ordinary materials to be found in the majority of even modest households.'[18]

13 Many contemporaries, of course, would have characterized the small farmer as part of the lower middle-class elite created by peasant proprietorship; Æ's refusal to accord the small farmer this middle class status was itself part of his ideology. **14** 'The future of the Irish aristocracy,' *Irish Homestead*, 1 Feb. 1908, pp 81–2. Also, see: 'The resignation of Lord Monteagle,' *Irish Homestead*, 28 Oct. 1905, p. 782. In this article, Æ praised Monteagle's performance as president of the IAOS and lauded him as one who brought to his public and philanthropic work 'the motto of his class, "Noblesse oblige".' **15** See 'Poultry societies,' *Irish Homestead*, 16 Apr. 1910, p. 310. In this instance, Æ lauded poultry and eggs as 'the great industries of the small farmer and cottagers.' **16** 'Labourers plots,' *Irish Homestead*, 18 July 1908, in Summerfield (ed.), *Selections*, vol. 1, p. 154. **17** 'At the roots of nationality,' *Irish Homestead*, 14 Apr. 1906, p. 282. **18** M.T.W., 'Plain fare made palatable,' *Irish Homestead*, 18 Mar. 1905, p. 218.

Clearly, one would expect to find the above sentiments reiterating the benefits of agricultural co-operation for the small farmer in a paper such as the *Irish Homestead*; large farmers stood to gain no advantage from such co-operation.[19] While this has to be recognized, Æ's concern to promote the well-being of the small farmer over his larger neighbour goes further than simply a rational understanding of how co-operation benefited the small rather than the larger farmer.

Æ's call to the Irish landlord class to work to better the future of Irish society drew on his belief in the merits of a hierarchical past. This past was underpinned by notions of reciprocal duties and rights between classes, where social relations were mediated through patronage and were premised on the concept of a moral economy.[20] Co-operation ensured a leadership role for the Anglo-Irish in the new Ireland. As early as 1899, Æ wrote that co-operation brought to the 'assistance of the simplest and poorest the intelligence and wealth of the rich and better educated, and yet without weakening the poorest members' feeling of self-respect'.[21]

Agricultural co-operation, as Æ promoted it, was designed at one level to create an alliance between the small farmer and the Anglo-Irish to ensure that the new rising class of shopkeepers and publicans were unable to gain an ascendancy in Irish life. By promoting an organized rural life through agricultural co-operation where the small farmer was led by a newly renovated Anglo-Irish ascendancy of culture and intellect, the nefarious influence of the gombeenman could be contained. The small farmer, less implicated in the commercial, modernizing world than his larger neighbour, was according to Æ's scheme, more amenable to Anglo-Irish leadership.[22] In 1906, he wrote that the rural district:

19 Liam Kennedy, 'Agricultural co-operation and Irish rural society, 1880–1914', unpublished PhD dissertation, University of York, 1978, p. 119. **20** The United Irishwomen, affiliated with the IAOS in 1910, would, he believed, foster a return to the social harmony of a bygone age, 'just as the aristocrat of three hundred years ago dined with all his retainers … the chief at the top of the hall and the swineherd at the bottom, but all happy and social …' 'The pleasures of eating', *Irish Homestead*, 15 Jan. 1910, p. 43. **21** 'Among the Societies', *Irish Homestead*, 7 Jan. 1899 in Summerfield (ed.), *Selections*, vol. 1, pp 48–9. **22** See Liam Kennedy, 'Traders and agricultural politics in pre-independent Ireland', in S. Clark and J. Donnelly (eds), *Irish peasants: violence and political unrest, 1780–1914* (Dublin: Gill and Macmillan, 1983), p. 347. Kennedy discusses how shopkeeper-graziers and other graziers improved their position in society at the expense of the rural smallholder and restricted the latter's attempts to achieve economic viability. David Jones also discusses how shopkeeper-graziers often improved their position at the expense of smaller farmers in the district by taking advantage of landlord facilitated free sale to increase their pasture acreage. See David Jones, 'The cleavage between graziers and peasants in the land struggle, 1890–1910, in Clark and Donnelly (eds), *Irish peasants*, pp 404–5. Frank Callanan contends that during the split in the Irish Parliamentary Party, 1890–1891, 'the ascendancy of anti-Parnellism in rural Ireland was a function of the political and social transformations wrought in the previous decade'. The barony of Tireagh in the west of Co. Sligo, a region 'deemed socially backward and politically undeveloped', produced a high Parnellite vote by contrast with the rest of the constituency during the 1891 Sligo bye-

affords the greatest opportunity to the man who wishes to make his mark.
It is here that the people are the most backward and most teachable. We
can imagine no more splendid ideal for a man to have than when he says
to himself, 'there are six hundred families in this parish were Providence
has placed me. They are poor, badly housed, badly fed, badly educated.
They are centuries behind other countries. I will read and study what
has been done elsewhere that I may know how to help them.'[23]

Æ's concern to promote the well-being of the small farmer through agricultural
co-operation had its literary manifestation in his creation of an Irish peasant, a
creation which can be seen not just in his poetry and fictional work but also in
the *Irish Homestead*. These 'created' peasants were small holders, primitive and
backward in the material needs of the life. Concurrently, they possessed an innate
dignity and willingness to be lead into the joys of an idealized rural way of life
that bore little resemblance to the realities of commercial farming in Ireland.[24]

Certainly, Æ's concern to distinguish between the small and the large farmer
mirrored the reality of the divisions within the farming community. A cleavage
between small farmers and the growing class of graziers existed as a continual
point of tension within the United Irish League in the early twentieth century
and came to the surface in the ranch war of 1906-1908.[25] On that basis, Æ's isolation of the small farming class as a specific interest group in Irish society was
rooted in a certain reality, but his vision of the Irish peasant was also highly ideological. His descriptions of the rural life that the small farmer ought to strive
for were, in many cases, literary constructs designed to act as a counter to what
he saw as the materialism of Catholic bourgeois Ireland.[26] 'There is no more
ideal life than the farmer's,' he wrote in 1899:

> no life which contains more elements of joy, mystery and beauty. He has
> always the scent of the earth in his nostrils, pure air and the perpetual

election. See Frank Callanan, *The Parnell split, 1890–1891* (Cork: Cork UP, 1992), pp 113–14.
Æ's focus on the smaller farmer and the inhabitants of the backward rural districts of the western seaboard was consistent with his desire to circumvent and contain the full scale consequence of social and political change in late nineteenth-century Ireland. **23** 'Local Organisation,' *Irish Homestead*, 7 Apr. 1906, p. 262. **24** David Jones contends that by 1900, 'commercial
production and a monetized economy were clearly evident even in the remote and infertile
areas of the west.' Jones, 'The cleavage between graziers and peasants,' p. 374. **25** Paul Bew,
Conflict and conciliation in Ireland, 1890–1910 (Oxford: Clarendon, 1987), p. 8. **26** In 1897, Æ
issued two pamphlet invectives against the despotism of Irish Catholicism: 'The awakening
of the fires' and 'Ideals in Ireland: Priest or hero,' both first published in the *Irish Theosophist*,
Jan.–Feb. 1897 and Apr.–May 1897 respectively. Æ's attitudes towards the religions of the
'grocer and the counting house' grew more strident as he got older. Talking the side of the
workers in the 1913 strike and lockout he saw himself in opposition to the Catholic church.
See Russell to Charles Weekes, [4 Nov. 1913], P 8389, NLI.

wonder of growing things. And it is so easy to make an earthy paradise around every cabin. A few lilac bushes, roses, creepers, a little paint on fences and on door and window and a pot of creamy whitewash over the walls, will make a home to allure the might ones of the earth from the palaces.[27]

This idealized rural life was always throughout the co-operative writings of Æ the alternative to the social and economic climate produced by gombeenism. Country towns, dominated by the activities of the gombeenman, he argued in *The National Being*, 'produce nothing and are mere social parasites;' creating no productive wealth, generating no civic virtues or intellectual life, such country towns were 'excrescences on the face of nature.'[28]

In 1912, Æ announced his belief after a holiday in the west of Ireland that:

the west Irish country folk are on the whole the happiest and most contented he has ever met or heard of. None of the political storms which are convulsing Ireland elsewhere had come near that quiet mountainy land. Even on the great question of the day he heard no more pronounced opinion than the oracular statement: 'If Home Rule be a good thing let it come. If it be not a good thing let it not come.'[29]

Indeed, Æ described himself, on holidays in Donegal, as staying at a small farmhouse using the quote 'a high windy place among distant hills,' which Summerfield suggests is misquoted from Synge's, *The Playboy of the Western World*.[30] This attempt to quote Synge suggests that Æ saw himself belonging with those within the Irish literary revival who idealized the Irish peasant class. Such idealization refused to credit the peasantry with material desires such as those evidenced by the growing Irish bourgeois classes. This attitude is highlighted strongly in Æ's *Irish Homestead* editorial of 14 May 1910, where he wrote:

the most interesting part of Ireland is the congested districts. There are compensations in the congested districts for their poverty. They are rich in human nature. We are reminded too, that the small farmer in the West of Ireland has the most imaginative, picturesque and literary speech in the world ... But the congested districts have out of their poverty developed something better than rich speech. They have developed, as all poor communities do, a rich humanity. The organisers of the IAOS find the best material for true co-operation in these poverty-stricken communi-

27 'The Irish cottage,' *Irish Homestead*, 29 Apr. 1899, in Summerfield (ed.), *Selections*, vol. 1, p. 50. **28** Æ, *The national being: some thoughts on an Irish polity* (Dublin: Maunsel, 1920), pp 42–3. **29** 'The obscurity of mandarin literature', *Irish Homestead*, 13 July 1912 in Summerfield (ed.), *Selections*, vol. 1, pp 318–19. **30** Ibid.

ties … In other parts of Ireland we organise industries more than men. In the West we organise the kindly, loyal, human feelings of the people.[31]

The editorial continued by arguing that a great responsibility rested with the members of the new Congested Districts Board because they had the power 'to fix the new social order.'[32] Æ's concern was to ensure that the Congested Districts Board in its attempts to better the material situation of the people did not in the process destroy what he considered their finer human qualities. In this context, he believed that people in these areas had to be weaned away from reliance on state aid and had to be educated towards self-help.[33]

Æ's concern for preserving the finer human qualities of the people of the west of Ireland bordered on patronizing. In the west of the country, the reality of life for many farmers was emigration. Donald Jordan's discussion of the ultimate failure to provide relief for the small farmers of Co. Mayo highlights the dismal realities of life on the land in one area on the western seaboard. Although following the Famine, small farmers broadened their economic activities to enter the cash market, Jordan contends that they still subsisted for the most part on the potato.[34] The threat of famine was therefore always a reality for the small farmers of Co. Mayo, especially in the peripheral areas where the land was unsuitable for crops other than the potato.[35]

Arguably for Æ to talk about the finer qualities of humanity in the face of such poverty and economically forced emigration was condescending and cavalier. His remarks must be seen in the context of his literary image of rural simplicity. Discussing the 'Back to the Land' movement in England, Alun Howkins writes that the:

> notion of returning to a purer, better and more natural life, was, of course not new. 'Agrarianism,' the idea of small producer units supported by some form of co-operation or communal production was a powerful part of English radical thought throughout the nineteenth century.'

Howkins contends that those who moved back to the countryside were 'not simply leaving a crowded or unsanitary urban area they were going to a rural

---

31 'The best place for co-operation', *Irish Homestead*, 14 May 1910, p. 399. **32** Ibid. **33** Æ's concern to promote self-help in the place of reliance is similar in many respects to the programme of constructive unionism. Constructive unionists were concerned, Andrew Gailey contends, with the shape democracy would assume in Irish society. By changing habits and mental attitudes through education and a focus on self-reliance, Irishmen would be taught the responsibilities of government and the unionist fear of demagogic politics alleviated. Andrew Gailey, *Ireland and the death of kindness: the experience of constructive unionism, 1890–1905* (Cork: Cork UP, 1987), pp 14–15, p. 18, p. 51, p. 309. **34** Jordan, *Land and popular politics in Ireland*, p. 200. **35** Ibid., p. 200, p. 207.

myth which they were creating. Central to that myth were ideas of a 'natural' or 'organic' social order and society'.[36] Æ's vision of a small peasantry whose finer human qualities count for more than mere material concerns clearly has to be seen in this context of a created rural myth.

Æ's engagement in the late nineteenth-, early twentieth-century pastoral versus tillage debate was on a cultural as well as an economic level.[37] In very literary terms, he asserted that tillage farming produced a more noble human beings than did pastoral farming:

> A man ought to know how to dig as well as write. He ought to be able to read the seasons as well as to read books. In short he ought to be able to drag from the earth her produce as well as cram his mind with the thoughts of others. Those of us who have engaged in digging know how well it stimulates our thinking power and nothing is better calculated to enable a man to concentrate his thoughts than ploughing ...
>
> ... But, of course, it is the hard work which is entailed by agriculture that the most valuable education lies. The man who tills is, in my opinion, much more superior in moral qualities to the man who is content with grazing ...[38]

Æ presented an image of rural life based on tillage farming which was arduous in its workload, modest, if adequate, in its material returns, but rich for its participants in nobility of life and inner strength of character.

This idyllic view of rural life was, of course, not unique to Æ or even to Irish rural commentators. Parallels can be made between his rural discourse and a tradition of English observers who created an idealized image of English rural life that was disconnected from the actual transforming fact of the historical moment. Such parallels reinforce the argument that Æ's vision was highly ideological.[39] William Morris wrote that there are 'few men ... who would not wish to spend part of their lives in the most necessary and pleasantest of all work – cultivating the earth.'[40] Similarly, Æ presented in the volumes of the *Irish Homestead* a liter-

---

36 Alun Howkins, *Reshaping rural England: a social history, 1850–1925* (London: Routledge, 1991), p. 225 and p. 231.   **37** During the first decade of the twentieth century, Æ was writing in the context of the sustained tension between ranchers or graziers and the small farmer. This conflict erupted in the 1880s during the land war and reached a height following the 1903 Land Act. Between 1906 and 1909, the conflict was so extreme that it was known as the ranch war. The rancher was able to acquire large areas of pasture at the expense of the smaller farmers, particularly among the impoverished small holders of the west of Ireland. Jones, 'The cleavage between graziers and peasants,' pp 381–2; Jordan, *Land and popular politics in Ireland*, p. 7.   **38** 'Agriculture in education.' *Irish Homestead*, 29 Dec. 1905, p. 934.   **39** See Raymond Williams, *The country and the city* (London: Paladin, 1975).   **40** William Morris, 'Useful work versus useless toil,' Asa Briggs (ed.), *William Morris: Selected writings and designs* (London: Penguin, 1977), pp 129–30.

ary image of Irish rural life where his concern was to foster a cultural dimension to rural life. 'We hope,' he wrote in 1908:

> in the next generation the then editor of the *Homestead* will find it possible, to print along with instructions of what seeds should be sown in the earth, the songs which the farmer might sing at his work. We have been in every country in Ireland and we never heard a song in the fields, or any suggestion of cheerfulness or lightheartedness in labour ... Song and labour, the soul and the body, are far apart in Ireland; but they may be brought closer, and a more lighthearted life be possible, if we can get our rural population educated to work more together, to be more social and to realise what they came to earth for, to live together and work together ...[41]

Of course, Æ himself never engaged in manual labour, and here he exemplifies what Newby and other writes on the English rural tradition have identified as the 'refusal to recognize the problem of rural poverty in the midst of this splendidly bucolic existence [the rural idyll].'[42] With a similar lack of true knowledge as to the hardships of rural labour, Æ praised the United Irishwomen's advocacy of gymnasiums for girls as well as boys and wrote:

> Little girls who have learned in the gymnasium how to use their limbs properly will not let themselves grow into despairing drudges bound down under a yoke that is too heavy. If they have to carry weights or do field work or, what may also be very laborious, heavy housecleaning and arranging, they will bring to it a science that will make it a delight at times and never a drudgery ...[43]

41 'Watertight compartments for ideals and actualities', *Irish Homestead*, 2 May 1908, in Summerfield (ed.), *Selections*, vol. 1, p. 145. Also, see: 'Singing and working,' *Irish Homestead*, 25 Nov. 1905, p. 865. In this article, Æ similarly argued for the necessity for song at work: 'We should have milking songs and a list for the carts bringing the milk, and a song when the milk is being separated, and a song for the dairymaid and one for the engine man.' **42** Howard Newby, *The deferential worker: a study of farm workers in East Anglia* (London: Allen Lane, 1977), p. 12. Brian Short writes of the belief that to be truly English at the start of the twentieth century was to be rural. 'But ... "rural" did not mean rural *people*, and especially not *poor* rural people, who might not fit the stereotypes of poverty by living in picturesque cottages. The countryside was made by working people, but the rural idyll of pastoral from the eighteenth to the twentieth century, itself an urban product, has largely banished them from the scene. The image was that of an outsider, often looking with a "tourist gaze" and seeking the landscape from a distance, not in detail, and not encompassing all its occupants.' Brian Short, 'Images and realities in the English rural community: an introduction,' in his *The English rural community: image and analysis*, pp 2–3. **43** 'Bessie Bobtail', *Irish Homestead*, 15 Apr. 1911, pp 288–9.

Æ's portrayal of the farmer who sings at his work or the girl who transforms her heavy field work into a delight exemplified those rural workers for whom, in the words of Howard Newby, 'metaphysical rewards have been deemed to be adequate compensation for … [their] labour'.[44] The picture of a rural organic community presented by Æ is an example of the idealized portrayal of rural life that Newby identifies in the English rural tradition.[45]

Roy Foster contends that when Yeats stressed the need for Ireland 'to become a country where, if there are few rich there shall be few very poor,' he anticipated the anti-materialistic image of Ireland that prevailed under de Valera in the 1930s and 1940s.[46] In the *Irish Homestead*, Æ himself referenced with approval this remark by Yeats, indicating clearly that his held the same ideal of rural adequacy and simplicity:

> We believe that we are going, perhaps first of all races in Europe, to have a real democracy, that is, a co-operative union of the inhabitants of the country with the ideal once stated by Mr Yeats, of a country where if nobody will be very rich nobody will be very poor, and our collective efforts will conduce to the happiness and well-being of the average man, and we will not be mere intellectual hewers of wood and drawers of water to enrich the holders of shares in great companies.[47]

Indeed, de Valera's often quoted and by now clichéd speech envisioning a countryside populated by athletic youths and comely women was pre-empted some three decades earlier by Æ. Again, one is looking at a literary image of rural simplicity:

> A fine life is possible for humanity working on the land, bronzed by the sun and wind, living close to nature, which bring about essential depth and a noble simplicity of character … We will move a hundred times more rapidly to national prosperity and happiness if we try to make our civilisation more predominately rural. There will be a better race in Ireland, stronger men and comlier women, and we will be less subject to the shock by the tidal ebb and flow of the industrial world, with its slumps in trade, its feverish and transient prosperities …[48]

Similarly, in *Co-operation and Nationality*, Æ wrote that the aspiration of a great nationality should be to 'beget youths, beautiful, gigantic, and sweet-blooded,

---

44 Newby, *The deferential worker*, pp 14–15.   **45** Ibid., pp 16–17.   **46** R.F. Foster, 'Thinking from hand to mouth: Anglo-Irish literature, Gaelic nationalism and Irish politics in the 1890s', in his *Paddy and Mr Punch: connections in Irish and English history* (London: Allen Lane, 1993), p. 74.   **47** 'What Ireland is aiming at', *Irish Homestead*, 27 Mar. 1915 in Summerfield (ed.), *Selections*, vol. 2, p. 466.   **48** 'Ireland, agriculture and the war', *Irish Homestead*, 20 Feb. 1915 in Summerfield (ed.), *Selections*, vol. 2, p. 459.

and their counterpart in comely and robust women.'[49] With this in mind, the image Æ placed in front of the *Irish Homestead* reader was that of the artist Millet's peasant. In short, the image was an artistic construct. Discussing 'The Woolcarder', Æ remarked how Millet captured in this painting the dignity of 'a life well spent in honourable labour.' Crucially, he believed that the appreciation of such fine art would develop a sense of aesthetic judgement in the Irish. Such judgement would enable them to express a preference for 'Millet over the cheap lithographs of a chubby child with two puppies sent round as an advertisement by the tea merchant.'[50] Such a statement indicates the manner in which commercial values were synonymous in Æ's thinking with vulgarity and lack of aesthetic taste.

Æ's created peasant was one who eschewed bourgeois tastes, was content with his modest lot and station in life, and did not seek to rise above it. In 1906, he declared that it was more important for the peasant to manifest an inner nobility of life 'than to change their social position or employment.' National Education system's role was to teach children 'to be fine men and women' rather than teaching them to aspire to move up the social scale.[51] The elemental hardiness of the peasant and his closeness to nature were the defining characteristics of Æ's ideal peasant, as exemplified in his the poem 'Survival' with its image of the digger:

> What pent-up fury in those arms,
> Red gilded by the sun's last breath!
> The spade along the ridges runs
> As if it had a race with death.
>
> The clods fly right: the clods fly left:
> The ridges rise on either side,
> The tireless fury is not spent,
> Though the fierce sunset long has died.
>
> The strength which tossed the hills on high,
> And rent the stormy seas apart,
> Is still within those mighty limbs,
> Still stirs the dreams of that wild heart.[52]

Æ's peasant was a stock figure, to use Raymond Williams' phrase, 'reduced … from human to "natural" status'.[53] The peasant's link with nature enabled him to establish a connection with the hidden world, the world of vision, which as

49 Russell, *Co-operation and nationality*, p. 72. **50** 'Another picture by Millet', *Irish Homestead*, 21 Oct. 1905. Also, see *Irish Homestead*, 4 Nov. 1905, p. 803; and 'The woodsawyers', *Irish Homestead*, 11 Nov. 1905, p. 820. **51** 'The Irish country girl', *Irish Homestead*, 3 Mar. 1906, pp 161–2. **52** Æ, 'Survival', in Æ, *Voices of the stones* (London: Macmillan, 1925), p. 9. **53** Williams, *The country and the city*, p. 310.

a theosophist Æ considered so essential to an Ireland lacking sufficient spirituality. This lack was manifested in the materialistically orientated mentality of the Irish who had no cultural or intellectual depth beyond that dictated by, in William Morris's phrase, 'the counting house'.[54] To counter the deficit of discerning intellectual inspiration in contemporary Ireland, Æ argued that Irish poets needed to return to writing of heroes and great men. The lack of such inspiration, he declared, created a situation where the huckster or gombeenman is taken as the representative type for all society to follow.[55] Indeed, for Morris, as for Æ, what was essential in life was linked with nature and divorced from vulgar materialism. What Morris referred to as 'wealth' was in many respects what Æ meant when he talked of spirituality. Castigating the production of 'articles of folly and luxury,' Morris declared that wealth was that given to man by 'Nature':

> The sunlight, the fresh air, the unspoiled face of the earth, food, raiment, and housing necessary and decent; the storing up of knowledge of all kinds, and the power of disseminating it; means of free communication between man and man; works of art, the beauty which man creates when he is most a man, most aspiring and thoughtful – things which serve the pleasure of people, free, manly and uncorrupted.[56]

Many of Æ's poems highlight what for him was the essential unity between the peasant and nature. The poem 'In Connemara' presents an image of an 'untroubled' peasant woman, carrying a creel of seaweed by day, but by night:

> Then she will wander, her heart all a laughter,
> Tracking the dream star that lights the purple gloom
> She follows the proud and golden races after
> As high as theirs her spirit, as high will be her doom.[57]

By night the peasant woman, therefore, seeks a mystical communication and the worlds of the spiritual planes of theosophical belief. Similarly, in 'An Artist of Gaelic Ireland,' discussing the works of Jack Yeats, Æ wrote of the peasant's link by night with the other worlds of his theosophist outlook:

> … it is only occasionally that the younger Yeats becomes the interpreter of the spirituality of the peasant. He is more often the recorder of the extravagant energies of the race-course and the market place, where he finds herded together all the grotesque humours of West Irish life. Yet in all these there is an ever present suggestion of poetry; and these people

54 William Morris, 'The lesser arts', in Briggs (ed.), *William Morris*, p. 103. **55** Æ, *The national being*, pp 13–14. **56** Morris, 'Useful work versus useless toil', p. 121. **57** Æ, 'In Connemara', in Æ, *The divine vision and other poems* (London: Macmillan, 1904), p. 70.

who laugh in the fairs will have after hours as solemn as the star gazer in the 'Midsummer Eve.[58]

Of course, the notion of the spiritual peasant with the ability to transcend material concerns and make a link with the spiritual world of Æ's theosophical beliefs in real terms meant little. In essence, what Æ's construct did was to remove the peasant from any connection with the realities of the small farmer's existence on the western Irish seaboard, where poverty, unemployment, emigration and potential famine were the harsh facts of life. Æ's removal of the peasant from the reality of his existence had similarities to the treatment of the poorer classes by English rural commentators. In such commentaries, real knowledge of the working countryman is missing; there is no sense in such accounts of the various degrees of skill and status, which existed in rural areas. Instead, the reader is presented with an archetypal rural dweller. As Brian Short states: 'Lob the countryman, with *all* the virtues of countrymen in general, is nothing more than a caricature.'[59] Similarly, Raymond Williams, discussing Edward Thomas's 'Lob' writes that:

> all countrymen, of all conditions and periods, are merged into a single legendary figure. The various idioms of specific country communities – the flowers, for example, have many local names – are reduced not only to one "country" idiom but to a legendary, timeless inventor, who is more readily seen than any actual people.[60]

If Æ's ploughman, in the poem 'The Earth Breath' looks 'Deep beneath his rustic habit and finds himself a king', it was because Æ considered contemporary Ireland squalid and lacking sufficiently in the noble and heroic values.[61] In his poem 'Exiles', Æ stressed the continuity of a noble tradition in the person of the Irish peasant:

> The gods have taken alien shapes upon them,
> Wild peasant driving swine
> In a strange country. Through the swarthy faces
> The starry faces shine.[62]

Declan Kiberd contends that the revival writers used the hero 'not as an exemplar for the Anglo-Irish overlords but as a model for those who were about to

58 Æ, 'An image of Gaelic Ireland', pamphlet reprinted from the *Freeman's Journal*, 23 Oct. 1901, p. 2. **59** Short, 'Images and realities in the English rural community', p. 4. **60** Williams, *The country and the city*, p. 308. **61** Æ, 'The Earth Breath', in Æ, *The nuts of knowledge, lyrical poems old and new by Æ* (Dublin: Dun Emer, 1903), p. 11. **62** Æ, 'Exiles', in Æ, *Voices of the stones*, p. 2.

replace them'. The English had dismissed the Celts as feminine and childlike and thus, necessitous of the ruling hand of their masculine conquerors. Using the heroes of the ancient Irish legends, in particular Cuchulain, the revival writers, Kiberd argues, 'provided a symbol of masculinity for Celts...'.[63] This is a positive reading of the role of the hero in the writings of the revival. Æ's use of the hero as a model for contemporary Ireland to follow has to be seen, however, in a more negative light. He held up the hero of ancient literature and the persona of the noble peasant for a new middle-class generation, which had no further aspirations than to share in the fruits of, as Æ saw it, base and soul-destroying commercial activity. This being said, however, Æ's statement when reviewing the paintings of Jack Yeats in 1901 suggests a lack of any true knowledge of the hardship of the life of the 'folk', as he called them. Lauding Jack Yeats's lack of intellectual patronage towards the peasants whom he painted, Æ wrote: 'I suggest Jack Yeats thinks the life of a Sligo fisherman is as good a method of life as any, and that he could share it for a long time without being in the least desirous of a return to the comfortable life of convention.'[64] Crucially, Æ created this exemplary peasant, closely linked to the natural world and dismissive of materialistic values, in his journalistic writings as well as in his literary work. The *Irish Homestead* was, consequently, a paper highly charged with the ideologies of the cultural revival. An understanding of the paper as a production of the cultural renaissance makes clear the manner in which the revival ethos was introduced into and permeated a wider contemporary social and economic discourse. Furthermore, the manner in which the *Irish Homestead* was presented as a farmer weekly allowed the spread of that ethos. The paper created possibilities for the reception the revival discourse amongst a wider society and allowed it to transcend the intellectual debates of a hermetically sealed Dublin-centred, intellectual clique.

63 Declan Kiberd, *Inventing Ireland* (London: Jonathan Cape, 1995), p. 25. **64** Æ, 'An artist of Gaelic Ireland', p. 1.

From manuscripts to street signs via *Séadna*: the Gaelic League and the changing role of literacy in Irish, 1875–1915

LIAM MAC MATHÚNA

This essay examines the balance between various types of literacy in Irish in the first phase of the revival movement. It addresses questions such as the fostering of basic learner competence, the ambition to create a modern literature and a modern journalism, as well as the public use of written Irish as a cultural symbol. The topic is a broad one and some of these aspects can merely be touched on.

Anticipating its abandonment as a community vernacular, the language had become virtually invisible in written form by 1875, as noted by Philip O'Leary:

> Many of the leading writers of the Gaelic Revival never read a book in the Irish language in their formative years. Some had not even imagined that such a thing was possible. Looking back on the language movement and his own involvement in it, one of the most prolific pioneers of modern Gaelic prose, 'Beirt Fhear' (Séamus Ó Dubhghaill) recalled: 'I myself never laid eyes on a book in Irish until I was twenty years old [i.e. 1875.].'[1]

O'Leary further observes:

> Surveying the linguistic / literary situation of 1882, the year the bilingual journal *Irisleabhar na Gaedhilge / The Gaelic Journal* was founded, Tadhg Ó Donnchadha wrote in 1909: 'If there were fifty people in all of Ireland at that time who could read and write Irish in the native script I'd say that that would be the total number.'[2]

However, it has to be said that this figure is at variance with other evidence, such as that provided in relation to Munster by John Fleming in an essay submitted to the Royal Irish Academy about 1874:

> As to the proportion of the people that read or write Irish, I cannot form an opinion. I know that in several districts in Waterford there are far more

---

1 Philip O'Leary, *The prose literature of the Gaelic Revival, 1881–1921: ideology and innovation* (University Park: The Pennsylvania State UP, 1994), p. 1. 2 Loc. cit.

Irish readers now than at any time heretofore, and the sale of Irish books
in Cork, Kerry and Clare show that the readers in the counties are many
... these readers are as a rule far below the Irish scholars of forty years
ago in their knowledge of the language. Those who can write Irish well
or even fairly are very few ...[3]

A broad brush-stroke approach to literacy in Irish in the year 1875 might be summarized as follows. Writing in Irish had had a remarkably rich manuscript tradition, dating back to the sixth century. This had continued strongly up to the eighteenth century, and persisted, albeit in attenuated form, as long as the language
was spoken traditionally. Printing had come late to Irish, delayed by the political
and social constraints on the Irish-speaking population. The initial works were
religious in content and Protestant in persuasion, the first being issued in Dublin
in 1571. Protestant interest publications, including the New and Old Testaments,
appeared fitfully between then and 1700. From the early seventeenth century, the
Franciscans published Catholic counter-Reformation devotional works on the
Continent, most notably in Louvain on. Again, production was low, approximately
twelve titles being issued over a period of some fifty years.

We know too that print runs were small, and that copies of the New
Testament could still be obtained from source almost thirty years after the initial publication. In the case of the Catholic works, manuscript production was
soon reverted to, with printed works being copied out by hand. The only texts
which could be said to have enjoyed extended popularity in printed form were
Gallagher's *Sermons* (1736 etc.) and Tadhg Gaelach Ó Súilleabháin's *Pious
Miscellany* (1802 etc.). Interestingly, the title page and general editorial notes of
both of these works were in English, and the font employed was Roman rather
the Gaelic script.

The manuscript tradition was strongest in Munster, as evidenced by the work
of several generations of the Ó Longáin family of Cork. A second area where the
scribal tradition lived on well was Omeath. However, even here the ability to
write within the Irish tradition was under threat, as shown by the 1825 Monaghan
Jail production of *Mac na Míchomhairle* in an orthography derived from English.[4]
This orthographic phenomenon was also quite common in Connaught in the
nineteenth century. This English-based phonetic writing shows firstly how wide
a gulf had opened up between spoken Irish and the Gaelic written tradition.
Secondly, it shows how familiarity with the norms of English was spreading
throughout the community, for popular literacy meant literacy in English, sustained by chapbooks and ballad-sheets distributed by itinerant hawkers.

3 Caoilfhionn Nic Pháidín, *Fáinne an Lae agus an Athbheochan (1898–1900)* (Baile Átha Cliath:
Cois Life, 1998), p. 141.   4 Seosamh Watson, 'An Scríobhaí mar Sheifteoir: Cás Ls Uí
Mhuirgheasa 16B', *Studia Hibernica*, 31 (2000–1), pp 257–75.

The Society for the Preservation of the Irish Language (SPIL) was established at the end of 1876 and is regularly held to have heralded the advent of a more vibrant approach to promoting the Irish language than that practised by the antiquarian, backward-looking associations which had preceded it. 'The object of the Society being the Preservation and Extension of the Irish as a spoken Language', a number of means was proposed for that end. Among these were: to publish cheap elementary works, from which the Language can be easily learned; to furnish same at reduced prices to Classes and Associations in connection with the Society; and to encourage the production of a Modern Irish Literature – original or translated.[5]

One may compare the aims of the Gaelic League, founded at a meeting held in Dublin in July 1893, where the following resolution was passed: 'That a Society be formed under the name of the Gaelic League for the purpose of keeping the Irish language spoken in Ireland.' However, the Objects of the new organization were soon identified as being twofold: the preservation of Irish as the national language of Ireland and the extension of its use as a spoken tongue; and the study and publication of existing Gaelic literature and the cultivation of a modern literature in Irish.

It can be seen immediately that the second object was also a binary one, wherein the promotion of a modern literature in Irish was to complement the study and publishing of the inherited tradition. The great store to be set on the printed word, albeit as an auxiliary to the promotion of the spoken language was clear from three of the eleven Means which elaborated on the Objects of the League:

> 6. The publication and distribution of books and pamphlets in Irish, or relating thereto.

> 7. The publication of the *Gaelic Journal*, a magazine devoted exclusively to the objects of the League and issued mainly in the Irish language.

> 11. The free grant of Irish books to branches of the League that cannot easily obtain them otherwise.[6]

When set against the background of the time, the twin objects of restoring the spoken language and creating a new literature in Irish were indeed revolutionary. The retreat of Irish as a vernacular in the second half of the nineteenth century was precipitate. Statistics on its decline were provided by the decennial census returns. Basing his analysis on the 1881 census, Garret FitzGerald has

5 Máirtín Ó Murchú, *Cumann Buan-Choimeádta na Gaeilge: Tús an Athréimnithe* (Baile Átha Cliath: Cois Life, 2001), pp 325–6. **6** Leabharlann Náisiúnta na hÉireann, *Athbheochan na Gaeilge. Doiciméid Staire* (Baile Átha Cliath: Leabharlann Náisiúnta na hÉireann, 1981), Doiciméad 6.

shown that the Irish-speaking proportion of the cohort of the population born
1861–71 had dropped to 13 per cent while the overall number of monoglots
had shrunk from 21 per cent of the Irish-speaking population in 1851 to 6.75
per cent of the Irish-speaking population in 1881.[7]

While these impersonal figures set out the big picture, they may be complemented by some anecdotal accounts included by Douglas Hyde in the published version of his seminal address, 'On the necessity for de-anglicizing the
Irish nation', originally delivered in November 1892. These illuminate the practical working out of the language shift from Irish to English which was proceeding at headlong speed in the western half of the country in the last decades
of the nineteenth century. In their own way they are more informative than the
array of statistics with which one is now familiar. The guilelessness of the second
account is truly remarkable, indicative as it is of the vagueness of the individual's appreciation of the mechanics of the language shift:

> I mention the case of a young man I met on the road coming from the
> fair of Tuam, some ten miles away. I saluted him in Irish, and he answered
> me in English. 'Don't you speak Irish,' said I. 'Well, I declare to God, sir,'
> he said, 'my father and mother hasn't a word of English, but still, I don't
> speak Irish.' This was absolutely true for him. There are thousands upon
> thousands of houses all over Ireland to-day where the old people invari-
> ably use Irish in addressing the children, and the children as invariably
> answer in English, the children understanding Irish but not speaking it, the
> parents understanding their children's English but unable to use it them-
> selves. In a great many cases, I should almost say most, the children are not
> conscious of the existence of two languages. I remember asking a gossoon
> a couple of miles west of Ballaghaderreen in the Co. Mayo, some questions
> in Irish and he answered them in English. At last I said to him, *'Nach
> labhrann tú Gaedheilg?'* (i.e., 'Don't you speak Irish?') and his answer was,
> 'And isn't it Irish I'm spaking?' 'No *a-chuisle,'* said I, 'it's not Irish you're
> speaking, but English.' 'Well then,' said he, 'that's how I spoke it ever'! He
> was quite unconscious that I was addressing him in one language and he
> answering in another … This is going on from Malin Head to Galway, and
> from Galway to Waterford, with the exception possibly of a few spots in
> Donegal and Kerry, where the people are wiser and more national.[8]

However, the situation with regard to the written Irish word was just as far-
reaching, as is clear from two other accounts of Hyde's that were included in his

7 Garret FitzGerald, 'Estimates for baronies of minimum level of Irish-speaking amongst successive decennial cohorts: 1771–1781 to 1861–1871', *Proceedings of the Royal Irish Academy*, 84,
C, no. 3 (Dublin: RIA, 1984), pp 117–55, at pp 127, 151.   8 Douglas Hyde, *Language, lore and
lyrics*, ed. Breandán Ó Conaire (Dublin: Irish Academic Press, 1986), pp 160–1.

groundbreaking survey and study, *A Literary History of Ireland*, first published in 1899:

> A friend of mine travelling in the County Clare sent me three Irish MSS. the other day, which he found the children tearing to pieces on the floor. One of these, about one hundred years old, contained a saga called the 'Love of Dubhlacha for Mongan', which M. d'Arbois de Jubainville had searched the libraries of Europe for in vain.'[9]
>
> These things are happening every day. A man living at the very doors of the Chief Commissioner of National Education writes to me thus: 'I could read many of irish Fenian tales and poems, that was in my father's manuscripts, he had a large collection of them. I was often sorry for letting them go to loss, but I could not copy the ⅟₂₀th of them … The writing got defaced, the books got damp and torn while I was away, I burned lots of them twice that I came to this country … I was learning to write the old irish at that time; I could read a fair share of it and write a little.'[10]

SPIL immediately set about providing intermediate school textbooks as well as more basic reading material for learners. By 1880 it had already issued Part I of *Tóruigheacht Dhiarmuda agus Ghráinne*, with Part II appearing the following year, both based on the 1858 edition of the tale, prepared by Standish Hayes O'Grady for the Ossianic Society. As Ó Murchú has observed, this was actually the first-ever school edition of an Irish-language text, and it has occupied a place on the secondary school syllabus ever since.[11] The Society had hoped soon 'to be in a position to publish a journal partly in the Irish tongue, for the cultivation of the language and literature of Ireland, and containing easy Lessons and Reports of the Transactions of the Society'.[12] This aim, however, was actually fulfilled by the establishment of the *Gaelic Journal / Irisleabhar na Gaedhilge* under the auspices of the Gaelic Union, an offshoot of SPIL, in 1882. There had of course been Irish-language sections, so-called Gaelic departments, in various Irish and Irish-American newspapers from the late 1850s. There had even been a succession of short-lived Irish-language journals, including *Bolg an tSolair*, printed at the Northern Star Office, Belfast, in 1795 and Mícheál Ó Lócháin's *An Gaodhal* in Brooklyn, New York, in 1881. However, the *Gaelic Journal* seemed to catch the temper of the times.

If the *Gaelic Journal* made an impact, which was recognized both by contemporaries and in retrospect, it was not until the Gaelic League was making headway that An tAthair Peadar Ua Laoghaire was prompted to embark on *Séadna*. This was immediately hailed as a major creative work. When the first

---

9 Douglas Hyde, *A literary history of Ireland* (London: Ernest Benn, 1967), pp 634–5. **10** Ibid., p. 635. **11** Ó Murchú, *Cumann Buan-Choimeádta*, p. 256. **12** Ibid., p. 326.

instalment of *Séadna* appeared on the pages of *The Gaelic Journal* in November 1894, it was introduced by the acting editor, Eoin Mac Néill, under the heading 'Munster Colloquial Irish': 'We wish to direct the attention of students to the following specimen of Munster Irish, one of the best examples, if not the very best, of Southern popular Gaelic that has ever been printed.'

Séadna first appeared in book form in 1904. Patrick Pearse welcomed it in an extensive review on the pages of *An Claidheamh Soluis*, 24 September 1904:

> But to receive 'Séadna,' whole and complete, into our hands was a new sensation. We read it straight through, commencing it on the top of a city tramcar, continuing it in a train bearing us swiftly westward, and finishing it on the slope of a Connacht mountainside; and when we had read the last line we longed for the presence of our friend of Oireachtas week, for, laying our hand on 'Séadna,' we should have said to him in triumph, 'Here, at last, is literature.'

> The appearance of 'Séadna,' marks an epoch, for with it Ireland has once again become creative … We have here, indeed, the everyday speech and beliefs of the folk, and yet we have something entirely different from the folk-tale. The folk-tale is an evolution; 'Séadna,' like all works of art, is a creation.

> … Before 'Séadna,' was written men thought that the way to produce Irish prose was to slavishly follow Keating: the lesson 'Séadna,' taught was that, in writing, your prime care must be, not to imitate this or that dead or living writer, but first and foremost to utter *yourself* …[13]

An tAthair Peadar explained in his autobiography *Mo Sgéal Féin* that he had noted the lack of any work in book form which could be put into the hands of young learners of Irish to teach them Irish. He had therefore determined to rectify this by writing *Séadna*. He then proceeds to note with evident satisfaction: 'Everyone, young and old, liked the book. It was read to the old folk and they liked it. They heard their own speech coming out of a book to them, something they had never heard before. The young people liked it because the Irish of that book was very like the English they themselves spoke.'[14]

While there was an almost inevitable reaction later against Séadna, a text which dominated the Irish language classroom for some two generations after its first appearance, it has to be acknowledged that the creative possibilities of a human striking a bargain with the devil continues to engage readers in many languages today. In fact, An tAthair Peadar's original work has a layered com-

13 Quoted in Peadar Ua Laoghaire: Liam Mac Mathúna (ed.), *Séadna* (Baile Átha Cliath: Carbad, 1987), pp xxv–xxvi. **14** Peadar Ua Laoghaire, *Mo Sgéal Féin* (Baile Átha Cliath: Brún agus Ó Nualláin, [1915]), p. 215.

plexity which was lost from view for many years, because the structured frame-work in which it was set (the telling of the story by a baby-sitting young teenage girl and the children's fireside discussion of the story as it unfolds) was edited out of the school version, *Scéal Shéadna*. Ironically, this had the effect of reduc-ing the tale to a more straightforward narrative, indeed going a long way towards restoring it to its folklore origins.

Although it still defies easy classification, *Séadna* was welcomed as a folk-novel. Writers in Irish also eagerly cultivated other modern literary genres. The short story in particular proved especially congenial, both Pádraic Ó Conaire and Patrick Pearse himself making lasting contributions. Ó Conaire's novel *Deoraidheacht*, urban and avant-garde, was the very antithesis of Pearse's and Ua Laoghaire's timeless rural settings. An tAthair Peadar's *Mo Sgéal Féin* (1915) is a memoir of the public man. The Gaeltacht autobiography genre, which was to overshadow almost all other creative endeavours, was still some time in the future, Tomás Ó Criomhthains's *An tOileánach*, not appearing until 1929.

The *Gaelic Journal* functioned as the premier forum for Irish-language writ-ing until it was superseded by the newspapers *Fáinne an Lae* and *An Claidheamh Soluis* almost twenty years later. Bernard Doyle set himself clear – and ambitious – aims for *Fáinne an Lae*, which he started to publish in 1898: 'The new journal will be a *bona fide* newspaper intended to supply in Irish a summary of news, and miscellaneous interesting matter as weekly reading for the ordinary house-hold. In fulfilling this purpose it will attain the great end of creating an Irish-reading public.'[15] However, the journal was not a commercial success and within three years had been amalgamated with a new Gaelic League newspaper, *An Claidheamh Soluis*. Functional written Irish was to experience a slow growth. Indeed, as Nic Pháidín observes, no Irish-language newspaper has yet succeed-ed in creating as big a market as Doyle had hoped for in 1898.[16] But the very fact that Irish was being written, could be written, was vested with symbolic significance, and soon became a powerful weapon in the language movement's crusade to gaelicize the administrative environment of urban areas.

Early in its existence the Gaelic League launched a popular initiative to raise public awareness about Irish-language place-names, while simultaneously har-nessing this awareness into pressure on the postal and local authorities to facil-itate their active use.

Candidates were lobbied in advance of the 1900 election to Dublin Corporation, and a majority of those subsequently elected had agreed to the inclusion of Irish on street nameplates. The Paving Committee initially drew attention to the great cost which would be involved by 'erecting bi-lingual street-name-plates at 8/- each – the ascertained price – in the different streets of the city, including those within the added area, will amount to a sum of £3,400, for

15 Nic Pháidín, *Fáinne an Lae*, p. 52. 16 Ibid., pp 83–4.

which of course, there is no provision in our finances'. The minutes of a subsequent Municipal Council meeting record that their report was adopted by way of amendment: 'That the report be adopted, and that in cases where street plates are renewed or new ones put up they shall be lettered bi-lingually.'[17]

And so, Dublin Corporation came to adopt a policy of bilingual street nameplates early in 1901. However, the implementation of this new policy cannot have been particularly swift, for we find Alderman Cole serving notice of the following motion in 1904:

> That this Council, desiring to meet the widely-expressed wishes of so many thousands of the citizens to have the streets of the entire city named in the Irish as well as in the English Language, direct that estimates be advertised for showing at what cost, and in what Irish material the names of the streets throughout the city could be affixed to the Electric Lamp Poles, and that a Special Sub-Committee of this Council be appointed to draw up a list of names in Irish to be so placed – the present names of the streets in English to remain as they are.[18]

This motion was ruled out of order, because the Council had already considered this matter and decided that when any new nameplates were being affixed they should be bilingual. We may note again how the process of bilingualization was couched in Cole's motion in such a way as not to challenge the existing names, the vast majority of which were of English-language origin.

By 1903, written Irish and the question of its status was increasingly finding its way into the public domain. There was continuous feuding between the League and the Post Office and railway companies over delays in the delivery of parcels and letters addressed in Irish. It was reported that a letter sent from Dublin to Béal Átha an Ghaorthaidh spent eight days touring Co. Cork before it was delivered.[19] Matters came to a head in 1904:

> In the Post Office two postmen were employed in Dublin to translate into English the names and places on the 4,000 Irish-addressed letters which they handled each week.

> In January, 1904, the Post Office printed a new rule: *'The address of a parcel must be clearly written in English characters in ordinary use in the United Kingdom. A parcel bearing an address otherwise written will not be accepted unless a translation of the address can be made.'* The rule was not put into operation until An

---

17 See Liam Mac Mathúna, 'Sráidainmneacha Bhaile Átha Cliath', in Breandán S. Mac Aodha (ed.), *Sráidainmneacha na hÉireann* (Baile Átha Cliath: An Gúm, 1998), pp 205–40, at p. 225. **18** Mac Mathúna, 'Sráidainmneacha Bhaile Átha Cliath', p. 226. **19** Pádraig Ó Fearaíl, *The story of Conradh na Gaeilge* (Baile Átha Cliath & Corcaigh: Clódhanna, 1975), p. 22.

Conradh sent several hundred parcels of *Seachtain na Gaeilge* literature to the G.P.O. to be posted. The parcels were refused. Three days later the parcels were brought back – by 150 members of Conradh na Gaeilge. Business in the parcel office was brought to a standstill, as officials argued with the members. Eventually all the parcels were posted in the letter box.[20]

An essential facilitating element in the gaelicizing of postal addresses was the publication of the two-volume bilingual gazetteer of Seosamh Laoide or J.H. Lloyd, the first volume of which (English-Irish) appeared in 1905: *Post-Sheanchas i n-a bhfuil Cúigí, Dúithchí, Conntaethe, Bailte Puist na hÉireann. Cuid I. Sacsbhéarla-Gaedhilg*, the second volume (Irish-English), *Cuid II. Gaedhilg-Sacsbhéarla*, followed in 1911.[21]

An Claidheamh Soluis had been publishing the Irish forms of anglicized surnames since 1900, while summonses by the Royal Irish Constabulary of people for having 'illegible' names on their carts were becoming more frequent. Ruth Dudley Edwards sets the scene for Pearse's one and only court case, effectively contrasting the diplomatic bent of Hyde with the younger man's desire for action: 'It was legally necessary for a cart-owner to put his name on his cart, and with the spread of the League's ideas on the use of Irish forms where possible, individual cart-owners began painting their Irish names in Irish characters. There were one or two prosecutions on this account, with small fines resulting.'[22] Hyde had 'wanted the placing of the Irish forms on carts to become so common that it could not be interfered with, and the government was not interfering'. However, Pearse appealed to the higher courts in the case brought against Niall Mac Giolla Brighde (Neil McBride) in 1905, and lost: 'Thus it was made illegal not only to have the name in Irish letters but to have it in any form except the correct English form.'[23] Pearse's own account of what transpired has quite a heroic ring to it:

> On Tuesday last the language movement marched boldly into the King's Bench Division of the High Court of Justice in Ireland, and for five hours counsel discussed with the Lord Chief Justice, Mr Justice Andrews, and Mr Justice Gibson, various questions ranging from the origin of the Irish alphabet to the position of the Pan-Celts with regard to the Irish language.
>
> We are only carrying out the spirit of the resolution of the Ard-Fheis when we advise all Gaels to simply ignore the British Law that makes it penal for them to use their own language to the exclusion of English. If they are summoned and fined, let them refuse to pay; if they are sent to prison, let them go to prison. The question can be brought to a head no other way.[24]

20 Ibid., p. 26. 21 Both volumes were published by Conradh na Gaedhilge, Baile Átha Cliath. 22 Ruth Dudley Edwards, *Patrick Pearse: the triumph of failure* (London: Victor Gollancz, 1977), p. 79. 23 Ibid., pp 79–80. 24 Ibid., pp 80, 81.

Mac Giolla Brighde lived in an Irish-speaking area and had been fined for having the Irish form of his name on his cart, the judge deciding that the Irish language had no standing in law. The Coiste Gnótha said that the court had, in effect, called Irish a foreign language. In another case, in an English-speaking district, Tomás Mac Seoin, was sentenced to a week's hard labour when he refused to pay a fine of one shilling on being summoned for having his name in Irish on his cart.[25]

A macaronic ballad-style song was composed celebrating one such encounter between a representative of the state, a policeman by the name of Thingyme, and the humble owner of an ass and cart. It tells how Mícheál an gabha, was accosted as he made his way across a bridge in Muileann na hAbhann:

> Ba ghairid go bhfaca mé asal a's trucail bheag,
> Chugainn ar a shodar faoi Mhícheál an gabha
> Siúd leis an Bobby 'This cart has no signature
> Only a lingo I cannot make out.'

> 'Your name my good man, and answer[ed] right quickly now.'
> 'Amharc ar an trucail an bhfuileann tú dall?
> Tá m'ainmse breacaithe i dteanga a thuigimse,
> Agus fógraím thusa go hIfreann lom.'

> 'Ten shillings with costs or a fortnight's imprisonment.
> Next on the list. Take this reprobate down.'
> 'Cuirtear faoi ghlasa mé feasta a ghlagaire,
> Pingin de m' sheilbh ní fheicfidh sibh ann.'

> [It wasn't long till I saw a donkey and a little cart,
> Coming towards us at a trot with Mícheál the smith
> Out steps the Bobby: 'This cart has no signature
> Only a lingo I cannot make out.'

> 'Your name my good man, and answer[ed] right quickly now.'
> 'Look at the cart, are you blind,
> My name is written out in a language I understand,
> And I damn you to the bareness of Hell.'

> 'Ten shillings with costs or a fortnight's imprisonment.
> Next on the list. Take this reprobate down.'
> 'Let me be locked up now you prattler,
> Not a penny of my money will you see there.'][26]

25 Ó Fearaíl, *The story of Conradh na Gaeilge*, p. 29. 26 Cumann an Ógra, An Ard-Scoil, Béal Feirste, *Abair Amhrán* (Béal Feirste: Comhaltas Uladh, 1989), pp 32–3.

The language movement was therefore engaged in a broad campaign, not only to reverse the shift in vernacular from Irish to English, but to confront the legal and administrative underpinning that had set the scene for that language change. Central to the project was the change from an invisible, private, apologetic role for Irish to a highly visible, public manifestation of a cultural revival, proclaimed from the sides of carts, from the names of train stations, from street name plates and from the addresses on letters and packages. This was undoubtedly an ideological stance, reacting against the reverses of several centuries.

The issuing of *Séadna* in book form came at a time when publishing by the Gaelic League in and about Irish was reaching new heights, under the general editorship of Seosamh Laoide. Hyde states that 'the work of producing publications was proceeding at such a rate that we had to put a particular editor in charge of them, who would read them and correct the text. We chose Laoide (J.H. Lloyd) for that. He had been editor of the *Gaelic Journal* until then.'[27]

Seosamh Laoide took up his new appointment on 1 January 1903. Throughout his time as the League's Publications Editor he seems to have been indefatigable. For instance, the year 1903 saw 37 volumes published, 31 followed in 1904 and 35 in 1905.

Irish may have had textbooks, produced under the auspices of SPIL and the Gaelic League, it may have had an embryonic modern literature, but it did not have a numerous, literate, book-reading public. Most of the learners inevitably would never progress beyond the less demanding works. More insidiously, the lack of a reading tradition in the Gaeltacht stunted the growth of a literature in Irish, which needed informed readers as well as competent writers.

The 1915 Ard-Fheis of the Gaelic League, held in Dundalk, is well-known for the clash about the constitutional change committing the organization to the ideal of 'a free Irish nation', led to Hyde's resignation from the presidency, but there were other tensions too. Due to lack of funds, the publishing enterprise had to be brought to a halt, effectively rendering Seosamh Laoide redundant. He was then fifty years of age. A bitter correspondence between Laoide and the Coiste Gnótha or Executive Committee ensued, when steps were taken to wind up the publishing activities and dispense with Laoide, because of the lack of sales. A trenchant letter which he sent, contained the following enumeration of the work he had accomplished:

Books written by myself from beginning to end	31
Books for which I provided vocabularies and references	36
Books which I read and edited	73
Original scripts of my own	68
Scripts to further learning	120

27 Dubhghlas de hÍde, *Mise agus an Connradh* (Baile Átha Cliath: Oifig Dhíolta Foillseacháin Rialtais, 1937), p. 102.

This gave a grand total of 328 publications, a very considerable achievement for the 13-year period 1903–15.[28]

Endorsing Durkacz's view that 'the alienation of language from literacy' was a critical factor in the decline of Irish, Gaelic and Welsh, Mary Daly sees this as part of a pervasive process, extending over several centuries:

> From the sixteenth century the Irish language was progressively exclud-ed from the worlds of commerce, politics, official religion, the professions and printed word as a result of complex socio-economic and political circumstances, and although Gaelic literature survived in oral and man-uscript form, the overwhelming majority of Gaelic speakers remained illiterate.[29]

Cullen grapples with the same problem for the period 1700–1850:

> The answers to the question as to why a living language with such an immense written culture … did not spawn printing lie along two lines. First, printing could only have succeeded in an urban context. However the towns represented the most anglicised aspect of Ireland … Secondly, printing … would have had to be sponsored actively in the seventeenth century, when modern means of communication and the penetration of law and legal forms to the masses were still in their early stages. Once these citadels were captured by a language, given the persuasive advan-tages not only of the written but of the printed word, the cause was lost.[30]

Pearse and others wished to proclaim Irish on the side of carts, as part of a grander design. Hyde initially wished to make the Irish present a rational con-tinuation of its past; soon he and others were striving to make the present and the future a continuation of a cultural past which should have been.

They marshalled a mass movement, lobbied the local authorities. They ensured that the reading and writing of Irish was central to its position in the schools, and a prerequisite for entry to the new National University and to a range of local authority employments. They created a literary milieu in which the language flourished. With regard to creative literature, Máirtín Ó Cadhain was of the view that writing in Irish was the clearest result of the work of the

---

28 See Liam Mac Mathúna, 'Seosamh Laoide, Eagarthóir', *Studia Hibernica*, 31 (2000–1), pp 87–103. **29** Mary E. Daly, 'Literacy and language change in the late nineteenth and early twentieth centuries', in Mary Daly and David Dickson (eds), *The origins of popular literacy in Ireland: language change and educational development, 1700–1920* (Dublin: Department of Modern History, Trinity College Dublin and Department of Modern Irish History, University College Dublin, 1990), pp 153–66, at p. 153. **30** L.M. Cullen, 'Patrons, teachers and literacy in Irish: 1700–1850', in Daly and Dickson (eds), *Origins of popular literacy*, pp 15–44, at pp 39–40.

Gaelic League on behalf of Irish. The printing presses that had been denied the language were now employed with zeal, making up for lost time and the neglect of centuries.[31]

Irish had achieved a symbolic public presence as well on Dublin street-name plates. However in 1915, the challenges remained daunting, especially that of making written Irish a meaningful, everyday language in the adult world of administration and commerce. To encourage the Irish-language communities to become active literates in their native language was still difficult, as witnessed by the on-off engagement with Irish as a creative medium even a generation later of one such as Liam O'Flaherty.

By 1915, the Gaelic League alone had issued some 300 books and publications in and about Irish. The works in Irish available to the public covered the full spectrum of modern literate life – primers, textbooks, dictionaries, poetry, novels, short stories, plays, journals, polemic. The constraints now were not those of official hostility, but rather the indifference of the market place. The invisibility of Irish had been replaced by a very public presence on letters, on parcels, on carts, on street nameplates. Indeed, the written medium largely was the message.

This essay has been concerned with investigating the balance aimed at and achieved between various types of literacy in Irish – the fostering of learner competence, the ambition to create a modern literature, to create a modern journalism, the use of written Irish as symbol. There are of course other areas of interest. There is, for instance, the question of the relationship with English, a relationship that encompassed code-mixing and macaronic composition, topics, which I have been examining elsewhere,[32] as well as the issue of the impact of English orthography on the native tradition. But more fundamentally, there are some underlying assumptions, which would merit discussion and challenge. For example, was the attempt to ape the development of literacy and literature in the major Western European languages the only path available to Irish? The whole oral-written dynamic in Irish should be opened up again to debate. There can be no gainsaying the vibrancy of the oral tradition in Irish in the nineteenth and preceding centuries. This contrasted with the neighbouring societies that had experienced the cultural upheaval, brought about by industrial revolution of the eighteenth and nineteenth centuries. A quotation from Canon Ulick Burke in his Academy essay of 1874 will show the complexity of the strands being woven together:

> [The] tales and traditions which are recited at the fireside by the peasants
> in the country villages are of two classes – Namely those which have

31 Máirtín Ó Cadhain, 'Conradh na Gaeilge agus an Litríocht', in Seán Ó Tuama (ed.), *The Gaelic League idea* (Cork and Dublin: Mercier Press, 1972), pp 52–62, at p. 57. **32** Liam Mac Mathúna, 'Irish shakes its head?: Code-mixing as a textual response to the rise of English as a societal language in Ireland', in Hildegard L.C. Tristram (ed.), *Proceedings of Celtic Englishes III, held in Potsdam, September 2001* (forthcoming).

been published by the Gaelic Society and by the Ossianic Society; – and secondly those not yet published:– Of this latter class – there are two sorts – those which have a literary status in Manuscript; and those which are still floating on the winds of mere oral tradition, and which yet have not been as far as the writer is aware committed to writing.[33]

Here, we have evidence for a three-fold interaction between print, manuscript, and oral transmission of texts. It was the interplay of these three strands that had set traditional Irish culture apart from the experience of the mainstream Western European languages. The period from 1875 to 1915 had seen writing in Irish thrust headlong into the modern world.

---

[33] Quoted in Meidhbhín Ní Úrdail, 'Oralisierung: Der Fall der Handschrift RIA 12 Q 13', in Hildegard L.C. Tristram (ed.), *(Re)Oralisierung* (Tubingen: Gunter Narr, 1996), pp 263–82, at p. 279.

American influence on the Gaelic League: inspiration or control?

ÚNA NÍ BHROIMÉIL

American support for Irish causes was common in the latter half of the nineteenth century. Leading Irish figures including Parnell, Davitt, W.B. Yeats, Pearse and de Valera, made the voyage across the Atlantic to convince the American Irish of the worthiness of their respective causes. The Gaelic League was no exception. It too pursued American support for its ideals and campaigns at home. When Douglas Hyde, the founder of the Gaelic League, visited the New York Gaelic societies in Manhattan, Long Island and the Bowery on his way home from a year's teaching in Canada in 1891, he acknowledged the example and the inspiration that the Irish Americans were giving to those at home.[1] And when finally the Gaelic League was founded in 1893 in Dublin, eyes turned very quickly towards America – Tír na nDollar – for financial support. Indeed, the money collected in America was essentially the lifeblood of the League in the early years of the twentieth century. As the paymasters of the movement it is pertinent therefore to ask if the Americans in fact exerted any control over the home organization.

Although one would imagine that the logical place for the beginning of a Gaelic revival was in Ireland itself, the Irish in America actually had a head start on the movement at home. Scholarly interest in the Irish language and literature in Ireland in the 1870s manifested itself through societies, such as the Society for the Preservation of the Irish Language (1876), The Gaelic Union (1879) and in the publication of the *Gaelic Journal* (1882); however, it was not until the foundation of the Gaelic League in 1893 that a practical program of de-anglicization was put into effect. Yet, long before the foundation of the Gaelic League in Ireland, Gaelic societies had appeared in the United States. As early as 1872–3 letters began to appear in the *Irish World* professing love for the 'fast dying language of our sires ... the only landmark left to distinguish our race from our cruel calumniators and oppressors'.[2] The first Irish class was founded by Michael J. Logan in Brooklyn in 1872, and the first society in the United States, the Philo Celtic Society of Boston, was founded in April 1873, 'to give free instruction in the Irish language to such of the children of the Clan-na-Gael as desire to take advantage of and be benefited by the opportunity.'[3] Many newspapers, includ-

---

1 Janet Egleston Dunleavy and Gareth W. Dunleavy, *Douglas Hyde – a maker of modern Ireland* (University of California Press: Berkeley and Los Angeles, 1991), pp 166–7. **2** Letter from 'Leix', *Irish World*, 26 Oct. 1872. **3** Ibid., 15 Nov. 1873.

ing the *Irish World*, the *Irish American*, the *Boston Pilot* and the *Boston Globe*, devoted space to reading material in Irish in their papers. The first edition of *An Gaodhal*, a monthly, bilingual journal was published by Logan in October 1881 as he argued that 'the preservation and cultivation of the Irish language was indispensable to the social status of the Irish people and their descendants and therefore of vital importance to Americans of Irish descent'.[4] By 1884, it was claimed in the *Irish World* that there were over fifty 'Irish' schools devoted to the study of the Irish tongue in the United States.[5]

In some ways this inclination towards the preservation of language in America is not surprising. Although one of the primary reasons for language shift in Ireland from Irish to English was emigration, there was a substantial body of Irish speakers in America.[6] Vaughan and Fitzpatrick estimate that 27.1 per cent of total Irish emigrants in the period 1851–5 and 24.4 per cent of total Irish emigrants in the period 1891–1900 were Irish speaking. Between 1856 and 1910, 49.3 per cent of all Irish emigrants to the United States came from those counties where the speaking of the Irish language was strongest.[7] And these Irish speakers in America tended to be concentrated in urban areas. Stiofán Ó hAnnracháin estimates that there were 40,000 in Philadelphia, 30,000 in Chicago and 20,000 in Yonkers at the close of the nineteenth century. David Doyle looks at New York and Boston where there were 70,000 and 30,000 Irish speakers respectively. Kenneth Nilsen and Seán de Fréine have documented the extensive use of Irish in Portland, Maine, at the beginning of the twentieth century.[8] But although these may have been Irish speakers they were also well versed in English. By 1910, 95 per cent of Irish immigrants claimed literacy in the English language.[9] If, therefore, the numbers show that there was little reason to support a language which had no place in the new world, the urge to preserve Irish in the English speaking United States must have been motivated by other considerations.

In the post-civil war United States, the Irish were still on a tentative footing as Catholic immigrants in a Protestant land. While Irish nationalism appeared to unite the Irish as a group, political nationalism was not its only manifestation. Irish music, history and language were held up as proof that the Irish were entitled to respect and status. Journalists reminded immigrants of the 'greatness' of

---

4 *An Gaodhal*, Dec. 1881. **5** *Irish World*, 12 Apr. 1884; 17 May 1884. **6** The 1851 census recorded one and a half million native Irish speakers; the 1891 census 700,000. Noel Mc Gonagle, 'Writing in Gaelic since 1800' in Thomas Bartlett et al. (eds), *Irish studies: a general introduction* (Gill and Macmillan: Dublin 1988), p. 108. **7** Counties which had at least 10 per cent Irish speaking population in 1891. W.E. Vaughan and A.J. Fitzpatrick, (eds), *Irish historical statistics: population, 1821–1971* (Royal Irish Academy: Dublin 1978), pp 261–353. **8** *Irish World*, 4 Mar. 1899, 29 Oct. 1898, 13 May 1899, quoted in Stiofán Ó hAnnracháin (ed.), *Go Meirceá Siar: Na Gaeil agus Meirceá:cnuasach Aistí* (Dublin, 1979), p. 10; Seán De Fréine, *The great silence* (Mercier Press: Dublin, 1965), pp 126–7; K.E. Nilsen, 'Thinking of Monday: The Irish speakers of Portland, Maine' *Éire-Ireland* 25:1, (1991), pp 6–19. **9** Chris Curtin, Riana O'Dwyer and Gearóid Ó Tuathaigh, 'Emigration and exile', in Thomas Bartlett et al., *Irish studies*, p. 68.

the old country and reiterated the idea that 'the Irish constituted a distinct and superior race complete with admirable traits and worthy characteristics'.[10] In 1884, the *Irish World* in an article about a musical performed in New York, *An Bard agus an Fó*, linked language and music with the self-respect of the Irish and their rights to nationhood: 'The more our language and music are understood the more claim can we lay on the educated mind to advance every struggle made for Ireland.'[11] Michael J. Logan reiterated this again and again in the pages of *An Gaodhal*. He urged his readers to support the Irish language so that they could be proud of their heritage and their race. This pride, he believed would contribute to an increase in their status and prestige as society recognized the Irish people in the United States as belonging to a nation with an ancient and glorious culture of its own. And while J.A. Fishman suggests that language was more likely to be a source of embarrassment and an obstacle to becoming true Americans, he does stress that language loyalty and language maintenance became aspects of consciousness for many immigrants as they became aware of their 'groupness'.[12] Therefore, in the Irish quest for assimilation to the host country a badge of ethnicity that indicated an ancient and glorious past rather than a demeaned and debased one could prove invaluable.

The American Irish in the years before the foundation of the Gaelic League were regarded as an inspiration to the Irish. They showed how societies could be founded for the revival of the language. They attended lectures on the revival and sent the proceeds to the Society for the Preservation of the Irish Language in Dublin. They bought the books. They offered prizes to Irish children for proficiency in the language. But there were no real links between them and 'home'. It was not until the foundation of the Gaelic League in 1893 that more formal links began to be established between the two movements.

And from the beginning the essence of this more formal link was money. What the Gaelic League in Ireland primarily wanted from the American societies was not inspiration but support in the form of financial assistance. With the foundation of the Gaelic League in Ireland the Gaelic societies in the United States became, in Irish eyes, useful tools for the promotion of the message of language revival in Ireland and a means of collecting money for that same revival. When the Gaelic League of America was founded in 1898 with headquarters at Madison Avenue in New York, it appeared that both Gaelic movements were as one in their ideals and objectives.[13]

And yet the Gaelic societies were slow to give money to the home organization. This was partly because their own numbers were small and they were not

10 J.P. Rodechko, *Patrick Ford and his search for America: a case study of Irish-American journalism, 1870–1913* (Arno Press: New York 1976). **11** *Irish World*, 29 Nov. 1884. **12** J.A. Fishman, *Language loyalty in the United States* (Arno Press: The Hague, 1966), p. 171. **13** Michael Funchion (ed.), *Irish American voluntary organizations* (Greenwood: Westport, Conn.), p. 132; *An Gaodhal*, Nov. 1898.

patronized by the wealthy. Their energies were focused on attending to their own members with picnics and balls and classes. A fund was set up by the *Irish World* in 1899 and by the Gaelic League of the state of New York in 1903 through the columns of the *Gaelic American* but by 1904, only $1,000 had been subscribed.[14] The Ancient Order of Hibernians had voted $2,000 to the Gaelic League in July 1902 'to be expended in Irish speaking districts' but the money was slow in arriving.[15] And Americans appeared confused as to what the Gaelic League was really about. Fr Peter Yorke, an Irish priest and nationalist in San Francisco, stressed the need for information on the aims and objectives of the League:

> The Gaelic League is not a mere literary movement, to be conducted in a lady-like manner by the speaking of pieces and the consumption of ice cream. It is not a mere language movement for the edification of scholars and the delectation of cranks. The Gaelic League is the national movement ... the Irish at home and abroad must know what they are aiming at and must see clear.[16]

It was in this context that the Gaelic League in Ireland decided to send three missions to the United States in 1906, 1910 and 1915. The first of these missions is probably the best known because Douglas Hyde was the main protagonist. Not only was he feted and well received in the States but he also collected $50,000 (£10,000) with the help of John Quinn, an Irish American lawyer and patron of the arts who lived in New York. It is on this mission that we see some effort of the Americans at control. Hyde made an agreement with the American collection committee that no more than £2,000 of this money would be spent by the Gaelic League in any one year. This meant essentially that although the amount of money collected was significant and badly needed that it was not going to be the saviour of the language movement at home and that more funds would soon be needed. Indeed as early as 1907, Hyde was again issuing appeals for money to the United States referring to the expenses of the League as being close on £700 a month This money was being spent on organizers and traveling teachers, twelve paid officers, maintaining its premises, publishing a weekly and monthly newspaper as well as books and pamphlets.[17] The Butte, Montana branch of the Gaelic League was even clearer about the way it wanted the money that it contributed spent: it promised to send as much money to Ireland each year as would keep one organizer in the field – an annual sum of £120.[18] However, while the spending of the money was circumscribed to some extent, most Leaguers felt that the cushion of the American money was enough to give

14 *Gaelic American*, 30 Apr. 1904. **15** *An Claidheamh Soluis*, 16 Aug. 1902. **16** *Chicago American*, 1 Sept. 1901, quoted in *An Claidheamh Soluis*, 28 Sept. 1901. **17** *Gaelic American*, 2 Mar. 1907. **18** *Gaelic American*, 16 Apr. 1907, 6 Sept. 1908, *An Claidheamh Soluis*, 15 June 1907, Sept. 1908, 2 Oct. 1909.

it the freedom to begin a campaign in 1908 to make Irish an essential subject for matriculation in the National University of Ireland and this campaign was successful when the university senate voted in favour in June 1910.[19] In this way it could be argued that the control of the American movement over the Irish Gaelic League was negligible but that the financial contributions allowed the League in Ireland to make significant advancements. And this sense of support was felt in America also. Under a front-page headline 'Splendid Victory for Essential Irish' in June 1910, the *Gaelic American* appealed for more funds to aid the Gaelic League to prevent Ireland becoming an English province.[20]

In the two later tours which were not as financially successful for the envoys as Hyde's tour – the 1910–12 mission netted $15,000 (£3,000) in eighteen months – that element of control was more evident. Fionán Mac Coluim was promised '$25,000 a year to be devoted to the payment of teachers and organizers in the old country' and conditions were specifically laid down by Judge Cohalan and Judge Keogh who were the treasurers of the finance committee: 'The condition must be rigidly adhered to viz. that the proceeds of American delegations shall be devoted to the upkeep of a system of traveling teachers of Irish.'[21] Having said that, the control disappeared somewhere over the Atlantic and Mac Coluim himself in his report to the executive committee in Dublin in 1914 not only castigated the committee for not acknowledging contributions but also stated that:

> Over $10,000 has been received from America since the bargain was made. On the basis agreed upon we should be able to point to at least 100 men in the field. In 1907 there were 125, in 1908, 140, in 1910 150. This year according to figures I have received there were only 76 or about one half of the number in 1910. This is unsatisfactory.[22]

And the solution was simple:

> There are thousands of too busy or too lazy well to do, fairly patriotic Irishmen, 'good fellows' who would never study Irish or attend meetings or do any organizing work but who would subscribe if approached provided they feel we can give them some distinction and adequate recognition of their subscriptions, supply them with periodical reports as to what we do with their money and give them some quid pro quo in the line of journals and literature as free gifts.[23]

19 Diarmuid Ó Cobhthaigh, *Douglas Hyde – An Craoibhín Aoibhinn* (Maunsel: Dublin, 1917), p. 92. **20** *Gaelic American*, 14 May 1910, 18 June 1910, 30 July 1910. **21** Fionán Mac Coluim to the Executive Committee of the Gaelic League, 11 February 1914 in Minute Book of the Executive Committee 1912–1917. Ms. 9,770, National Library of Ireland (NLI). **22** Ibid. **23** Ibid.

But this was not done and MacColuim who was on the ground in the United States could see the effect this was having on contributions to the Gaelic League as only $1,703 was collected in 1914. The Americans were exerting control in the most obvious way open to them – through closing their pocketbooks.

The people who were contributing to the Gaelic League were part of the problem. Those who were regularly giving money to the language movement were ordinary workers who were contributing small amounts of cash. Of the $826.50 collected in 1914 in New York, $600 was collected in the form of $5–$25 contributions primarily through a card system inaugurated by Diarmuid Lynch.[24] Collection cards were issued to Irish American societies to be distributed among their members and a person who collected or contributed a minimum of $5 would receive a Gaelic Alliance membership card issued in Dublin and signed by the president of the Gaelic League. While big names like Bourke Cockran and Daniel Cohalan may have fronted the fundraising, these ordinary American Irish did not carry much clout with their small denominations. Even during Hyde's successful mission friction was evident between those who were members of Gaelic societies whom John Quinn scornfully dismissed: 'I mistrust enthusiasm very much on general principles. Most enthusiasts want to belong to "committees" and go to "banquets".'[25] While the Gaelic societies regarded the visit of Hyde as recognition of their efforts over the previous thirty years, Quinn and Hyde focused on courting the wealthy as the money needed to be collected and this caused friction between the societies and the mission. Hyde remarked:

> But the more I see and hear the more convinced I am that it is not through public speeches, no matter how good they may be, or applauding meetings, no matter how loud the applause, that the money will come in; but through personal appeals to men who are well disposed and at the same time, wealthy.[26]

It could therefore be said that the American Irish had no control over the Irish language movement. And yet, the moral support and imprimatur of the American Irish was of great significance for the Gaelic League. When the *Playboy* controversy erupted in America in 1911, many supporters of the League including John Devoy condemned the Gaelic League for appearing to endorse the production because of its links with Lady Gregory and Yeats. The *Gaelic American* carried lengthy protests from various Gaelic societies condemning the play and recorded resignations from the Gaelic society in Washington when Lady Gregory was invited to address the members.[27] Devoy complained about Hyde's inaction on the *Playboy* to Daniel Cohalan:

24 Subscriptions to Gaelic League Fund (United States) 1911; 1912; 1913; 1914, Ms.9,770, NLI.   25 John Quinn to Douglas Hyde, 27 Oct. 1905, Ms.17,299, NLI.   26 Douglas Hyde to 'A Chara' (a Gaelic Leaguer in Ireland), 29 Nov. 1905, Ms.18,253, NLI.   27 *Gaelic American*,

Many things have chilled my enthusiasm for the Gaelic league. The worst is that Yeats has managed to fill every American editor with the ideas that his theatre company is a product of the Gaelic League, had Hyde's endorsement and, by inference, that he approves the *Playboy*. It is repeated almost every day … and we are being lectured as being 'out of touch' with Ireland by people who never knew Ireland. Until he comes out with a denial I will personally do no more for the Gaelic League.[28]

Straightaway, Hyde sent a cable to the United States dissociating the Gaelic League from the Abbey production and Fr Ó Flannagáin, one of the League's envoys, issued his own statement:

Neither Lady Gregory nor W.B. Yeats were [sic] ever elected to the governing body of the League. Neither of them has ever been present at a National Convention of the League. Not one of the authors whose plays are being staged in New York is recognized in Ireland as a prominent Gaelic Leaguer.[29]

The panic that ensued among the Leaguers at home and abroad when it appeared that support, both financial and moral, would be withdrawn from the Gaelic League is telling. They needed the wider context of the Americans to prove to the world that they were not mad and that emigrants, who had no practical, linguistic need of the Irish language, were supportive of the movement. Thus, both Lady Gregory and Yeats, two of the most steadfast friends of the League at home, were rejected in the United States to appease the Americans. This indeed was control but imposed more by the Irish than by the Americans.

The American Gaelic societies were parts of a larger process by which assimilation into American society also involved the embrace of a distinctive ethnic identity, though they rarely acknowledged that this was the case. As societies they were neither organized nor powerful enough to exert control over the home movement. Indeed, in spite of resolutions supporting the aims of the Gaelic League in Ireland their focus was firmly on the United States and on their need for asserting a distinctive and cultured identity there. Equally, the Gaelic League in Ireland formed part of a bigger nationalistic picture, which would become more evident at the 1915 Ard Fheis. The movements meant and constituted different things in both countries.

A great deal of the Gaelic League's energies was focused on the United States at the turn of the century. While the Irish were painfully conscious of the poten-

14 Oct. 1911, 25 Oct. 1911, 25 Nov. 1911. **28** John Devoy to Daniel F. Cohalan, 29 Nov. 1911, quoted in Charles Callan Tansill, *America and the fight for Irish freedom, 1866–1922* (Devin-Adair: New York, 1957). **29** *Gaelic American*, 9 Dec. 1911.

tial that was America whether in the form of cash or moral support, the Gaelic League more often ignored than met the needs of its most consistent supporters there for some form of recognition. This blithe dismissal of the ordinary contributors in the United States lead to receding returns at a time when other, more immediate, political issues diverted attention from the language question. In the few years when substantial contributions flowed to the Gaelic League from the American missions American money provided a shield and a buffer for the League campaigns. Yet, American influence on the direction and objectives of the Gaelic League in Ireland was minimal.

A song to sweeten Ireland's wrong: music education and the Celtic Revival

MARY STAKELUM

> When there was talk amongst the people that the Government was going
> to found schools to teach them under their own rule, he understood
> instantly that treachery and evil were going to be practised against them
> and he advised the people not to touch them at all.[1]

At varying levels and in various guises, three traditions of musical life were reflected in the National system of education from its inception in Ireland in 1831.
Put simply, these were music of the Western art tradition, Anglo-Irish music and
music in the oral Irish tradition.[2] The purpose in this essay is twofold – to explore
the extent to which policy and comment on music in school navigated through
these currents; and to show how the Gaelic League was a reflection of the growing tide in one direction.

   Set up in the early part of the nineteenth century, the National system of
education was established during a period when Britain promoted administrative efficiency, economic growth and the physical and educational welfare of the
Irish population. Within this context, the National system of education's role
was to reform the poor of Ireland by providing a non-denominational education that emphasized numeracy and literacy.[3] It has been argued elsewhere that
the aim of this was to serve the expanding administrative needs of the imperial British state rather than the improvement of the local agrarian economy.[4] The

---

1 Douglas Hyde, *Songs ascribed to Raftery* (Shannon: Irish UP, 1973) p. 21. The introduction of
the national system of education to Ireland was in the hands of the National Board. Membership
of the Board was comprised of commissioners. For an account of the members, see Donald
Akenson, *The Irish education experiment: the national system of education in the nineteenth century*
(London: Routledge and Kegan Paul, 1970), pp 124–7. Davis described those on the Board as
'dry, ungenial men, ignorant of our history, in love with English literature and character, impe-
rialists to the core' in 'Popular education' in Thomas Davis, *Essays and poems with a centenary
memoir 1845–1945* (Dublin: Gill, 1945), p. 79. See also Thomas Durcan, *History of Irish education
from 1800 with special reference to manual instruction* (Bala, North Wales: Dragon, 1972).   2 For a
comment on earlier documentary evidence for music education practices in Ireland, see Fergal
McGrath, *Education in ancient and medieval Ireland* (Dublin: Special Publications, 1979), pp 224–33.
3 For a survey of the background, see Gearoid O Tuathaigh, *Ireland before the Famine, 1798–1848*
(Dublin: Gill and Macmillan, 1990), pp 97–108.   4 See John Hutchinson, *The dynamics of cultural nationalism, The Gaelic League and the creation of the Irish nation state* (London: Allen and
Unwin, 1987), p. 264; and Oliver MacDonagh, 'The economy and society 1830–1845', in W.E.

agency for this educational implementation was the Board of National Education. In the case of music, the Commissioners sent representatives to Battersea College in London to study the method of instruction in use in the English system of education.[5] The Wilhem-Hullah method arose from the adaptation by John Hullah of the 'method of instruction in vocal music invented and applied by M. Wilhem of Paris introduced by the Government into all the schools, of whatever description, in France.'[6]

The importation of the Wilhem-Hullah method unaltered had implications for the flavour of music education in Ireland. Insofar as the method centred on the development of music literacy, music education became equated with a skills-based practice, with an emphasis on vocal music. In supporting the Wilhem-Hullah method, the British Committee of Council on Education would have read the account by Hullah of the effects of singing:

> One of the chief means of diffusing through the people national senti-ments is afforded by songs which … preserve for the peasant the tradi-tions of his country's triumphs, and inspire him with confidence in her greatness and strength … The national legends, frequently embodied in songs are the peasant's chief source of that national feeling which other ranks derive from a more extensive acquaintance with history.[7]

The case for the presence of music in school was strengthened by the view that:

> if vocal music were generally taught in the National schools, the songs learned would supercede those that the humbler classes now generally sing, which are for the most part vicious trash, hawked about by itiner-ant ballad singers: in times of political excitement often seditious and fre-quently obscene and demoralizing.[8]

Traditionally, in Ireland, the hedge school master had contributed to this corpus of ballads, on themes described by Crofton Croker as treasonable, amatory and laudatory,[9] and those songs served a function 'both as an expression of the singers' and listeners' feelings or opinions but also a form of propaganda'.[10]

Vaughan (ed.), *A new history of Ireland, Ireland under the Union*, vol. 1 (Oxford: Clarendon, 1998), pp 232–41. **5** For an account of the Battersea institution, see Bernarr Rainbow, *Music in edu-cational thought and practice, a survey from 800 B.C.* (Aberystwyth: Boethius, 1989), pp 185–97; and, Bernarr Rainbow, *The land without music* (London: Novello, 1967). **6** 'Prefatory Minute of the Committee of Council on Education (i) Singing School for Schoolmasters in Exeter-Hall', in John Hullah, *Wilhem's method of teaching singing, adapted to English use* (London: Parker, 1841), p. i. **7** John Hullah, *Wilhem's method*, p. 4. **8** Stated by Inspector Newell in: *Twentieth Report* of the Commissioners of National Education in Ireland (1853), p. 113. **9** Thomas Crofton Croker, *Researches in the south of Ireland* (London, 1824), p. 329. See also Graves et al. (eds), *Thomas Davis, Selections from his prose and poetry* (Dublin: Talbot, n.d.), pp 209–31. **10** Georges-Denis Zimmermann, *Songs of Irish rebellion. Political street ballads and rebel songs, 1780–1900* (Dublin: Allen

In adapting the method to the English system, Hullah had been careful that:

> the spirit of the method should be preserved but that, while this was effect-
> ed, it should acquire a national character ... and [observed that] this has
> been attempted by the introduction of many of the best specimens of those
> old English melodies which deserve to be restored to popular use.[11]

Because the National system was founded on the desire to ensure literacy, the
oral transmission of songs was overshadowed by the cultivation of songs, which
were notated. This, coupled with the absence in the syllabus of tunes from the
'great heritage in the national music which had every excellence and every variety',[12] resulted in the principles and practices of music education becoming less
reflective of the lives of the people. Music education became more a monument
to the ideals of the reforming state. Furthermore, Hullah outlined the process
by which he combined words and music:

> in order that the restoration of this national music may be facilitated,
> words have been adapted to it, intended to associate it with the customs
> of the people, and with healthy, moral and religious sentiments, which
> may be intelligible and congenial to the minds of the children who are
> to sing them.[13]

When importing this system to Ireland, it is evident that the National Board over-
looked this practice of underlining the national character. While the Hullah manual
contained songs which arguably were suited to the national character of England,
the content and sentiment were less relevant to the Irish setting, as exemplified
by the inclusion in the manual of Hullah's setting of 'The English Child'.[14]

   In addition to prescribing the syllabus, the National Board introduced a training scheme and while this served to improve the standard of teaching, by now
perceived to be 'inferior in point of competency' by the Commissioners,[15] it also

Figgis; repr. Dublin: Four Courts, 2002), p. 12. **11** Ibid. **12** Graves et al. (eds) *Thomas Davis,*
p. 228. **13** Ibid., p. ii. **14** Ibid., pp 33–4. Described in the manual as a song which contained
'no interval greater than a fourth, nor any note shorter than a crotchet,' the value of the melody
as a pedagogical aid clearly outweighed any consideration of the effect the sentiment expressed
in the text might have in the Irish setting. The text is reads: 'I thank the goodness and the
grace/ That on my birth have smiled/ And made me in these Christian days/ A happy English
child./ I was not born as thousands are/ Where God was never known:/ And taught to pray
a useless prayer/ To blocks of wood and stone./ My God, I thank Thee who hast planned/ A
better lot for me/ And place me in this happy land/ Where I may hear of Thee.' **15** As evidenced in the exchange between the Revd Carlile, a Scottish presbyterian minister (resident
commissioner, 3 Mar. 1837) and the lord president. Responding to the question as to the quality and calibre of the teachers in Ireland posed by the lord president as follows: 'What is your
opinion of the teachers in respect of their competency and moral character?', Carlile states: 'I

ensured that the teaching community would become controlled and exclusive. It ensured too that those ballads and songs, which were widely circulated on broadsheets, were discouraged.[16] In the past, the hedge school master occupied a prominent position in the parish. He was next to the landlord and the priest, and his level of knowledge afforded him legitimacy in the community. His popularity ensured his continuance in employment. Under the new centralized system, however, his position was less certain and was contingent upon satisfying the requirements of the Board.[17]

In a framework such as this, knowledge is seen as external to teachers (at least initially) and becomes embodied in textbook and syllabus. Teachers become more readily interchangeable, members of a homogenous community, sharing a common practice bias. In the context of music in the National system, the content from the outset elevated the status of notated music and so defined music as product-led, where the process of music-making was secondary.[18] The teacher may be seen as conduit of an 'alien' culture to a group of people thought ready to assimilate it and appreciate it, namely the pupils. Inspector Keenan recognized that Hullah's manual 'contains tunes that are not of a class which recommends themselves to the ears of Irish children. They are tunes that were prepared entirely for English schools and in the whole book there is not a single Irish air.'[19] It

think upon the whole their moral character is respectable: in point of competency many of them are very inferior. We have had no opportunity yet of training teachers: we have been obliged to take the masters already to be found in the Country, trained or not trained, and they are upon the whole a very inferior class of teachers. This arises I believe, chiefly from their extreme poverty.' *Report from the select committee (of the House of Commons) on foundation schools and education in Ireland*, Part 1. Minutes of Evidence taken before the Committee, p. 19.   **16** See Maura Murphy, 'The ballad singer and the role of the seditious ballad in nineteenth-century Ireland: Dublin Castle's View', *Ulster Folklife*, 25 (1979), pp 79–102.   **17** The system of training began with the establishment of the Board of National Education. After some three months a certificate of competence were issued to those teachers who had mastered the skills necessary to implement the prescribed syllabus. Initially criticized, the initiation process became more elaborately organized as the century progressed. See Dowling, *A history of Ireland: A study in conflicting loyalties*, pp 116–27.   **18** That music literacy was to become the basis for music education was endorsed by the Powis Commission (1868–70) in John Coolahan, *Irish education, history and structure* (Dublin: Institute of Public Administration 1981), pp 24–30. The system whereby the role and practice of the teacher was constrained by national prescription was supported by the Payment by Results scheme, introduced by Robert Lowe in Britain some decades earlier. For a comprehensive account of how it impacted upon education in Ireland, see Durcan, *History of Irish education*, pp 42–3. A revised program was introduced in 1899. It came about from the Belmore Commission. See Coolahan, *Irish education*, p. 34; and Aine Hyland and Kenneth Milne, *Irish educational documents, a selection of extracts from documents relating to the history of Irish education from the earliest times to 1922*, vol. 1 (Dublin: Church of Ireland, 1987), pp 142–8. In the revised program, the status of music literacy was reaffirmed, and the role of vocal music endorsed by the Commissioners who held that it had a 'cheering effect' in schools. See Appendix to Sixty-seventh Report of the Commissioners of National Education in Ireland (1900), p. 76; and Appendix 11 in Durcan, *History of Irish education*, pp 247–9, for 'Programme in singing for the national schools' in 1900.   **19** *Royal*

was felt too, under this policy that the technical aspects of music were accorded more attention than the aesthetic and artistic: 'The introduction of Hullah's system into the country brought into use a series of melodies, constructed with no idea as to melodic excellence but to illustrate the intervals, sharps, flats scales, marks of expression etc. to be met with in music.'[20] Furthermore, the policy of importing songs did nothing to cultivate the relationship between popular and learned cultures. As Zimmermann notes, in the case of the oral tradition, the song becomes 'more than a text and a melody which can be recorded or printed, examined and criticised'.[21] By the end of the century, policy and practice were out of step with each other. While the policy had succeeded in mirroring 'what is prescribed in the programmes of elementary schools throughout the whole civilised world',[22] the practice of music in schools in Ireland was cause for concern. It was practically an unknown art, especially 'in remote areas that were outside the towns',[23] with singing taught 'only in one school in every seven, and this in a country which has some of the best Celtic melodies in the world'.[24]

That the Irish language had suffered a similar fate under the national system was lamented by Hyde. Believing the National Board to be responsible for the decline in the language, he stated:

> This board, evidently activated by a false sense of imperialism, and by an overmasterly desire to centralize and being itself appointed by government chiefly from a class of Irishmen who have been steadily hostile to the natives, and being perfectly ignorant of the language and literature of the Irish from the first with unvarying pertinacity the great aim of utterly exterminating this fine Aryan language.[25]

With the emphasis by the Celtic Revival on regeneration, music in education came to be perceived as a prime source for linking the past with future nationalistic aspirations.[26] In so doing, music both reflected and defined the notion of

---

commission of inquiry, primary education, Ireland, vol. III (1870), p. 88. Patrick Keenan was appointed as resident commissioner in 1871 and was a keen advocate of the system of Payment by Results. **20** Appendix to *Twenty-second report of the commissioners of national education in Ireland* (1855), p. 73. **21** Zimmermann in *Songs of Irish rebellion*, p. 12. **22** Reported by Inspector Goodman in: *Sixty-eighth report of the commissioners of national education in Ireland* (1901), p. 147. **23** *Seventy-first report of the commissioners of national education in Ireland* (1904) p. 4. **24** Graham Balfour, *Educational systems in Great Britain and Ireland* (Oxford: Clarendon, 1898), p. xxix. **25** Douglas Hyde, *A literary history of Ireland from earliest times to the present day* (London: Ernst Benn, new edition 1967, originally published 1899), p. 630. Other critics of the previous system of education included Pearse who held that 'had the education of the country been sane and national for the last hundred years, there would never have been a necessity for the language movement' in 'The Education Question' *An Claidheamh Soluis* 13.8 (1904), p. 6. **26** This point is developed in Marie McCarthy, 'Music education and the quest for cultural identity in Ireland, 1831–1989' (unpublished PhD, 1990), p. 212.

polarization and revival.[27] For its part, the Gaelic League 'was not opposed to the appreciation of the music of the great masters ... but it insists upon our national treasures getting the due attention that would be paid to them were they possessed by any other nation of the world'.[28] There was a perception that music in the oral tradition did not receive the attention it merited, as implied in this contemporary account of two music traditions, side by side in a locality:

> the one performed in a school hall festooned with evergreens and the walls bedecked with tissue paper of various colours ... with a platform ... erected at one end and thereon ... a polished mahogany piano, the other in an obscure smoky hovel, ... with a woman of seventy Nellie Dhubh, sitting on a stool by the little turf fire that is just kindling into flame.[29]

In the same account, the reporter describes that the difference in the repertoire was also considerable:

> In the first, the performance included two songs by Moore, being respectable and arranged for the piano, in English words of course. The remainder of the songs are English sentimental ditties, dreamy love songs with a roaring English sea song in praise of Jack Tar thrown in. The second performer speaks a barbarous patois of broken English, at which her neighbours jeer. But she also speaks Irish, and speaks it well and fluently. And she sings too, or did sing, before her voice became so thin and trebly. She can still give [the reporter] some faint idea of the exquisite old Irish airs that were the common property of the countryside sixty years ago.

He outlines the difficulties facing the collector of songs in the oral tradition:

> She has the songs yet – the words I mean. I have time to write down three of them and I find them exquisite Irish poetry, the most tuneful

27 Harry White draws on the paradigm of cultural polarizition to explain the particular case of the history of music thus; '[f]irstly it identifies the function of music in Ascendancy thought as a dislocated articulation of two cultures: secondly it explains the fundamental preoccupation with music as a resource in the development of Irish political consciousness: thirdly it confronts the advancement of the native musical repertory as a symbol of renascent Irish civilisation' in Harry White, *The keeper's recital: music and cultural history in Ireland, 1770–1970* (Cork UP, 1998), p. 6. **28** Denis Moonan, 'The spirit of the Gaelic League', *Gaelic League pamphlets*, no. 33 (Dublin: Gaelic League, n.d), p. 7. **29** Reported by P.T. Mac G. in 'Derryflat and Derryard', *An Claidheamh Soluis* 3.2 (1900), p. 744. The extent to which this account is distilled in a nationalism both cultural and political can be seen by placing it in the context outlined in D.G. Boyce, *Nineteenth century Ireland: the search for stability* (Dublin: Gill and Macmillan, 1990), pp 154–84.

songs in the world. And yet the elite of the district who patronised the English songs and were satisfied, consider her little better than a barbarian. A few short years and she will pass away and even this feeble reminder of what they have lost shall no longer disturb the generation of the National schools, and the piano and the English songs. Even the Gaelic League, active as its members are, cannot secure all the treasures of this sort of writing, and there are very few to write the music.[30]

The Gaelic League saw the connection between preserving the customs and practices of the locality and the celebration of national character. This concern to stem the tide of loss was shared by Hyde who recognized the urgency of preserving or reviving the status of music, noting that 'if Ireland loses her music she loses what is, after her Gaelic language and literature, her most valuable and most characteristic possession. And she is rapidly losing it.'[31] The difficulty was that access to it was denied to those without Irish. '[A]ll these traditions are so inextricably bound up with the tongue in which they are preserved.'[32] Hyde's hope was that the Gaelic League would bring about:

> … the revival of our Irish music hand in hand with the revival of Irish ideas and Celtic modes of thought so that the people may be brought to love the purity of Siubhail Siubhail or the fun of the Moddereen Ruadh in preference to 'Get your Hair cut' or Over the Garden Wall' or even if it is not asking too much, of 'Ta-ra-ra boom-de-ay'.[33]

In addressing the wealth of songs and stories in every locality, he advocated that 'whoever will take the pains to examine them will find them remarkable for a generosity of sentiment and an absence of vulgarity, which have done much to leave their impress upon the character of our nation'.[34] In effect, he called for a review of the practice of propagating those songs introduced by the National Board which served as a reminder of imported ideals. In a move to bring about the revival of 'our Irish music', the Gaelic League supported a culture of performance, in the form of two festivals, the Feis Ceoil and the Oireachtas [35]

---

30 Ibid. Compare these circumstances with those encountered by Petrie in 'George Petrie as a musician and amongst his friends' in A.P. Graves, *Irish literary and musical studies* (New York: Books for Libraries, 1914) pp 232–3. **31** Douglas Hyde, 'The necessity for de-anglicising Ireland', in Breandán Ó Conaire (ed.), *Language, lore and lyrics* (Dublin: Irish Academic Press) p. 167. **32** Douglas Hyde, 'The unpublished songs of Ireland' in Ó Conaire (ed.), *Language, lore and lyrics*, p. 72. **33** Douglas Hyde, 'The necessity for de-anglicising Ireland', p. 168. **34** For an account of Hyde's definition of songs, see his 'Gaelic folk songs', in Ó Conaire (ed.) *Language, lore and lyrics*, pp 104–21. **35** These festivals were modelled on the Welsh Eisteddfod. See Marie McCarthy, 'Music education', pp 190–1. The Feis Ceoil aimed to promote the study and cultivation of Irish music, to promote the general cultivation of music in Ireland, to hold an annual musical festival or Feis Ceoil and to collect and preserve by publication the

Although both events originated from a fervent commitment to promote Irish music, differences emerged in how they realized their aims. One difference lay in the manner in which the term 'Irish music' was understood and interpreted by each group. For the Feis Ceoil, it referred to 'all music which is characteristically Irish, whether of the remotest antiquity or of today, whether the simplest tune or the elaborate work of the artist, whether Irish from intrinsic peculiarities or from the instrument on which it is meant to be played'.[36] For the Oireachtas, however, it meant 'the old songs sung by the old people in the old way'.[37] When it came to choosing pieces for inclusion in its syllabus, the differences became obvious. In defining its role in two ways, namely 'to preserve and often to restore to its medieval purity our own incomparable old music ... while at the same time fostering a modern school of Irish music',[38] the Feis Ceoil made no distinction between high art and national art. Since there was a dearth of this variety of music available that was of a sufficiently high standard and the notion of having 'our exquisite folk music harmonized and blared out on orchestras'[39] was resisted, the Feis Ceoil Committee took to the practice of setting pieces from abroad. Criticism was levelled at this policy of offering prizes in musical styles 'rather more representative of Florence or the Fatherland than of Ireland'.[40] Edward Martyn defended the policy. He argued that allegiance to the process and the product in music involved attending to the art of making music as well as to the act of preserving it: '[O]ur musicians ... will never be able to compose choral and orchestral music if they are not made familiar with the world's masterworks of unaccompanied choir singing and orchestral symphony. For before people can create an art they must know what art is.'[41] This sentiment was echoed by George O'Neill, who lamented the fact that there were no composers to write music that was both high art and national art. O'Neill asserted that: 'Irish musicians ... are not such fools as to trouble about writing music (Irish music anyhow) for orchestra. Why? Because there are in Ireland no orchestras.'[42] In contending that it was necessary to move away from

---

old airs of Ireland (as stated by the editor in 'The Feis Ceoil', *An Claidheamh Soluis*, 27.4 (1899), p. 166); while the Oireachtas acted as the nucleus around which the language movement with all its phases and developments collected itself and included among its aims the maintenance of their social traditions; the folktale, the folksong, the old traditional style of singing, the fine old dances, the harper, the piper – all those elements which go to make up the cultured social life of Irish speaking Ireland', as noted by the editor in 'The Oireachtas: Work for the Branches', *An Claidheamh Soluis*, 24.2 (1900) p. 792.   **36** George O'Neill, 'The work of the Feis Ceoil Association: A history and an appeal', in *Irish Ecclesiastical Record*, 4th series, 8 (June–Sept. 1900), p. 347.   **37** As noted by the editor in 'The Oireachtas', *An Claidheamh Soluis*, 3.3 (1900), p. 808.   **38** Attributed to Edward Martyn in 'The Feis Ceoil', *An Claidheamh Soluis*, 27.5 (1899) p. 166.   **39** Stated by Edward Martyn in 'The Feis Ceoil', *An Claidheamh Soluis* 4.5 (1901) p. 123.   **40** Edward Martyn, 'The Feis Ceoil', *An Claidheamh Soluis*, 27.5 (1899), p. 166.   **41** Stated by Edward Martyn in 'The Feis Ceoil', *An Claidheamh Soluis* 4.5 (1901), p. 123.   **42** George O'Neill, 'The work of the Feis Ceoil', *An Claidheamh Soluis*, 25.5 (1901), p. 170. For

the existing repertoire and develop the new, he argued that it should be possible to be both a member of Conradh and an inheritor of the art treasures of the human race:

> We should still remain (many of us) musicians, capable of being delighted and elevated by the creations of a Beethoven, a Brahms or a Gounod, and of fifty others, to whose works we find nothing analogous in our own country. Do you tell us we must shut our ears to these? You might just as reasonably insist upon our shutting our eyes to Raphael and Titian, and bid us throw into the fire Homer, Dante and Shakespeare.[43]

The Oireachtas Committee made no such compromise and insisted on the exclusive use of Irish language songs, directing that all set pieces in the singing competitions be Irish language songs. There were few publications of songs in the Irish language, and in an effort to make them available, the committee organized the publication in *An Claidheamh Soluis* of 'Irish songs with music in Tonic Sol-fa notation'.[44] Although it was an effort by the committee to preserve 'the old songs sung by the old people in the old way',[45] their project inevitably became embroiled in the problem and found itself the object of criticism. In those songs published by *An Claidheamh Soluis*, the emphasis was on the language, and words were put to melodies adapted from tunes of old collections. The emphasis on the written word, while lending itself to songs in the Irish language, meant a concomitant lack of attention to other aspects of music. Furthermore, the shortcomings inherent in the practice of committing songs in the oral tradition to notation were known to the Gaelic League: 'We recognise the value of the tonic sol-fa system, and encourage it as a means of popularizing Irish music, but the last thing in the world we desire is to see the tonic sol-fa system, or any other system, interfering with the traditional style of singing common throughout the Irish-speaking parts of Ireland.'[46] Since the traditional style of singing relied for its authenticity on the style and interpretation of the individual singer, subtleties and nuances were not likely to be captured in notated versions, nor were they easily replicated in schools. Cultural national-

---

a more optimistic account, see Aloys Fleischmann, 'Music and society, 1850–1921' in W.E. Vaughan (ed.), *A new history of Ireland*, pp 517–18. **43** Ibid. **44** As reported by the editor in: 'Irish songs and music', *An Claidheamh Soluis*, 30.12 (1899), p. 664. Publication began with 'Banchnuic Eireann O' and 'Is trua gan peata an mhaoir agam', being the songs prescribed respectively for boys' and girls' choral singing at the Leinster Feis. The songs were arranged by Brendan Rogers and presented in tonic sol-fa, characteristic of the Curwen method, as opposed to staff notation introduced in the Hullah manual earlier. Coldrey describes how the Christian Brothers appear to have supported the feiseanna right from their inception in the late 1890s in: Barry Coldrey, *Faith and fatherland: the Christian Brothers and development of Irish nationalism, 1838–1921* (Dublin: Gill and Macmillan, 1988), pp 189–207. **45** See note 37 above. **46** Ibid.

ists who sought to compile Irish music for use in schools balanced their collections between Irish language songs and Anglo-Irish ballads and songs. Examples
include Goodman's 'The Irish Minstrel'[47] and Breathnach's publications.[48] That
this union of written and oral traditions would compromise the music was
expressed by Richard Henebry[49] who believed that the collections of music contain outlines and much would be left to the interpretation by the performer.
Arguing against the practice of 'filling in' the tune from the score, which was
the practice in those collections intended for school use, Henebry stated:

> in a more complicated tune, say a reel, I fear that neither I nor anybody
> else could restore the whole score from the printed skeleton. Because
> neither the exact phrasing, not the minute accentuation, nor the tonali-
> ty on which the original phrasing of the tune was constructed, nor its
> general carriage is there adequately represented.[50]

He was similarly opposed to arrangements of melodies for forces other than those
for which they were originally intended. He believed that 'the loss between a
phonographic reproduction of one of those melodies and, say, a rendering by a
modern violinist or flute player from a skeleton score, such as is used in making
our "collections" of printed music, is so great as to constitute a change in identity'.[51] Classes in singing[52] were subjected to the same disdain. When Henebry commented that 'this habit of English has a physical effect on the speaking organs, and
destroys the full, soft, and mellow Irish voice so necessary for singing',[53] he may
well have been witnessing the effects of the 'common modern teachers in towns
… [where he found that] the colour was completely gone from the voice, and the
power glide and the complicated graces so dear to music'.[54] The interest in promoting the language was such that these considerations went largely unheeded in
the education policy under the newly formed Irish Free State: 'In the administration of Irish education, it is the intention of the new government to work with
all its might for the strengthening of the national fibre by giving the language, history, music and tradition of Ireland their natural place in the life of Irish schools.'[55]

---

47 Peter Goodman, *The Irish minstrel: a collection of songs for use in Irish schools* (Dublin: M.H. Gill
and Son, 1907). It was sanctioned by the Commissioners of National Education in Ireland and
included airs from Petrie, Joyce and Horncastle as well as songs in the Irish language and some
of Moore's melodies. Its exclusive focus on Irish songs and airs may be interpreted as a response
to the demands of cultural nationalists. **48** Most notably: Padruig Breathnach, *Ceol ar Sinsear*
(Dublin: Browne and Nolan, 1913); and Padruig Breathnach, *Songs of the Gaels; a collection of
Anglo-Irish songs and ballads* (Dublin: Browne and Nolan, 1922). Both collections presented the
songs in tonic sol-fa. **49** Henebry was a member of the Irish folk music society and professor
of Irish in University College Cork. **50** Richard Henebry, *A handbook of Irish music* (Cork UP,
1908), p. 49. **51** Ibid. **52** Including those organized by the Gaelic League; see Annie Patterson,
'The interpretation of Irish music', *Journal of the Ivernian Society* (Sept. 1901), pp 31–42. **53**
Richard Henebry, *A handbook of Irish music*, p. 57. **54** Ibid. **55** From 'Minutes of the pro-

O'Neill's plea to 'make the average Irish man a better musician'[56] was not taken up by the new government, which appeared to be more intent on making the Irish man a better nationalist. Eoin MacNeill, a founding member of the Gaelic League, strengthened this resolve when he asserted that 'the chief function of Irish educational policy is to conserve and develop Irish nationality'.[57]

It can reasonably be concluded then, that the music was given priority not for educational or aesthetic reasons but for nationalistic ones. The zeal with which this was embraced by teachers in the schools led to the proposal that in some schools, singing was to be taught solely through the medium of Irish and all songs were to be in the Irish language.[58] Music in school would become the servant of language, be used as a means to progress the Irish language, and lead to the formulation of a motto such as 'to our language through our music'.[59] To an extent, this legacy has survived in Ireland to the present day where the challenge in contemporary practice is towards recognizing the value of vocal music both as an art form of an intrinsically expressive nature and as an act of expressing the extra-musical.[60]

In summary, the template imported from England set in motion the construction of nationhood. It was a template where the child was seen as being inducted into a standardized culture based on the norms and requirements of the political centre. Arguably, this induction would imply a consequential estrangement from the informal languages, from the dialects, beliefs, and customs of his kindred and locality. In short, it would produce an alienation of the young from the traditions of their parents and locality[61] In lamenting this 'anglicisation', and suggesting that we are a nation of imitators, lost to the power of native initiative and alive only to secondhand assimilation,[62] Hyde might well have been describing the very foundation of music education in Ireland where

ceedings of the commissioners of national education at their special meeting on Tuesday, the 31st January, 1922', pp 2–3. Ó Brolchain's statement was typical of the strength of feeling with which the sentiments of the Gaelic League were expressed in the newly formed Irish free state. **56** George O'Neill, 'The work of the Feis Ceoil', p. 170. **57** Eoin MacNeill, 'Irish educational policy – II', *Irish Statesman*, 24.10 (1925), p. 200. **58** As expressed at their conference in 1921 by members of the Irish National Teachers Organisation (INTO) in *National programme conference, national programme of primary instruction* (Dublin: Educational Company of Ireland, 1922), p. 4 . See also T.J. O Connell, *History of the INTO, 1868–1968* (Dublin, privately printed, n.d.) p. 344. **59** Appearing as a caption in *The teachers' work*, 18 (Nov. 1927), p. 119. **60** See Government of Ireland, *Primary school curriculum, music* (Dublin Stationery Office, 1999), pp 5–6. **61** See Elie Kedourie, *Nationalism* (Oxford: Blackwell, 1966), pp 98–105. Also, in emphatically censuring the National Board for 'the painful skill with which they have cut from every work in their schools the recognition of the literature, antiquities and state of Ireland,', Davis held that their policy of developing literacy meant, in the Irish context that 'the materials and books provided, though models of general information and literary finish, are empty of Irish statistics, history and hopes'; see Thomas Davis, *Essays and poems*, pp 79–80. **62** Douglas Hyde, 'The necessity for de-anglicizing Ireland', in Ó Conaire (ed.), *Language, lore and lyrics*, p. 169.

'a French method of music teaching designed for use in a monitorial system was imported via an English adaptation into Ireland'.[63] Practices introduced under the National system of education served to further the ideals of the reforming state and enjoyed an uneasy relationship with the existing practices. This led to a compromise where aspects of an imported system were grafted onto the traditional landscape. The ideals of the Gaelic League regarding revival of music became concerned less with the problem of losing the national treasures than with the manner in which they would be restored. Until the relationship between music and cultural identity is resolved in the field of education, music in Ireland will continue to struggle. The struggle involves both the advancement of artistic and educative aims and the perception of music as an art form that is at once a process and a product.

63 Marie McCarthy, 'Music education', p. 82.

Revivalist archaeology and museum politics during the Irish Revival

ELIZABETH CROOKE

The Irish Revival of 1880s–1920s has been characterized as a time when art met propaganda with the politicization of language, sport, literature, and theatre providing the evidence. Each of these movements drew from an imagination of the Irish past, a past littered with the spirit of heroes and the belief in a glorious past that could provide inspiration for the future. Incorporated into these aspirations was an interest in the archaeology of the Irish landscape and the material remains that it revealed – this provided stimulation for Irish antiquarians, the basis for important collections, and was placed on public view in the Dublin Museum of Science and Art, which opened on Kildare Street in 1890. The history of collecting and exhibition building in Ireland exposes these practices as vehicles for the cultural and political propaganda that dominated Irish nationalism in the nineteenth and early twentieth centuries. This essay is an evaluation of how some of the characteristics associated with the Irish Revival also shaped the archaeological and museum movements in Ireland.

Of the characteristics that the archaeological and museum movements in Ireland shared with the Irish Revival, two will be explored in this essay. Firstly, the way Ireland's past was understood and celebrated and, secondly, the tensions arising from the influence of Britain on Irish culture and institutions. In the case of the former, the idealization of the Irish past that inspired the language and literature movements also stirred people to collect and exhibit archaeology for public benefit. In relation to the second point, it was a matter of distrust in Britain and a belief in its lack of understanding of Irish culture, which sustained the various conflicts regarding the development of the Dublin museum and its collections. Although this essay considers mainly examples of activity during the revival of the 1880s–1920s, they should not be isolated from the pursuits of antiquarian and cultural movements earlier in the century.[1] The later period is, however, particularly relevant; it was when almost a century of interest in the creation of a national museum for Ireland culminated in the Dublin Museum of Science and Art.

The imagining of ancient Ireland during the revival was a product of versions of cultural nationalism and a century of politicization of the past. Since

---

[1] Some of the themes of this essay are put in this wider context in Elizabeth Crooke, *Politics, archaeology and the creation of a national museum in Ireland: an expression of national life* (Dublin: Irish Academic Press, 2000).

the time of O'Connell's meeting on Tara Hill, and the writings of Thomas Davis and the Young Ireland movement, archaeology had been incorporated into the nationalist campaign and was used in the writing of key propagandists. Firmly established in popular writing was a belief in the unique nature of the Irish past, represented in ancient writing, folklore and antiquities. Ireland was represented as having a long established tradition, encapsulated in historical and archaeological sources, and it was the preservation of this heritage that was used as one of the arguments to justify the drive for independence.

Many who were prominent in the late nineteenth-century revival built upon this popular perception of the Irish past and promoted the preservation of archaeology and antiquities as part of the national endeavour. The romantic vision of the past, promoted by revivalist activity, fuelled interest in Ireland's archaeology and a belief that the collection and display of antiquities was an expression of public duty. For cultural nationalism, the material presence of archaeological sites, monuments and objects provided a tangible link with Ireland's golden age. The founder of the Gaelic League, Douglas Hyde, referred to Ireland's folklore as the 'golden legends of far-off centuries',[2] which reconstructed the mind of 'Prehistoric man'.[3] Collecting the ancient folk songs and stories of Ireland was presented as an essential part of recalling Irish nationality, which had long been under threat from external influences. In an address delivered in New York, Hyde declared his interest in 'going here and there throughout the entire island and gathering, here and there, every relic of the past upon which we can lay our hands and gathering them together into one great whole and building and enshrining every one of them in the temple that shall be raised to the godhead of Irish nationhood'.[4] The novelist, George Moore, believed that the 'ancient architecture, whether in palace or cottage is beautiful; all of the coins, weapons and pottery of the ancient world are beautiful'.[5] Historian Alice Stopford Green wrote of the grandeur of Irish archaeology; in her mind, 'no jeweller's work was ever more perfect than the Ardagh Chalice', the 'fame of Tara was in the heart of every Irishman'. To her, these were 'national relics', 'memorials of ancient life', and should be preserved.[6]

Archaeological remains were perceived as tangible links that encapsulated the memories of a glorious past, and this gave them political value. Nationalist and author William O'Brien described archaeological monuments as the homes of the Irish nation and the Irish landscape as an historic entity 'woven inextricably around the Irish heart'. For O'Brien, archaeology inspired patriotism, which he

2 Douglas Hyde, 'The unpublished songs of Ireland' (1885), in Hyde, *Language, lore and lyrics,* ed. B. Ó Conaire (Dublin: Irish Academy Press, 1986), p. 73.   3 Hyde, 'Irish folklore' (1889), in O'Conaire, *Hyde,* p. 3.   4 Hyde, 'The Gaelic Revival' (1905), in O'Conaire, *Hyde,* p. 184. 5 George Moore, 'Literature and the Irish language', in Lady Gregory (ed.), *Ideals of Ireland* (London: At the Unicorn, 1901), p. 50.   6 Alice Stopford Green, *Irish nationality* (London: Williams and Norgate, 1911), pp 12, 17, 143, 239.

defined as 'the weird voice we hear from every graveyard where our fathers are sleeping, for every Irish graveyard contains the bones of uncanonized saints and martyrs' and their ruins were 'the most eloquent schoolmasters, the most stupendous memorials of a history and a race that was destined not to die'. Archaeological monuments were described as 'majestic shrines in which the old race worshipped ... the voice of Ireland's past'.[7] This sense of worshipping the remains of antiquity was a constant theme in such popular writing. In 1881, Standish O'Grady wrote about how the history of Ireland clung to and grew from Irish barrows, so that the history of one generation became the poetry of the next. For O'Grady, the monuments of Ireland were the material representation of Ireland's legends; the legends provided the 'names, pedigrees, achievements and characters' of the 'massive cromlechs and great cairns'. These were the remains of 'prehistoric times and nations'. In his typical style, O'Grady damned the 'scientific' development of archaeological practice that did not adopt his more imaginative approach. He criticized archaeological 'explorers' for destroying the 'noble sepulchral raths' and unearthing our bones and ashes of kings and warriors, 'laid there once by pious hands'. He disapproved of those who hoarded and made fruitless a treasure of 'stone celt and arrow-head, of brazen sword and gold fibula and torque'.[8]

What such writers had in common was a spiritual relationship with archaeology that elevated ancient artefacts and sites to the status of national relics or shrines to be worshipped. This sentiment defined and sustained some of the essential beliefs of Irish nationalism – the golden age waiting to be reborn and the national space of the Irish landscape and its archaeology. This environment symbolized Irish nationality, archaeology had long been established as a national emblem – both monuments, such as the round tower, and portable remains were frequently used to illustrate national life. The membership card of the Repeal Association, for instance, was decorated with a harp against a sunburst with Bronze Age artefacts in the foreground – a sword, horn, or trumpet, axehead and penannular brooch. Later in the century Irish architecture and design reused these motifs, which became representative of the Celtic Revival. The arts and crafts movement took inspiration from the patterns of the ancient past: the Tara Brooch was frequently reproduced; the Book of Kells provided templates for embroidery and lace work; and the gold of Bronze Age Ireland was the stimulus for new work in silver.[9]

Many of these inspirational works of art and artefacts were held in the Royal Irish Academy collection under the care of the antiquarian George Petrie

---

7 William O'Brien, *The Irish national idea* (Cork: Young Ireland Society, 1886), p. 7. **8** 'Celt' is an antiquarian term used in reference to stone or bronze axes, it is no longer in use. L. Flanagan, *A dictionary of Irish archaeology* (Dublin: Gill and Macmillan, 1992), p. 54. **9** See discussion in Jeanne Sheehy, *The rediscovery of Ireland's past: the Celtic Revival, 1830–1930* (London: Thames and Hudson, 1980). See page 28 for an image of the membership card and chapter four for the use of images of archaeology in art and architecture.

(1789–1866), among others. During his time in the Academy, the collection was ordered into the Three-Age system of stone, bronze and iron; a catalogue was produced (the final form was compiled by William Wilde); and a vast collection of gold artefacts, most famously the Tara Brooch, was secured for the nation.[10] Well before the popularization of Irish language and literature stirred the Anglo-Irish later in the century, a sense of national pride and inspired interest in Irish antiquities is evident among the members of the Royal Irish Academy. In 1851, T.R. Robinson, president of the Academy, declared the pursuit of literature and antiquities as the main source of their national influence and in true harmony with their duty to their country.[11] The mathematician and astronomer Sir William Rowan Hamilton claimed the study of antiquities as the 'guardian of the purity of history – the history of nations and mankind'.[12] In 1856, the president of the Royal Irish Academy, the Revd James Todd spoke of the importance of 'our national antiquities' because it 'brings to light the manners and customs of our forefathers; it makes known to us the origin of our noblest institutions ... [and] it connects, as by a golden chain, the present and the past'. Many of those who contributed to the creation of this important collection of Irish archaeology, such as those named above, can be described as cultural rather than political nationalists. Although the language of the antiquarians, in relation to prehistory, may have resembled that of their nationalist political contemporaries, the former did not necessarily agree with the politics of the latter. The antiquarians did, however, have a political or cultural agenda. When the members of the Royal Irish Academy created their museum of Irish antiquities, which they considered as being provided for public and national benefit, they were not only providing a display about the Irish past but were building themselves into that story. They were exhibiting their own aspirations as well as Ireland's history.

These themes of collecting, displaying and building museums as being as much about the self, as about the object, are important in any consideration of the history of museums and is an essential part of the story of the museum on Kildare Street. This museum today still reflects the description of the role of a national museum provided by the one-time director, George Noble Count Plunkett. Plunkett, appointed director in 1907, was already an established political figure and was active in the Royal Irish Academy and Royal Society of Antiquaries of Ireland. His position in the museum came to an end in 1916 because of the involvement of his son, the revolutionary Joseph Plunkett, in the Easter Rising. Count Plunkett's politics no doubt shaped how he understood the purpose of the museum in Dublin. In 1912, speaking to a meeting of the Museums

10 G.F. Mitchell, 'Antiquities', in T. O Raifeartaigh (ed.), *The Royal Irish Academy, a bicentennial history, 1785–1985* (Dublin: The Royal Irish Academy, 1985), pp 93–165. 11 T.R. Robinson, 'Presidential address to the Academy', *Proceedings of the Royal Irish Academy* 5 (1851), p. 109. 12 W.R. Hamilton, 'Presidential address to the Academy', *Proceedings of the Royal Irish Academy* 1 (1838), p. 117.

Association of Britain and Ireland, held that year in Dublin, he declared 'no community, however small and insignificant, considers itself properly provided for unless it has a museum'. For Plunkett, a museum went beyond classifications and systems; rather, a museum was 'part of the national life, it is an expression of the national life and of the higher qualities of the people to whom it belongs. It is something which locally has struck its roots, and we may expect from it such flowers and fruit as belong to the nature of the place.'[13] This statement from Plunkett reveals the belief held by many emerging and new nations that a museum could be used as one of the locations to forge a shared identity and present a view of history endorsed by the new political regime. However, the Dublin Museum, when it was founded in 1877 and opened in 1890, did not reflect 'national life' in the way for which Plunkett and followers of Irish cultural nationalism would have perceived it. A truer description of the early days of the museum is provided by Professor A.B. Meyer, a visiting academic from Dresden, who in 1905 said that the museum 'like the one of the same name in Edinburgh, is copied more or less after the South Kensington Museum' and added that 'this uniformity of the museums in the Island Kingdom corresponds to the uniformity of life there'.[14] What these points recognize is that despite the fact that the Dublin museum emerged from a century of cultural nationalism and that the artefacts it contained provided inspiration for that ideology, the museum's initial form was not true to such thinking. It is the tension over what a national collection and museum should be, at a time when Ireland's cultural identity was being so hotly debated, that provides the subject of the remainder of this essay.

The creation of the Museum of Science and Art was one of the most prominent additions to the cultural landscape of late nineteenth-century Dublin. Passed in 1877, the Museum Act initiated collecting and the appointment of a director. An architectural competition for the museum building was launched in 1881, followed by a second competition in 1883, and the first stone of the building was laid in 1885. In 1890, the doors opened to the new building on Kildare Street. From its foundation until 1899, the Museum was under direct administration of the Department of Science and Art, South Kensington, London. After 1899, the museum became the responsibility of the newly formed Department of Agriculture and Technical Instruction in Dublin. For many, the new institution contravened the ideal of a museum provided for the celebration of Ireland's past and managed by and for the Irish people. The tensions arising from this are evident in various reactions to stages in the Museum's history, most clearly concerning the new museum building, the display of archaeology within it, and the ownership of a collection of antiquities known as the Broighter hoard.

---

13 Count George Noble Plunkett, 'Presidential address delivered at the Museums Association Dublin conference', *Museums Journal* 2:12 (1912), pp 33–9. **14** A.B. Meyer, *Studies of the museums of the United States and Europe* (Washington: Government Printing Office, 1905).

When the officials of the Department of Science and Art became interested in developments in Ireland, their aim was to improve and guide public education throughout the island within a framework defined for both Britain and Ireland. To investigate pre-existing provision, in 1876, a parliamentary commission was established to gather information and make a recommendation for the improvement of science and art instruction. When in Dublin the commissioners met with two proposals: the creation of a national museum of archaeology and the establishment of a 'Royal Irish Institute'. What is essential about these proposals is that both institutions were to be independent of the London Department and have a distinctively Irish character. The proposal to create a national museum of archaeology, supported by public funds, came from the Royal Irish Academy. The Academy had long recognized that it had not the financial means or the physical space to maintain its collection, which had been growing in size and importance. The Academy had, as a result, been looking for an opportunity to create a large-scale public institution worthy of their museum. In 1868, when the idea of a new cultural institution for science and art instruction was mooted at a parliamentary enquiry, the president, the Revd J.H. Todd, proposed the foundation of a separate 'National Museum of Irish Antiquities and Historical Monuments'.[15] On the same occasion, William Wilde referred to the need to establish a 'great national collection of antiquities properly housed, safely guarded, scientifically arranged and displayed in a great Celtic museum', led by the Royal Irish Academy.[16]

The second proposal that was presented to the commissioners came from those involved in the development of Irish industry. This interest was channelled into the proposal for a 'Royal Irish Institute', which would do the equivalent work of the Department of Science and Art in London but as an independent body. Those proposing the new institute visualized the creation of a 'national museum' within or on the site of the 1853 Exhibition Palace that had been built on Merrion Square. The purpose of the institute would be to develop and design technical education among the 'middle and lower classes in Ireland', and it would include a permanent exhibition of Irish art, design and manufactures. It would be an amalgamation of services already provided by the Royal Dublin Society and the Museum of Irish Industry, which had existed in Dublin in various forms since 1852. The significance of this new institute was that it would be independent from the Science and Art Department in South Kensington, which was already leading developments in England, Scotland, and Wales. John Prendergast Vereker, secretary of the proposed new institute, speaking at a parliamentary commission that was put in place to investigate the development of science and

15 Todd, Report from the commission on the Science and Art Department in Ireland 21 (1868–9), p. 337.   16 William Wilde, *Report* from the commission on the Science and Art Department in Ireland 24 (1868–9), p. 461.

art instruction in Ireland, suggested that under no circumstances could a London body adequately direct training in Ireland. His desire was to see a body managed 'completely under the control of Irishmen who have no object dearer to their heart than the promotion of the industry and the manufactures and the progress of their own country'. He argued, 'I don't think Irishmen would have any confidence in an institution that was dependent on South Kensington'.[17] This mistrust was, Vereker added, based on the 'strong feeling [which] still obtains among the people that the ignorant prejudices which formerly induced England to destroy Irish manufacturing industry are still in existence'.[18] Vereker's purpose was 'the founding in Ireland of a great national institute, governed in Ireland, responsible to the Irish government alone'.[19]

The Department's response to these proposals was mixed: it recognized the sentiment of the Irish appeal but would not give way to the more long-term implications of independent provision. With regard to the Academy, they agreed on the importance of the Irish antiquities collection. Sir Henry Cole, director of the Department of Science and Art, even went so far as to suggest that the creation of a new institution in Dublin, which would properly care for this collection, would do justice to Ireland and contribute to the debt England owed to Ireland. This was necessary, Cole claimed, because Ireland is 'the nation towards which we pursued in former times an policy that ought to make us blush'.[20] However, the commissioners concluded that the creation of an entirely independent Department of Science and Art for Ireland 'would be detrimental to the interests of Science and Art in that country'.[21] Instead, they recommended the establishment of 'a General Industrial and Fine Arts Museum in Dublin' so that the people of Ireland 'would then obtain the fullest opportunity of improvement in the cultivation of the Industrial and Decorative Arts by the Study of approved models and objects'.[22] The letter from Lord Sandon, the vice-president of the Science and Art Department, to the Royal Irish Academy declared that 'the time has now arrived when the wants of the community at large have outgrown the useful action of private societies', and so 'a thorough rearrangement and consolidation of existing institutions have become an essential condition precedent for further progress'. The Department's interest was to develop a common museum network or infrastructure administered from London, of which Ireland was to be a part. Lord Sandon announced that, in keeping with the rest of the kingdom, 'their Lordships propose to build … a Science and Art

17 John Prendergast Vereker, *Report* from the commission on the Science and Art Department in Ireland 24 (1868–9), p. 56. Vereker was not alone in this opinion, many others at the same enquiry voiced similar views. **18** Ibid., p. 56. **19** Ibid., p. 73. **20** Henry Cole, *Report* from the commission on the Science and Art Department in Ireland 24 (1868–9), p. 120. Cole here acknowledges that he is quoting Sir Stafford Northcote, cabinet minister. **21** *Report* from the commission on the Science and Art Department in Ireland 24 (1868–9), p. i. **22** Ibid., p. iv.

Museum for Ireland, somewhat similar to that now existing in Edinburgh for Scotland.'

The Department of Science and Art in South Kensington had initiated the merger of the Dublin institutions, although they were aware that the Royal Irish Academy would strenuously oppose the move. By collaborating with the new institution, the members feared that the collections of science, art, and industry would distract from the importance of antiquities. Samuel Ferguson's fear was that this would lead to a derogation of the scholastic and scientific supremacy of the Academy. In their response to the Department of Science and Art in South Kensington, the Academy referred to the proposed transfer as an act of subordination.[23] Their objections were based on a number of factors. In the first place, the Academy was certain of the importance of having a museum that regarded collecting the antiquities of Ireland as one of their main purposes. In previous years, the Academy had made the decision to give Irish antiquities prominence; they had donated their geological collections to the Royal Dublin Society and had taken non-Irish antiquities off display.[24] Repeatedly, successive presidents of the Academy had spoken of the importance of Irish antiquities for national and cultural life within Ireland, and many felt the collection had achieved a prominent place in European archaeology.[25] Lord Sandon's advice, however, was for the Academy to accept the merger: by 'declining to become a branch of the South Kensington Establishment, the Academy would show a selfish inclination to stand in the way of the creation of a great Science and Art Museum in Ireland'.[26] Rather than the creation a new independent institution, Ireland was being further drawn into the imperial model of museum education defined in London.

From the passing of the Museum Act in 1877, the new Science and Art Museum was destined for the cultural core in the Leinster Gardens area composed of the National Gallery, the Natural History Museum and the Royal Dublin Society buildings. The earliest proposal was that the Museum should be located on the Leinster Gardens, but Lord Pembroke objected to the loss of his flowerbeds;[27] henceforth, the new buildings were planned for Kildare Street. When the first architectural competition for the new Museum buildings, launched in 1881, resulted in a shortlist that did not include any Irish architects, past discontent returned. *Hibernia* announced to its readers: 'we regret to announce that the new museum of Science and Art in Dublin is not to be the work of an Irishman'. This was described as 'a serious error detrimental to our interest as Irish men, and an unmerited reflection upon our intellectual status

23 Lady Ferguson, *Sir Samuel Ferguson in the Ireland of his day* (Edinburgh: William Blackwood, 1896), pp 298–9. 24 Recorded in the Minutes of the Antiquities Committee, 1855. 25 The pioneering Danish archaeologist J.J.A. Worsaae visited the collection in 1847 and the British Association for the Advancement of Science visited it in 1857. 26 Sandon, Minutes of the Royal Irish Academy Council, 14 Feb. 1876. 27 Report of Department of Science and Art 37 (1881), p.xxii.

has been committed by the Department of Science and Art under the very cover of doing us service'.[28] The *Irish Builder* added to the debate, declaring that 'we have not much faith in the good intentions of South Kensington officials respecting Ireland or matters Irish'.[29] The newspaper warned that London was bearing a negative influence over the cultural institutions in Ireland. The Royal Dublin Society was accused of surrendering to the 'sister kingdom'; the Royal Irish Academy had been 'swallowed' and 'its splendid collection of antiquities, literary and art treasures were hungered for by the rapacious maw of South Kensington'. The *Irish Builder* promoted the idea that the Irish people should not be answerable to London officials by stating 'we believe in these matters the Irish people are the best judges of their own wants, and should be allowed to exercise their undoubted rights'.[30] The *Irish Builder* was not alone in their objections to the integration of the Academy with this new museum. In the *Gaelic Journal*, William O'Brien condemned the Academy for being 'languid in spirit' and 'surrendering to a South Kensington collection of curiosities, the inestimable relics of Celtic antiquity bequeathed to them by the pious patriotism of generations of Hudsons, Hardimans and Wildes'.[31]

It is evident from both the foundation and history of the Museum that there were a number of competing interests in this new cultural institution. The Department in London wanted to guide, define and control of art and technical instruction in Ireland and draw the Irish sector into the framework being developed across Britain. Those involved in Irish industry wanted to be charge of their own public education. Those committed to the preservation and display of the archaeology of Ireland were principally interested in the development of a national museum in which archaeological collections would take prominence. The tensions between these groups continued even after the museum doors were opened to the public.

Tensions between London and Dublin were also very much evidence in relation to the dispute that arose concerning the ownership of the Broighter hoard. The hoard was found in 1896 during ploughing in Broighter townland, Co. Londonderry. The hoard comprised a tubular gold collar, two bracelets, two necklaces, a gold bowl, and a gold boat complete with oars. Once found, the hoard was sold by the landowner to a dealer. The dealer sold it to the British Museum, which placed the items on display. When the Royal Irish Academy became aware the hoard was in the possession of the British Museum, they appealed for its return by insisting that under treasure trove law the rightful place for the hoard was in their collection and that the British Museum was holding the hoard illegally. In 1897, a bill was brought to parliament to enable its return, but this failed. In 1898, a committee was established by her majesty's treasury to

---

28 *Hibernia* 2 Jan. 1882, p. 108. **29** *Irish Builder* 15 Nov. 1882, p. 326. **30** *Irish Builder* 15 Jan. 1883, p. 17. **31** William O'Brien, *Gaelic Journal* 4:43 (July 1892), p. 164.

investigate the ownership of the hoard. The committee recommended the return of the hoard to Ireland on long-term loan, but again the British Museum refused. Consequently, in June 1903, the crown brought the British Museum to court to investigate whether or not the hoard was treasure trove and, based on that, to establish its legal ownership. When the case came to conclusion, Justice Farwell declared that, 'the articles in question are treasure trove belonging to His Majesty by virtue of the prerogative royal'.[32] This meant that the British Museum was holding the collection illegally and, in 1906, the hoard was returned to Dublin.

The intensity of the debate concerning the hoard reveals the tensions that could easily arise between cultural institutions in Ireland and England. The director of the British Museum, Sir Edward Thompson, argued that the 'ornaments' were very valuable for the British Museum.[33] Indeed, the collection of Irish antiquities was considered relevant to the museum because the museum 'represents the Empire. It is not a London Museum, it is not an English Museum, it is a British Museum.'[34] The idea of the British Museum representing the empire as justification for it keeping the Irish collection was also voiced by C.H. Read, the keeper of British and medieval antiquities and ethnography, and Sir John Robinson, fellow of the Society of Antiquaries in London. Viscount Dillion, the president of the Society, argued that London, as the capital, was the best location for the objects because he considered the people of England, Scotland and Ireland 'as being all members of one nation'. He described the loss of the collection from Ireland as 'not a national calamity ... particularly as, after all, Ireland is part of England'.[35] In Dublin, the *Evening Herald* responded in anger. It described the retention of the collection by an English museum as 'a flagrant violation of one of the few national rights of Ireland that has been allowed to us'.[36] The hoard became representative of the struggles of Ireland with its near neighbour. If the return of the hoard can be considered as granting of a national right, one must consider the paradox inherent in the point that it was returned only because it was declared the legal property of the crown.

The return of the hoard to Ireland in the early twentieth century came at a time when the Dublin Museum was involved in a slow transformation towards the character described by Count Plunkett when he addressed the Museums Association in 1912. In 1899, the museum, for the first time, came under Dublin-based administration through the establishment of the Department of Agriculture

32 Justice Farwell in *Law Reports Supreme Court of Judicature Chancery Division 1903*, vol. 2 (London, 1903), p. 614. 33 Sir Edward Thompson, cited in 'Report of a committee appointed to inquire into the circumstances under which certain Celtic ornaments found in Ireland were recently offered were recently offered for sale to the British Museum and to consider the relationships between the British Museum and the museums of Edinburgh and Dublin with regard to the acquisition and retention of objects of antiquarian and historic interest' 77 (1899), p. 699. 34 Ibid., p. 702. 35 Viscount Dillion, Ibid., p. 24. 36 *Evening Herald*, 8 Dec. 1897.

and Technical Instruction. Horace Plunkett stated that the new Department would set about 'encouraging national freedom, aiming at distinctive national qualities having at hand, as part of its inspirations, the beautiful and suggestive objects of the Museum'.[37] Shortly after Count Plunkett was appointed as director of the Museum, its title was changed. Previously referred to as the Dublin Museum of Science and Art, it became known as the National Museum of Science and Art, Dublin; later in the century, it was to become known by the now familiar title, the National Museum of Ireland. The introduction of the word 'national' in the title was considered more appropriate to a 'Museum of Ireland and treasury of Celtic antiquities'.[38] Count Plunkett also set about rearranging the museum, by giving the museum less consideration of 'foreign objects'. Irish antiquities and objects illustrative of Irish arts and industries were now allowed more prominent display space than previously awarded to them. With these changes, the museum was beginning the process of becoming an expression of national life.

The history of the National Museum provides a new and vital dimension to understanding the significance of the Irish Revival of the 1880s–1920s to Ireland's cultural history. The nature of the interests in Irish archaeology, in collecting and in the creation of a national museum in Dublin brings greater depth to our knowledge of the political nature of engagement with the past. Throughout its history, the museum on Kildare Street has provided a venue for the expression of national and cultural aspirations. The objects, displays and the building itself gathered meanings from the political context in which they were exhibited. The politicization of archaeology and collecting spanned the nineteenth century but gathered pace over the debates on the creation of the museum and the ownership of the Broighter hoard. The examples of these cases reveal that the tensions in the literary and language revivals also materialized in other aspects of Irish cultural life. The Abbey Theatre may have been a better-known cultural venue in Dublin in the early twentieth century, but the National Museum was another stage on which similar political conflicts were acted out. In both the literary and the museum movements an Irish ideal was being constructed and challenged.

37 Horace Plunkett, Report of the Department of Agriculture and Technical Instruction 20 (1902), p. 541. **38** Horace Plunkett, Report of the Department of Agriculture and Technical Instruction 22 (1908), p. 14.

Embroidered spectacle: Celtic Revival as aristocratic display

JANICE HELLAND

A large and boisterous demonstration marked the countess of Aberdeen's departure from Dublin in August 1886. She celebrated her devotion to Ireland and her penchant for home rule by wearing a dress of pale azure Irish poplin (St Patrick's blue) trimmed abundantly with Limerick lace complemented by a bonnet decorated with shamrocks.[1] The rousing street cheers for Aberdeen and her husband, the departing viceroy, mirrored the silence of Dublin's elite. According to *Lady's Pictorial's* regular column 'Society in Dublin', the Aberdeens had offended loyalists with their flagrant support for home rule. Lord Aberdeen, for example, had openly declared his sympathy for home rule at a Castle dinner party in July: he had announced 'with a bland smile, that he hoped and believed that all at the table were of his way of thinking; he was answered by one of his most prominent guests – a well known Chief Justice – that his assumption was hardly correct, as in all probability only himself, and, perhaps, his footman, were disposed to follow Mr Gladstone's rule'.[2]

Conversely, *The Times'* Dublin correspondent applauded the Aberdeens: 'If it were possible, the majority of people in the country would desire to see the Viceroyalty retained by Lord and Lady Aberdeen, who have done more to make the office popular with the masses than any of their predecessors.' They overcame prejudices, continued *The Times*, 'by their unfailing and unbounded kindness and generosity' and gave help whenever needed 'without distinction of creed or party'.[3] A few days later, *The Times* published a much more critical description of the departure from Ireland in the form of a letter to the editor in which the Aberdeens were chastised for their support of Irish nationalism: 'Certainly Lord Aberdeen and his amiable Countess did receive a popular ovation. None will dispute this. None will also, with truth, deny that the ovation was a thoroughly "National" one.'[4] According to this Dublin observer, 'green was everywhere, and the chief banners were green flags' with a crownless harp and American and French flags. The Aberdeens represented home rule and the cheer

1 *Lady's Pictorial*, 14 Aug. 1886, p. 127. 2 *Lady's Pictorial*, 31 July 1886, p. 75. 3 *The Times*, 22 July 1886, p. 7. 4 *The Times*, 6 Aug. 1886, p. 7. For a discussion of the complicated relationship between lords lieutenant and Irish nationalism, see James Murphy, *Abject loyalty: nationalism and monarchy in Ireland during the reign of Queen Victoria* (Washington, DC: The Catholic University of America Press, 2001).

ing crowds that greeted the viceregal entourage as it made its way through the Dublin streets signified, according to some, a 'demonstration of Separatists'.[5]

Affection for Ishbel Aberdeen herself remained as contradictory as the mixed responses to the viceroyalty. One columnist sarcastically reported upon the collection of subscriptions for a farewell gift for the countess: although money was 'not flowing in with extraordinary rapidity', it was expected that 'the lady philanthropist' would 'make up all the deficiencies herself' and, regardless, loyalists would not 'turn up for the farewell reception'.[6] This disparaging view of Lady Aberdeen's activities contradicted frequent praise for her dedication: she was consistently both belittled and acclaimed.[7] Sir Horace Plunkett described her as a 'goody goody rebel', and she was often lampooned in the press as 'Blowsy Bella' and later as 'Lady Microbe';[8] others commended her as 'seemingly ubiquitous … continually occupied in promoting good and useful work'.[9]

The 1886 spectacle of departure neither began nor ended Ishbel Aberdeen's controversial relationship with Ireland. Similarly, the dress she selected for the occasion was one of many that articulated her keenness for displaying Irish cloth and Celtic motifs on her own body. As Elizabeth Wilson suggests, fashion, because it is related to fine art and popular culture, is 'a kind of performance art'; it is, according to Wilson, 'a mass pastime, a form of group entertainment' that acts as 'a kind of a hinge between the élitist and the popular'.[10] If, as Wilson proposes, fashion is performance, then Lady Aberdeen regularly and dramatically showed her support for Irish industry and art, publicly and privately, at Court drawing rooms, at exhibitions and on the street.

Aberdeen first conflated her own body with Celticness when she appeared as Aoife, the twelfth-century Irish bride of Norman invader, Strongbow, at a lavish viceregal garden party organised to promote home manufacture.[11] Thus, in a spectacular event the *Lady's Pictorial* called 'the most brilliant national festival that has, perhaps, ever been held in Ireland',[12] Lady Aberdeen brought aristocratic pleasure together with Celtic revival. All the invited guests had been told to wear Irish costumes made of Irish materials and, as the *Irish Times* wrote:

5 *The Times*, 6 Aug. 1886, p. 7. The lord mayor of Dublin insisted the Aberdeens' popularity followed from their 'sympathy with the political desires of the Irish people' (*The Times*, 14 Aug. 1886, p. 8). 6 *Lady's Pictorial*, 31 July 1886, p. 75. 7 In her study of nineteenth-century philanthropy in Ireland, Maria Luddy confirms this dichotomy. See *Women and philanthropy in nineteenth-century Ireland*, (Cambridge UP, 1995), p. 190. 8 Nicola Gordon Bowe and Elizabeth Cumming, *The arts & crafts movement in Dublin and Edinburgh, 1885–1925* (Dublin: Irish Academic, 1998), p. 87. 9 *Lady's Pictorial*, 10 Apr. 1886, p. 314. 10 Elizabeth Wilson, *Adorned in dreams: fashion and modernity* (Berkeley: University of California Press, 1987), p. 60. See also, Janice Helland, 'The performative art of court dress' in B. Elliott and J. Helland (eds), *Women and the decorative arts, 1880–1935: the gender of ornament* (Aldershot, Hants.: Ashgate 2002), pp 96–113. 11 See, for example, *Irish Textile Journal*, 15 May 1886, p. 58, for a discussion of the relationship between the Garden Party and encouragement of Ireland's poplin industry. 12 *Lady's Pictorial*, 22 May 1886, p. 497.

'No element was wanting that could contribute to the pleasure and success of the occasion' which was 'both picturesque and patriotic.'[13] The *Illustrated London News* considered the garden party 'pleasant and picturesque' with costumes that were 'romantic and fantastic' as well as 'humourous and popular'.[14] Approximately 2000 guests circulated throughout the afternoon, while 'on the outer side of the deep ditch or sunken fence which forms the boundary between the public and the viceregal grounds, many spectators had also assembled'.[15] At three o'clock in the afternoon, after having greeted their guests, the earl and countess appeared on the terrace and, to the tune of the National Anthem, moved toward the reception. Ishbel Aberdeen's costume created a stir and garnered attention in every press review of the occasion. She personified her support for a particular kind of Ireland by wearing a 'robe and mantle of the richest ivory-coloured Empress poplin, beautifully embroidered by hand, in gold, with interleaf decorations' based upon designs in the Book of Kells.[16] The costume, designed by Major Robert McEniry, the curator of the Irish Academy, was, according to the *Lady's Pictorial*, 'that of "Strongbow's Bride", copied exactly from the picture by Maclise, and manufactured by Mary Sims, of Dawson-street, for the occasion'.[17] To complete her Celtic masquerade, Lady Aberdeen wore a richly embroidered mantle fastened by a Tara brooch and a gold-embroidered shoulder-piece fastened by fibula brooch. To complete her performance as promoter of Ireland and keeper of harmony, she carried a bouquet of roses, thistles and shamrocks.[18]

Two aspects of Ishbel Aberdeen's performance signify a Celtic revival circumscribed by Anglo permutations: the embroidered Book of Kells motifs and the replication of the twelfth-century Irish 'princess', Aoife.[19] Each must be considered separately and interstitially, as idiosyncratic allegiances expressed by a late nineteenth-century aristocrat and as indicators of emergent nationalism. As Neil Harris, among others, has suggested, craft revival in the late nineteenth century frequently was linked with national or ethnic identity and as such 'helped to evoke historic pasts and dreams of independence'.[20] The embroidery on Aberdeen's dress, although worked by women in the Royal Irish School of Art Needlework, owed its inspiration to the Donegal Industrial Fund renowned for

13 *Irish Times*, 24 May 1886, p. 5.   **14** *Illustrated London News*, 5 June 1886, p. 600.   **15** *Irish Times*, 24 May 1886, p. 5.   **16** *Illustrated London News*, 5 June 1886, p. 600 and *Irish Times*, 24 May 1886, p. 5.   **17** *Lady's Pictorial*, 20 May 1886, p. 497. McEniry's design was not 'copied exactly' but rather represents an amalgam of costumes and symbols used by Maclise to signify Ireland. Major Robert McEniry (the *Irish Times* mistakenly referred to him as Major MacHenery) was resident museum curator from 1872 to 1890. I thank Siobhán O'Rafferty, Librarian, Royal Irish Academy, for this information.   **18** *Irish Times*, 24 May 1886, p. 5 and *Illustrated London News*, 5 June 1886, p. 600.   **19** The picture now hangs in the National Gallery of Ireland as Daniel Maclise, *The marriage of Strongbow and Aoife* (1854).   **20** Neil Harris, 'Selling national culture: Ireland at the world's Columbian Exposition' in T.J. Edelstein (ed.), *Imagining and Irish past: the Celtic Revival, 1840–1940* (Chicago: David & Alfred Smart Museum of Art, 1992), p. 93.

its trademark use of Kells embroidery and for its determination to revive specifically and uniquely Irish crafts. Lady Aberdeen ardently shared this determination, and any discussion of her Celtic dresses must be linked to the activities and reputation of the Donegal Industrial Fund.

Alice Hart introduced Kells embroideries to exhibition viewers soon after the Fund's inauguration in 1883.[21] By 1885, the Fund had been awarded a gold medal at the International Inventions Exhibition in London for Kells embroideries including, for example, a pair of portière curtains of Irish woollen cloth decorated with 'a singularly bold design taken from a Celtic illumination of the seventh century'.[22] Work exhibited at the Inventions captured the interests of press and viewers alike and, because both the marchioness of Waterford and the princess of Wales supported the 'tiny shop' located at 'Ye Signe of ye Rose and Shamrock', aristocratic glamour complemented its popularity and appeal.[23] Concomitantly, in July 1885, the Fund participated in 'an exhibition of Irish lace and cottage industries' held in the Royal School of Art Needlework under the patronage of the princess of Wales.[24] By early 1886, when Ishbel Aberdeen went to Ireland, she would have been very familiar with the Fund's activities and awards.

Londoner Alice Rowland Hart[25] had established the Donegal Industrial Fund after a visit she and her physician activist husband had made to Donegal in 1883. Typically liberal and concerned, the Harts responded intensely to the increasingly frequent accounts of Irish misery and famine that proliferated during the early 1880s and, in preparation for their trip to view the situation themselves, they read a series of books, pamphlets, published speeches and reports 'with ever increasing interest, mingled with feelings of pain, shame and indignation'.[26] Alice Hart, in a speech she gave in London, told her audience that as she read Irish history, she 'felt for the first time ashamed of being an Englishwomen'.[27] She blamed England for 'willingly and knowingly' destroying the glass and woollen industries of Ireland; she denied the commonly voiced characteristic of Irish 'idleness' by insisting that the population wanted employment; and she decided 'that the most practical thing to do would be to revive the old Cottage Industries, and to develop and improve the ancient arts of spinning, weaving, knitting, sewing and embroidery'.[28] Her main concern was to provide work for an agricultural, rural population during the long winter months, thus supplementing the meagre income they earned during the growing season. To this end, she founded the Donegal Industrial Fund for the encouragement of Irish Home Industries and the benefit of Irish workers.[29]

21 A short article in *The Times*, 8 Dec. 1885, p. 4, dates the founding of the Donegal Industrial Fund to Dec. 1883. **22** *Queen*, 20 June 1885, p. 655. See also, Alice Hart, *The cottage industries of Ireland, with an account of the work of the Donegal Industrial Fund* (London: Hamilton, Adams, 1887). **23** *Queen*, 9 May 1885, p. 477. **24** *The Times*, 17 July 1885, p. 4. **25** Alice Rowland (1848–1931), daughter of a mercantile family and student of medicine, married Ernest Hart in 1872. **26** Alice Hart, *Cottage industries and what they can do for Ireland* (London, 1885), p. 3. **27** Ibid. **28** Ibid., p. 12. **29** Alice Hart, *Cottage industries*.

For almost two years, Hart operated out of a London storefront in New Cavendish Street. During this time, she sought commissions for Irish goods from businesses such as Debenhams, and Freebody and Marshall and organized and operated highly successful stalls in large international exhibitions. She arranged for the teaching of classes and dissemination of information in Irish and attempted to convince Irish entrepreneurs to buy Irish goods; to do otherwise, she considered 'not a patriotic thing to do'.[30] In December 1885, Hart opened the doors to her new storefront, Donegal House, in Wigmore Street 'for the exhibition and sale of goods which have been manufactured by the Irish peasantry'; everything on display was 'manufactured by hand' and included homespun tweeds, friezes and woollen fabrics, all of which had been made from undyed or vegetable dyed wool, woven on hand looms.[31] Concurrently, the more decorative objects of the Donegal Exhibition Fund appeared in a month-long exhibition at Howell's and James's Art Exhibition Galleries on Regent Street. The stars of this 'art exhibition' were the Kells embroideries based upon designs from seventh-century Celtic manuscripts and 'ancient architectural decorations'[32] when Ireland, according to Hart, 'was in questions of art far in advance of England'.[33] The *Magazine of Art* told its readers that Hart's designs 'taken either from Irish monuments or Irish manuscripts' represented 'patriotic objects' and thus could be 'regarded as a genuine attempt to revive the art as well as the industries of Ireland'.[34]

Touted as a 'new and original type of artistic hand work' and directed toward consumers who were identified as 'lovers of art', Kells embroideries, made with dyed polished flax threads of Irish manufacture worked on various linens, became the hallmark of the Donegal Industrial Fund; they also represented objects that expanded the Fund's image to include more than wearable goods and reified the Fund's identity as a producer of 'Celticness'.[35] Hart's intent 'was to create a new Irish industry with Irish materials, and worked by Irish workers.'[36] Years later, Hart described her amazement when she first turned the pages of the Book of Kells in the library of Trinity College: 'it revealed to me', wrote Hart, 'a mine and storehouse of design. In a few square inches of these wondrous pages there was more design and more suggestion than in sheaves of original drawings turned out from South Kensington'.[37] The production of Kells embroideries was for

30 'Mrs Ernest Hart's Lecture', *Irish Times*, 18 June 1888, p. 3. In 1883, Hart circulated letters to 30 Irish newspapers seeking assistance from 'the ladies of Ireland' skilled in embroidery to teach peasant girls. See, Mary Jeune, 'Irish Industrial Art', *Woman's World*, 2 (1889), pp 160–1. **31** *The Times*, 8 Dec. 1885, p. 4. **32** 'Exhibition of Kells Embroideries at Messrs Howell and James's', *Queen*, 5 Dec. 1885, p. 631. **33** Alice Hart, 1885, p. 14. **34** *Magazine of Art*, Dec. 1886, p. xi and Jan. 1889, p. xv. **35** Alice Hart, 'The old Celtic manuscripts as sources of design, *House Beautiful*, Jan. 1904, pp 22–3. 'Kells' embroideries were rather more eclectic than the name implies often including Hart's love of Japanese art mingled with Celtic interlacing. **36** Jeune, p. 161. **37** Alice Hart, 'The old Celtic manuscripts as sources of design', pp 22–3.

Hart a statement of Irishness – that is, a reification of Irish culture and art in the reality of famine and hardship. It was these elegant designs combined with Hart's commitment and energy that probably attracted Lady Aberdeen to her cause; they remained united in their commitment to Irish arts and industries until Chicago's 1893 World Columbian Exposition.

Lady Aberdeen's involvement with the revival of cottage crafts, like Alice Hart's, had begun as early as 1883 when an 'exhibition of industry and art' opened in Aberdeen under the patronage of the earl and countess;[38] her connection with Irish crafts began immediately upon her arrival in Dublin in 1886, when she assumed the position of president of the committee formed 'for the purpose of organising a stall to represent the industries pursued by women in Ireland in the forthcoming International Exhibition, to be held in Edinburgh'.[39] 'Curiously enough', wrote Aberdeen in her reminiscences, 'this Committee had been organised by Lady Carnarvon (during Lord Carnarvon's brief viceroyalty) at the request of Lady Aberdeen and Lady Rosebery, as Joint Convenors of the Women's Section of the Edinburgh Exhibition'.[40] Aberdeen enthusiastically embraced her new activities in Ireland and, in her search for objects that would grace the Irish stalls in Edinburgh, she encountered numbers of women already connected with cottage crafts. If, despite Hart's high profile as an advocate of domestic arts, Aberdeen had not met her in London, she soon met with her in Dublin. According to the *Queen, the Lady's Newspaper*, in April 1886, the 'Lady Lieutenant' paid an official visit to Alice Hart 'to inspect the beautiful Kells embroideries, laces, dresses, and Irish tweeds, of the Donegal Industrial Fund'[41] and ordered a dress 'decorated with Kells embroidery' that first was exhibited in Donegal House (London) and then sent to the Liverpool International Exhibition.[42] The *Liverpool Daily Post* described the costume as 'conspicuous among articles shown'; the front of the dress was so solidly embroidered with the 'finest coloured threads that not an inch of the original material is seen'.[43] The coloured embroidery establishes this dress as different from Lady Aberdeen's white and gold garden party dress but confirms Aberdeen's connection to Alice Hart. (She ordered at least three dresses from the Fund between 1885 and 1888.) The extensive press coverage of Hart's organization establishes Kells embroidery as a virtual trademark of the Donegal Industrial Fund – a trademark that reified

38 *Queen*, 6 Jan. 1883, p. 9. **39** *The Times*, 8 Mar. 1886, p. 7. **40** *'We twa': Reminiscences of Lord and Lady Aberdeen*, vol. 1 (London, 1925), pp 253–4. **41** Alice Hart and Mary Power Lalor organized an exhibition of cottage crafts 'in one of the most elegant apartments' in Dublin's Shelbourne Hotel (*Irish Times*, 7 Apr. 1886), p. 5. According to *Queen*, 'the rank and file of Irish fashion' including the Princess Saxe-Weimar, Lady Guinness and Lady Hamilton, followed Lady Aberdeen's 'excellent example' and attended the show and sale (*Queen*, 24 Apr. 1886), p. 435. **42** *Queen*, 24 Apr. 1886, p. 451. **43** *Liverpool Daily Post*, 14 May 1886, p. 3. **44** See, for example, Paul Larmour, *The arts & crafts movement in Ireland* (Belfast: Friar's Bush Press, 1992).

a revival of ancient Celtic arts as interpreted by Alice Hart and worn by Lady Aberdeen. Thus, any discussion of the embroidered panels of Aberdeen's dress, although worked by the Royal Irish School of Art Needlework, must be linked to the Donegal Industrial Fund's distinctive and specific revival project as well as to the revival project of what would later become the arts and crafts movement.[44] Similarly, because the Robert McEniry's design for the costume owes its inspiration to Maclise's picture, the dress must be considered alongside the painting. The sumptuous embroidery signalled a revival of interest in ancient Irish art specifically related to a liberal concern for economic and political conditions in Ireland. The costume itself signalled a mid nineteenth-century interpretation of twelfth-century Irish history.

When Daniel Maclise's picture debuted as *Strongbow's Marriage with the Princess Eva* in London's 1854 Royal Academy Exhibition, *The Times* considered it 'of all others' most likely to 'first fix the attention of the spectator'; it occupied 'nearly one side of the middle room' and represented 'the most elaborate and ambitious' work Maclise had 'ever presented to the public view'.[45] The *London Illustrated News* likewise thought Maclise excelled 'in invention' and considered the picture rivalled only by Frith's *Life at the Sea-side*.[46] Lord Northwick purchased Maclise's large painting for his 'splendid gallery at Thirlstane-house, Cheltenham' for the 'large sum of £4000'.[47] After Northwick's death in 1859, the picture sold at auction for substantially less than he had paid for it and was exhibited off and on in London until, finally, it remained on permanent view at the Aquarium.[48]

When the picture again came up for auction in 1879, Sir Richard Wallace (of Wallace Collection fame) purchased the picture and presented it to the National Gallery of Ireland.[49] By 1879 the painting had acquired a much longer and more descriptive title: *The Marriage of Richard de Clare, Earl of Pembroke, surnamed 'Strongbow', with the Princess Eva, daughter of Dermod Macmorrogh, King of Leinster*. The scene, according to *The Times*, was 'crowded with figures, Strongbow in the centre, placing the ring on the finger of the beautiful Eva, attended by her maidens, while on the battlefield, surrounded by his Norman soldiers, with Irish chieftains laying down their arms at this feet and the dead and dying lying around.'[50] Maclise represented a dramatic, if fictitious, historical simultaneity and thus captured a series of events in one immense framed tableau. John Turpin called the picture 'a form of public historical theatre analogous to the historical novel and costume drama concentrating on heroic and tragic themes'; he also suggested that it represented 'a grandiose sweep of historical narrative, with precise antiquarian-

45 *The Times*, 29 Apr. 1854, p. 12. **46** *Illustrated London News*, 6 May 1854, p. 421. **47** *The Times*, 12 July 1879, p. 6. **48** Ibid. **49** Wallace was a member of the Board of Governors and Guardians in the National Gallery of Ireland at the time. He presented the picture to the Gallery because of its Irish content. I thank Sighle Bhreathnach Lynch for this information. **50** *The Times*, 12 July 1879, p. 6.

ism of costume and accessories'.[51] As Hilary O'Kelly suggested in her essay on 'Reconstructing Irishness', it is virtually impossible to reconstruct Irish dress from that period;[52] thus it is unlikely Maclise's picture reproduced 'precise' dress and accessories. The artist would not even have had access to Eugene O'Curry's *The Manners and Customs of the Ancient Irish*, which was not published until the 1860s and, although he may have seen Joseph Cooper Walker's *An Historical Essay on the Dress of the Irish* published in 1788,[53] it would not have helped with the reconstruction of Aoife's dress for the painting. Thus, Fintan Cullen's insistence that, 'This is not nationalistic sympathy but metropolitan interest in anthropological detail. Equally, this is not history as such but entertainment',[54] is probably more precise than Turpin's sympathetic reading of the picture.

However, for late nineteenth-century viewers such as Ishbel Aberdeen and Robert McEniry, Maclise offered rare and precious insight into twelfth-century costume. For Aberdeen, the picture's narrative of romantic unification after dispute and destruction might have complemented her Gladstonian liberal desire for peaceful home rule. Although the first volumes of Goddard Henry Orpen's expansive study of Ireland under the Normans were not published until 1911, Orpen had been studying, researching and writing about this period of Irish history for some time, and he quite likely knew McEniry as well as Aberdeen. In the first volume of his published magnum opus, he discussed Aoife's historical marriage to Strongbow as well as Maclise's 'imaginative' interpretation of the event:

> Far be it from me to question the prescriptive right of the painter to treat his subject in an imaginative way, and to introduce any setting that serves to help out his thought; but in view of the statements of recent historians it is almost necessary to remark that Maclise's picture is not a contemporary record, and cannot be used, as the Bayeux Tapestry has been used, to fill up the gaps of contemporary writers. There is no other authority for this scene, which on the face of it is utterly improbable.[55]

Orpen suggested that the marriage took place in the Christ Church of the Holy Trinity at Waterford some days after Strongbow took the town. He also indicated that Gerald of Wales (late twelfth century) in one 'heavily loaded Latin

51 John Turpin, 'Irish history painting', *Irish Arts Review* (1989–90), p. 240. **52** Hilary O'Kelly, 'Reconstructing Irishness: dress in the Celtic Revival, 1880–1920' in J. Ash and E. Wilson, eds., *Chic thrills* (London: Pandora, 1992), pp 75–83. **53** See Mairead Dunlevy, *Dress in Ireland* (London: B.T. Batsford, 1989), for a discussion of Cooper's eighteenth-century essay as well as insight into the lack of evidence for clearly understanding twelfth-century women's dress. **54** Fintan Cullen, *Visual politics: the representation of Ireland, 1750–1930* (Cork UP, 1997), pp 48–9. **55** Goddard Henry Orpen, *Ireland under the Normans, 1169–1216,* vol. i (Oxford UP, 1911), p. 198.

sentence' conflated a series of events that included battles, the building of a gar-
rison, the signing of a treaty and the marriage (among others).[56] Thus Orpen,
having criticized Maclise, alluded to how Maclise may have constructed his historical simultaneity. However the events fell out historically, Maclise did construct the image of a potential albeit fictitious harmony between England and
Ireland consecrated by the love and sanctity of marriage. Ishbel Aberdeen, cat-
egorically supportive of home rule, must have found the picture romantic (marriage as healer of enmity) and promising (the descendents of Aoife and
Strongbow might potentially erase differences). She may even, in flights of imagination, have fancied herself a modern-day Aoife, filled with the desire for a non-
conflicted relationship that might celebrate a rich and colourful Celtic past along
with a productive and bountiful future. Whatever images or stories passed through
her mind as she prepared for the garden party, Aberdeen's selection of that particular dress from that particular painting signifies the visualization of a legendary
Irish woman and the representation of a turbulent Irish history. The dress that,
like her bouquet, played well to an enthusiastic audience, illuminated Irish arts
and industries but camouflaged political undercurrents in much the same way
Maclise's picture romanticized a love conceived upon defeat.

Ishbel Aberdeen's departure costume, while not as overtly Celtic as the garden
party dress, used colour to establish her connection with Ireland (St Patrick's
blue) and accoutrements (Limerick lace and shamrocks) to ensure the message
was understood. Soon after leaving Ireland, the Aberdeens set out upon extensive travels spending much of 1887 in Australia and Canada, returning to England
late that year with their political preferences still intact. Lady Aberdeen's appearance at Queen Victoria's first Drawing Room of the 1888 season in a dress flam-
boyantly embroidered with Celtic motifs must have surprised many of the elite
while it confirmed her commitment to Ireland and to its cultural heritage even
as she helped to construct and authenticate that heritage. If, as Jane Schneider
and Annette Weiner suggest, cloth can communicate 'the wearer's or user's ideological values and claims',[57] then Ishbel Aberdeen's clothing consistently demonstrated her politics and her beliefs. Like her replicated twelfth-century costume,
her Court dress was made from cream imperial poplin embroidered with gold;
however, the decoration was much more lavish, and the costume included the
compulsory Court train: the tablier, front of bodice, and the border around the
train of the 'richest ivory double poplin' lined with satin were 'embroidered in
gold from Celtic designs copied from old Irish manuscripts'.[58] This was apparel she favoured; she wore it again in 1893 to the first Drawing Room of the

56 Orpen's sources were the late twelfth- or early thirteenth-century writings of Gerald of
Wales and the thirteenth-century *Song of Dermot*.   **57** Jane Schneider and Annette B. Weiner
(eds), *Cloth and human experience* (Washington: Smithsonian Institution, 1989), p. 1.   **58** *Queen*,
3 Mar. 1888, p. 258 and *Lady's Pictorial*, 3 Mar. 1888, p. 221. The Irish School of Art Needlework
did the embroidery; Mary Sims of Dawson Street made the dress.

season in Dublin Castle[59] when she visited Ireland to gather objects and support for her proposed Irish Village at the Chicago World's Fair. *Queen* featured a photograph of Lady Aberdeen wearing the dress on the cover of one its 1896 issues;[60] and panels from the dress were worked into the costume she wore at Canada's Victorian Era Ball in 1897.[61] She was also photographed wearing her garden party dress and, in keeping with her support for Irish industry, she posed as spinner for a fiction that proposed Aberdeen as Celtic Ireland and keeper of domestic tradition.[62] The image of Lady Aberdeen elegantly posed with her hand on the spinning wheel, her gaze directed at the yarn, personified her promotion of Ireland at the Chicago World's Fair, where she established an Irish village in competition with her former colleague, Alice Hart. The two proponents of Irish art fell out over the Chicago exhibition and instead of the one village Lady Aberdeen desired, two faux villages offered Ireland to America. Alice Hart's village featured her 'famous Kells embroideries' along with a 'half-size reproduction of the ruins of Donegal Castle', imitations of Celtic jewellery and copies of illuminated manuscripts.[63] Ishbel Aberdeen replicated Blarney Castle (to two thirds its size) and constructed a 'series of cottages each based upon an original in Ireland' including one based upon her own cottage near Queenstown; she would live in the replicated cottage for weeks at a time.[64] Thus the frequently reproduced photograph of the aristocrat with a spinning wheel complemented her Chicago activities while it represented the Celtic. The image also reified Ishbel Aberdeen as founder of the Irish Home Industries Association. This was the persona she cultivated and maintained even after she moved to Canada in 1893 and then revitalized when she returned to Ireland in 1905.

Ishbel Aberdeen's use of her own body as a device to support Irish art and industry followed a pattern of aristocratic patronage that, by 1885, was celebrated even in literature: Rosa Mulholland, a character in *Marcella Grace*, insisted upon cloth woven in Dublin for her 'castle train' even though her *modiste* wanted Lyon velvet.[65] In 1886 Queen Victoria wore Irish lace to her Drawing Room as an attempt to help revive the industry.[66] Lady Londonderry frequently wore dresses trimmed with lace or incorporating embroidery made by Irish women: she wore a costume of Irish poplin when she arrived in Dublin as vicereine,[67] and

59 *Gentlewoman* described the dress and published a small drawing of it (18 Feb. 1893, p. 216). **60** *Queen*, 21 Nov. 1896, p. 945, cover photograph by Lafayette. **61** Lord Aberdeen has been appointed governor-general of Canada in 1893. For a discussion of the Ball and Lady Aberdeen's role in it, see Cynthia Cooper, *Magnificent entertainments: fancy dress balls of Canada's governors general, 1876–1898* (Hull, Quebec: Canadian Museum of Civilization, 1997). A photograph of Lady Aberdeen in her Ball costume is reproduced on page 102. **62** This photograph is frequently reproduced. For example, see Bowe and Cumming, p. 88, or Doris French, *Ishbel and the empire: a biography of Lady Aberdeen* (Toronto & Oxford: Dundurn, 1988), p. 78. **63** Harris, p. 90. **64** Ibid., p. 96. **65** As quoted in Murphy, *Abject loyalty*, p. xx. **66** Alice Hart, 'The women's industries of Ireland', *Queen*, 18 Dec. 1886, p. 742. **67** The marquess of

a dress trimmed with Irish lace to her first Drawing Room;[68] an 1888 costume was embroidered by the Royal Irish School of Art Needlework;[69] an 1897 Court dress was 'embroidered with lilies and love knots in tinted silks by the students at Viscountess Duncannon's Garry Hill School of Needlework'.[70] Lady Cadogan, when she was vicereine, also patronized local arts. She wore a spectacular pale green satin dress decorated with a 'rich trail of green velvet shamrocks down each side of the skirt, fastening in a drapery of fine Limerick lace' to a Flower Ball at Dublin Castle (embroidered at the Royal Irish School of Art Needlework);[71] and a black and white dress 'studded with pearls and diamonds' worked at Lady Duncannon's Garry Hill School to a London fancy ball hosted by the duchess of Devonshire.[72] Even Mary, princess of York, wore a dress of Irish poplin with a deep yolk 'of exquisite gold thread and sequin transparent embroidery' made by Lady Duncannon's cottage workers,[73] and another dress embroidered at the Royal Irish School of Art Needlework and trimmed with Carrickmacross lace when she visited Ireland in 1897.[74]

None, however, embodied Irishness and epitomized the Celtic revival with such extravagance and splendour as Ishbel Aberdeen. She sought to encourage Irish art and manufacture and to urge consumers to buy Irish rather than seek goods from elsewhere – she insisted that lace on dresses should be Irish, not French nor Italian, and that embroidery should be done by Irish women on Irish cloth. (Alice Hart introduced a 'flax on flax' type of embroidery that incorporated Irish thread as well as Irish fabric.) She also promoted Irish designers and dressmakers – Aberdeen time and again commissioned Mary Sims or Harriet Manning, both Dublin dressmakers. Her own image moved beyond this to overtly promote the Celtic – a revival of ancient Irish art as interpreted in the nineteenth century. Her patronage is a blatant form of benevolent colonialism but one that shifts and, in many ways, disrupts such a definitive label. Her boundaries are mercantile rather than military, directed toward self-help rather than external control: this does not erase a problem but it does complicate an issue. Ishbel Aberdeen sold Celtic-ness and, particularly in America. This had consequences beyond her liberal desire for home rule; she sought Irish identity in ancient symbols that she then performed on her own aristocratic body and this, too, surpassed her own philanthropic benevolence. She personified and reproduced Irish revival as display and pleasure, as spectacle and desire, and thus as sought after and replicated. Her attentions and motives remain suspect in an atmosphere of colonialism, but her patronage leaves a legacy of complexity not

Londonderry followed the earl of Aberdeen as lord lieutenant of Ireland. See, for example, *Illustrated London News* (28 Aug. 1886, p. 229) for a descriptive account of the new appointment. **68** *Lady's Pictorial*, 12 Feb. 1887, p. 162. **69** *Lady's Pictorial*, 5 May 1888, p. 487. **70** *Queen*, 15 May 1897, p. 962. **71** *Ladies Field*, 26 Mar. 1898, p. 55 and *Irish Society*, 19 Mar. 1898, p. 354. **72** *Queen*, 10 July 1897, p. 76. **73** *Gentlewoman*, 21 Aug. 1897, p. 7. **74** *Queen*, 18 Sept. 1897, p. 542.

easily disentangled from late nineteenth-century Irish history. Neil Harris, in his discussion of Aberdeen at the Chicago World's Fair, suggested that she 'married theatre to shopping'; if this is true, she also wed Celtic Revival to English court and to American fantasy in an enduring albeit an uneasy exchange.[75]

NOTES

I should like to thank Cynthia Cooper, Sighle Bhreathnach Lynch and Siobhán O'Rafferty for their suggestions, and Betsey Taylor FitzSimon for her helpful editorial comments. My thanks also go to the Social Sciences and Humanities Research Council of Canada whose support funded the research for this essay.

75 Harris, p. 100.

Crafting a national identity: the Dun Emer Guild, 1902–1908

ELAINE CHEASLEY PATERSON

The home arts and industries associations of late nineteenth-century Ireland sought to bring together the exhibition and sale of beautiful objects with improved living and working conditions for Irish peasants and rural labourers. Directed by educated middle-class women, these ventures successfully intertwined art, entrepreneurial activity, and philanthropy, with an unusual brand of nationalism.

One such venture was the Dun Emer Guild established at Dundrum, Co. Dublin, in 1902 by three middle-class Irish women, Evelyn Gleeson (1855–1944) and the Yeats sisters, Lily (1866–1949) and Elizabeth (1868–1940), and developed into a thriving industry by 1908. The objectives of the Guild were to provide work for Irish women crafting art objects using exclusively Irish materials and to educate working women 'in the hope that they might eventually become teachers to others' so that similar industries could develop throughout Ireland.[1] The Guild specialized in weaving, embroidery and printing on a hand press.

The objectives of the Dun Emer Guild were in line with those of the larger home arts movement, which included: making beautiful objects available to the mass of the people, and not just the few; making the home the centre of interest and attraction; reducing the exodus of workers from country to town; reviving local village industries; and holding classes where voluntary teachers would give instruction in arts and handicrafts, both design and execution, to artisans and labourers. In the 1885 *Magazine of Art*, the movement's founder, Eglantyne Jebb, wrote that home arts and industries associations should help workers lead happier lives and have 'lighter hearts, tidier children, cleaner cottages, and a better moral tone all round'.[2] Thus the unofficial goal of most home arts industries was social reform through education, as much as art production. At Dun Emer, another specifically nationalist objective was to offer work to young women in a 'poor district' where, without such employment, these young women 'habitually emigrated'.[3]

1 Dun Emer Guild prospectus (1903), Evelyn Gleeson Papers (EGP), Trinity College, Dublin. 2 E.L. Jebb, 'The Home Arts and Industries Association', *Magazine of Art* (1885), pp 294–8. See also *The Amateurs' Art Designer* (later *Home Art Work*), 1884–1891; and Alfred Harris, 'Home Arts and Industries', in *Transactions of the National Association for the Advancement of Art and its Application to Industry: Edinburgh Meeting, 1889* (London: 1890), pp 421–33. 3 Draft of Guild

In an essay intended for the Irish Literary Society, Evelyn Gleeson proposed 'to those who are Gaelic Leaguers' the possibility of nationalizing others 'through the eyes as well as through the ears'. Referring to the success of art industries like Dun Emer, she explained that 'the people themselves must be interested in the work, enthusiastic if possible, otherwise the scheme is a failure, not merely financially but educationally. This enthusiasm is aroused by appealing to local patriotism.'[4] According to social anthropologist Ernest Gellner, part of the discourse generated in the formation of modern nations is the discovery of 'folk roots'. This emergent nationalism is also based on the assumption that the 'folk' has a residual presence in existing rural communities.[5] Although the Dun Emer Guild can be viewed as a revival of traditional Irish 'folk arts', it is important to identify the ways in which the founders of this industry appealed to 'local patriotism' in order to negotiate and originate, rather than merely preserve, an Irish cultural identity.

This biographical sketch of an art industry must examine the social networks of these three women since, as sociologist Liz Stanley points out, lives make more sense when located through participation in a range of overlapping social groups. Stanley claims 'ideas' are the products of socially shared understandings reworked in different ways within particular cultural settings.[6] The complex intersection of the home arts movement and the Irish Revival produced the specific cultural setting of Dun Emer. Gleeson and the Yeats sisters were personally and professionally involved in these groups and creatively combined the social, political and artistic understandings of both in their Guild.

Evelyn Gleeson met Lily and Elizabeth Yeats through her involvement with the Irish Literary Society of London founded by their brother, the poet WB Yeats, in the 1890s. All three women shared an interest in craftwork and a need to contribute in some practical way to the Irish Revival – a movement concerned, in part, with culturally validating a separate Irish identity.[7] Both Lily and Elizabeth Yeats were trained at the Metropolitan School of Art (Dublin), and Evelyn Gleeson had studied design at the South Kensington Museum (London). Gleeson's focus had been on hand-woven carpets and several of her designs were sold commercially. Elizabeth Yeats had taught and lectured on art professionally in London, while Lily Yeats had been an assistant to May Morris in the embroidery department of Morris & Co. at Kelmscott House. To prepare for her work on a hand press at Dun

prospectus intended for potential shareholders, EGP, Trinity College, Dublin. **4** Fragment of draft essay by Evelyn Gleeson intended for the Irish Literary Society (*c.*1907), EGP, Trinity College, Dublin. **5** Ernest Gellner, *Nations and nationalism* (Oxford: Basil Blackwell, 1983), p. 57. **6** Liz Stanley, 'On auto/biography in sociology', *Sociology*, 27:1 (Feb. 1993), pp 41–52. **7** Eugene O'Brien explains that 'Irish Revival' is often used as an umbrella term to include the Gaelic revival, the Celtic revival, and the Literary revival. ('"What ish my Nation?": towards a negative definition of identity', *Minerva*, 2 (Nov. 1998), p. 3 (journal online); available from http://www.ul.ie/~philos.

Emer, Elizabeth Yeats had also taken a hand-printing course at the Women's Printing Society in London.[8] All this artistic training led the three women to the idea of developing an Irish art industry, but the passion for it was Evelyn Gleeson's.

Evelyn Gleeson's nationalist sympathies, intertwined with her feminist beliefs as a suffragist, fed her desire to found an establishment in Ireland for the artistic training and employment of young women. In her correspondence with several newspapers, her developing interest in the movement for the emancipation of women is clear. To the editor of the *Weekly Sun* she writes: 'It has been my fortune to meet most of the leading women among the "shrieking sisterhood" and also to have spent many years among the "womanly" women who believe in the perfect rounding of the "sphere" and the divine right of man to keep his foot on their necks.'[9] Her wish to contribute in a useful way to the Irish nationalist cause is also evident in her letter to the *Irish Independent*. She writes: 'Whether women will ever obtain the franchise or not is a moot point, a great many of us think that it is, like home rule, merely a question of time. "National Politics" may not be the "métier" of Irish women, but they love their country very dearly and they claim the right with or without your correspondent's permission, to labour in its cause, as heartily … as their brothers.'[10] Historian Anne McClintock has argued that women are typically constructed as the symbol of the nation, but are denied any direct relation to national agency.[11] I suggest, however, that the women of Dun Emer did participate in nationalist discourse through a process of visual political argument, carefully developed within the boundaries of acceptable women's work. National participation was inextricably linked to, and limited by, the gendered social roles prescribed to these middle-class women.

Cultural representations do not simply 'reflect' experience or embellish it with aesthetic form, but significantly alter and shape the ways people make sense of their lives. To engage in cultural activity in circumstances where a culture is being effaced, or even to assert the existence of a civilization prior to conquest, is to make a political statement.[12] This transformative power of culture, so effectively harnessed by the Irish Revival, is evident in the Dun Emer Guild. A particular Irish cultural identity was cultivated at the Guild, through the works produced and in the organizational structure of the industry – one in which it was possible for Irish people of different traditions to feel themselves at home. Set within the Revival, the Guild was nevertheless an attempt to move away from

8 EGP, Trinity College, Dublin. 9 *Weekly Sun*, Newspaper clipping book, EGP, Trinity College, Dublin. 10 *Irish Independent*, Newspaper clipping book, EGP, Trinity College, Dublin. 11 Anne McClintock, *Imperial leather: Race, gender and sexuality in the colonial contest* (New York: Routledge, 1995). 12 Luke Gibbons, 'Race against time: racial discourse and Irish history', in Robert Young (ed.), 'Neocolonialisms', *Oxford Literary Review*, 13 (1991); and *Transformations in Irish culture* (Cork UP, 1996), p. 8. Gibbons claims that race entered Irish nationalist rhetoric by 'defining an untouched, pure Celtic past – before the colonizing English polluted it – and forming the base on which the distinctive culture of Ireland' was supposedly founded.

the 'fixed centrality of the Irishness of the Revival,' where different qualities became commodities that were associated with Irishness, to the exclusion of all others.[13] The inclusiveness sought by Gleeson and the Yeats sisters was meant to broaden the scope of 'Irish identity' and appeal to a group other than their own, as middle-class Irish women.

With Gleeson as the driving force, the Yeats sisters readily agreed to bring their special skills to her project. Her plan for the industry already worked out, Evelyn Gleeson went to Dublin in 1902 to take a house and commence work.[14] The Dun Emer venture was funded largely by Evelyn Gleeson's inheritance, and the Yeats sisters were salaried assistants. Although the sisters were unable to contribute money to the enterprise, they were well-connected and offered considerable experience and expertise in their crafts.[15] Gleeson undertook substantial responsibility for financing the Guild by paying the rent for the first two years and guaranteeing the Yeats sisters salaries of £125 each per annum. Additional support for the industry came in the form of a £500 loan from Evelyn Gleeson's close friend, Dr Augustine Henry, as well as several grants over the course of the venture from the Irish government's Department of Agriculture and Technical Instruction.[16] As well as the sale of articles made by the members of the Guild, other income was expected from the sale of vegetables, fruits and flowers from its garden, and from art lessons given by its members.

With this financial plan in place and using the medieval workshop model favoured by the Arts and Crafts Movement, the Dun Emer Guild was installed in a large home in the Dublin suburb of Dundrum.[17] The embroidery, tapestry and weaving workrooms were on the upper floor of the house in a large room, while the printing press was set up in a separate room. The Yeats sisters lived with their father some twenty minutes away, but Evelyn Gleeson lived at Dun Emer. Every Thursday, the workrooms were opened to the public for viewing, along with a display room exhibiting finished works. At Dun Emer, public and private spaces were conflated as industry and the buying public converged inside one woman's home.

Within this unusual space, each woman was in charge of a particular craft and given complete independence in her own department: Evelyn Gleeson in

13 Eugene O'Brien, 'Towards a Negative Definition of Identity', pp 4–11. **14** Liam Miller, *The Dun Emer Press, later the Cuala Press* (Dublin: Dolmen, 1973). See also Paul Larmour, *The arts and crafts movement in Ireland* (Belfast: Friar's Bush, 1992) and 'The Dun Emer Guild', *Irish Arts Review*, 1:4 (Winter 1984), pp 24–8. **15** Lily and Elizabeth Yeats were familiar with many key figures of the Irish Revival (for instance, J.M. Synge and Augusta Lady Gregory) through family connections. Both of their brothers, Jack B. Yeats (1871–1957) the painter and William B. Yeats (1865–1939) the poet, made significant contributions to the Revival. **16** Dun Emer Guild Articles of Association, EGP, Trinity College, Dublin; and Henry-Gleeson Letters, 1879–1930, National Library of Ireland. **17** For more on the workshop as an organizational model, see Elizabeth Cumming and Wendy Kaplan, *The arts and crafts movement* (London: Thames and Hudson, 1991).

tapestry and carpets; Lily Yeats in embroidery on Irish linen; Elizabeth Yeats in printing on a hand press. The Guild's Articles of Association indicate that these three crafts were chosen on the grounds that they were 'little known and afforded scope for artistic powers'.[18] Art production was therefore an important aspect of this endeavour from the very beginning.

The artistic and social ideals of the three founders are defined in the Guild's 1903 prospectus:

> The idea is to make beautiful things; this, of course, means materials honest and true and the application to them of deftness of hand, brightness of colour, and cleverness of design.
>
> Everything as far as possible, is Irish: the paper of the books, the linen of the embroidery and the wool of the tapestry and carpets. The designs are also of the spirit and tradition of the country.
>
> The education of the work-girls is also part of the idea, they are taught to paint and their brains and fingers are made more active and understanding.[19]

The Guild was successful in educating and sending out teachers. The records show that women came in for a few months of training and then departed to teach the craft they had learned, the most successful of these being May Kerley, who left the Dun Emer Guild to become the teacher and manager of the Glenbeigh Industry in Co. Kerry.[20] Also, by choosing to use exclusively Irish materials, the Guild supported other local industries.

The organization and output of this home art industry interlaced feminist and nationalist politics in concrete ways. Through their participation in the home arts movement, Gleeson and the Yeats sisters were able to present their political ideals. Involvement in this movement provided them with personal as well as group authority. Set against an industrial profile (low wages, sweated work at home for pennies), this artistic revival of Irish industries redefined women's crafts as art and provided the women working in them with an alternative to these harsh conditions.[21] A critique of art and labour under industrial capitalism was implied in the Guild's prospectus, which also conveyed a patriotic message to its patrons:

18 Dun Emer Guild Articles of Association, EGP, Trinity College, Dublin. **19** Dun Emer Guild prospectus (1903), EGP, Trinity College, Dublin. **20** EGP, Trinity College, Dublin. See also Gifford Lewis, *The Yeats sisters and the Cuala* (Dublin: Irish Academic Press, 1994). In 1905, other women training at the Guild included Dora Griffiths from Kilkenny who took a 6-week weaving course; Delia Larkin from Beaufort, Co. Kerry who trained for 2 months; and Miss Brodigan who studied tapestry and weaving (Dun Emer Journal 1903–1905, Cuala Press Archive, Early Printed Books, Trinity College, Dublin). **21** For more on this see Maria Luddy, *Women and philanthropy in nineteenth-century Ireland* (New York: Cambridge UP, 1995); Eileen Boris, *Art and labor: Ruskin, Morris, and the craftsman ideal in America* (Philadelphia: Temple UP, 1986).

Things made of pure materials, worked by these Irish girls must be *more lasting and more valuable* than machine-made goods which only serve a temporary purpose. All the things made at Dun Emer are beautiful and *have cost thought and care.*

There is no limit to the number and kind of things that could be well made in Ireland if designers and workers could *depend upon a certain market.* It is indisputable that the talent for artistic hand-work is widely spread amidst the Irish people.'[22] [Emphasis added]

By praising the ability of Irish craftworkers and advocating support for local industries, the Guild linked craft revival with the economic self-sufficiency and collective self-consciousness promoted by Irish Revivalists as a necessity for Ireland to become competitive in world markets.

The Dun Emer women put these ideals to practical use not only in the organization, design and craftwork of their industry, but in their everyday lives – supporting other home industries by purchasing items made in Ireland under the auspices of the home arts movement. For instance, Lily Yeats owned a dress and veil made of Limerick lace produced at Florence Vere O'Brien's Limerick school.[23] The adopted daughter of the Irish chief secretary (W.E. Forster), O'Brien successfully revived the craft of handmade lace and exhibited her industry's products at most of the major arts and crafts and art industry exhibitions in Ireland from 1890 to 1920.[24] Fashion historian Elizabeth Wilson claims that dress links the biological body to the social being, and private to public. Fashion can serve as a means of expressing individual identity while also securing social solidarity and imposing group norms, while deviations in dress are usually experienced as shocking and disturbing.[25] The personal act of dressing in Irish handmade lace reflected a particular tactic of consumption, one that lent a political dimension to an everyday practice.

In her writings on Irish dress, Evelyn Gleeson mused, 'how interesting and full of colour our streets could become if our people had a national dress and wore it proudly'.[26] Celtic dress was also praised by the weekly Gaelic League newspaper. In an illustrated article entitled 'A Costume for Irish Ladies' the journalist explained the many useful ways the outfits might be worn, while concluding that 'the most conscientious Irish Irelander may now be blissfully happy' wearing such an outfit.[27] Indeed, Celtic costume was an established way for the

22 Dun Emer Guild prospectus (1903), EGP, Trinity College, Dublin. **23** Last Will and Testament of Susan Mary (Lily) Yeats of Churchtown, Dundrum, Co. Dublin, 5 Jan. 1949. Lily bequeathed the Limerick lace dress and veil to her niece, Anne Butler Yeats. **24** *The Amateurs' Art Designer* (Sept. 1889). **25** Elizabeth Wilson, *Adorned in dreams: fashion and modernity* (University of California Press, 1987). **26** Draft letter to the editor of *Evening Herald*, EGP, Trinity College, Dublin. **27** 'A costume for Irish ladies', *Sinn Féin*, 5 Mar. 1910, quoted in Elizabeth Cumming and Nicola Gordon Bowe, *The arts and crafts movements in Dublin and*

upper classes in Ireland to show an acceptance of Irish patriotism. Lady Aberdeen famously dressed her children in Celtic attire and insisted that guests at several of her garden parties wear only Irish-made clothing.[28] Mary Colum's recounting of her own experience wearing Celtic costume provides an interesting contrast to this: '[It] was all right for the Abbey Theatre or Gaelic League dances, but once when myself and a friend … walked together down a street where the fisherwomen were selling their fish, we were openly derided.'[29] By clothing herself in Limerick lace, a handmade Irish material available in limited quantities, Lily Yeats clearly marked herself as a middle-class Irish woman, home arts supporter, and Irish Revivalist. Though still a display of class difference and privilege, this particular outfit deviated from the norm of Victorian fashion in that it produced a different set of references and meaning, ones grounded in the cultural nationalism of the Revival, as well as the social activism and aesthetic sensibilities of the home arts movement.

Many nineteenth-century social reformers were committed to the idea that rich and poor share a common culture and heritage that were physically realized in art objects. This shared culture was meant to help transcend class divisions and to foster a unified nation.[30] At Dun Emer, a sense of pride in Irish culture was evident in the design and material of every object. This sentiment was also conveyed to the local women workers through Irish language, music, dance, acting, painting, and drawing classes provided by the Guild. By encouraging local women to develop their cultural knowledge, Gleeson and the Yeats sisters performed a kind of educative nationalism. Yet, as educators, they laid claim to this culture and controlled how it was presented to the pupils. Representations of the middle-class background of the teachers and the working-class status of the students were harnessed together in a collaborative experiment. Students at Dun Emer won prizes in various competitions (language, music, dancing, drawing). For example, Rosie Gallagher of the Dun Emer Guild won the senior language contest at a Gaelic League competition held on the Dun Emer grounds. These women also helped produce the handmade journal of the Guild, by contributing poetry, short stories, drawings, and designs. Every woman working at the Guild was named at the beginning of each journal and news of the Guild was reported enthusiastically at the end of it, listing prizes won by particular women

Edinburgh, 1885-1925 (Dublin: Irish Academic Press, 1998), p. 122. **28** Evelyn Gleeson knew Lady Aberdeen socially and was invited to at least one of her garden parties. She was also aware of Lady Aberdeen's ability to draw attention to an industry. This is evident in a letter from Augustine Henry where he advises Gleeson to 'get Lady Aberdeen out' to Dun Emer for it 'increases profits' (Henry-Gleeson Letters, 1879–1930, National Library of Ireland; and EGP, Trinity College, Dublin). **29** Mary Colum, wife of the poet Padraic Colum, as quoted in Cumming and Bowe, *The arts and crafts movements*, p. 122. **30** Seth Koven, 'The Whitechapel picture exhibitions and the politics of seeing', in Daniel Sherman and Irit Rogoff (eds), *Museum culture: histories, discourses, spectacles* (Minneapolis: University of Minnesota Press, 1994), pp 22–48.

at specific exhibitions.[31] While the women workers certainly took pride in their learning and accomplishments, they also seem caught between a desire to share in the culture and ideology presented to them in these classes and the economic reality of their lives which materially excluded them from it. The products of the Guild were beyond the means of most of the working-class women who produced them.

The popularity of the Irish Revival meant this concern for Irish culture traversed all aspects of the arts in Ireland. One important institution of the Revival, the Gaelic League, was described as 'an organisation composed of all classes of Irishmen, without distinction of religious or political belief, aiming at development of the distinctive culture of Ireland and the betterment socially and industrially of the Irish people'.[32] Though carefully avoiding religious and class distinctions, the League nevertheless fostered a particular ideology based in these very differences. As Timothy Foley and Sean Ryder explain in *Ideology and Ireland in the Nineteenth Century* (1998), unresolved contests between Gaelic and English cultural values, between peasantry and gentry, between Protestant and Catholic were such highly visible conflicts in late nineteenth-century Ireland that ideology found itself continually in a state of exposure and confrontation, unable to 'naturalize' itself and achieve hegemonic invisibility.[33] Homi Bhabha claims that an important feature of colonial discourse is its dependence on the concept of 'fixity' in the ideological construction of otherness, in this case Irishness, with the stereotype as its major discursive strategy.[34] The spontaneous and visible recognition characteristic of the stereotype allows both colonizer and colonized to create a fixed reality where the other is entirely knowable. Yet in this 'metropolitan colony', whose subject population was both 'native' and 'white' at the same time, visual recognition had to take on new forms as physical difference was not sufficient to legitimate difference and power.[35] Given this, it is not surprising that the need for some kind of undeniably Irish character in art and design, as proposed by the Irish Revival, was a common theme at the turn of the century and was repeatedly praised by critics and commentators.

Celtic ornamentalism, found in ancient manuscripts such as the Book of Kells, was viewed as the ultimate expression of an Irish national art. In its 1903

31 Cuala Press Archive, Early Printed Books, Trinity College, Dublin.   **32** Newspaper clipping book, EGP, Trinity College, Dublin. The Gaelic League was founded in 1893. Its object was the encouragement of the Irish language and of Irish culture. The League spread throughout the country, recruiting Irish teachers and holding competitions in Irish speaking, music and dancing. See Jeanne Sheehy, *The rediscovery of Ireland's past: the Celtic Revival, 1830–1930* (London: Thames and Hudson, 1980), p. 98.   **33** Timothy P. Foley and Sean Ryder (eds), *Ideology and Ireland in the nineteenth century* (Dublin: Four Courts Press, 1998).   **34** Homi Bhabha, 'The other question', *Screen*, 24:6 (1983), pp 18–36.   **35** Catherine Hall (ed.), *Cultures of empire: colonisers in Britain and the empire in the nineteenth and twentieth centuries* (New York: Routledge, 2000). I believe Hall's use of the term 'metropolitan colony' best describes Ireland's location within the British empire.

prospectus, the Dun Emer Guild's designs were described as in keeping with the tradition of Celtic ornament while still being new and innovative. These designs were a rethinking of tradition, as it manifested itself in a country with a fractured, colonial past.[36] The reworking of traditional elements in these designs was the visual key to an earlier historical moment imagined to be noble, distinguished and artistically sophisticated. The newspapers commended this 'manifestation of the Celtic spirit as [one that] makes for peace, for practical effort, [and] for progress in the arts. [The] spirits of poetry, patriotism and true craft have joined hands at Dun Emer.'[37] This unproblematic continuity with tradition, which the press mistakenly assigned to the products of the Guild, papered over a disruptive history as well as current tensions. As early as 1903, the *Irish Homestead* wrote: 'Miss Gleeson and her colleagues deserve well of the Irish public, not only for what they have done, but for that sentiment of allying industry to art, and both to patriotism, which runs as a triple coloured thread ... through all their labours.'[38] Reclaiming Irishness and 'proving' Irish authenticities were common themes of late nineteenth-century Irish cultural nationalism. By this time, the role of authenticity had shifted from that of signifier of Irish cultural 'incapacities', to that of marketable sign of value.[39] The aura of intangible value that the press associated with the production of newly revived 'traditional' Irish craftwork demonstrates how authenticity was a profoundly political pretext for evaluation. The newspapers presented the products of the Guild as a form of consumable Irishness with its accompanying illusion of a uniform national identity.

The women of Dun Emer, on the other hand, sought to develop a new national art by originating works that combined the use of traditional craft skills and design motifs, to signal a pride in Ireland's past, with a more subtle, innovative artistic style that expressed hope for the present and future of the country. While references to a 'traditional' Irish past conferred a level of 'authenticity' upon the Guild's products, innovative and original designs and technical skills offered the craftworkers an opportunity to express their own creativity and draw upon current theories of art as well as nationalism. In a letter of 1904, Evelyn Gleeson writes, 'as the work at Dun Emer is all original, our methods are also those we have evolved from our own experience and they are in accordance with the best modern theories'.[40] At Dun Emer, authentic Ireland was made modern and new.

The best-known products of the Dun Emer embroidery department were twenty-four banners made for St Brendan's cathedral in Loughrea, Co. Galway.

36 Gibbons, *Transformations in Irish culture*, p. 5.   **37** 'An Artistic Industry', *c.* 1903, Newspaper clipping book, EGP, Trinity College, Dublin.   **38** *Irish Homestead*, 9 May 1903, p. 392.   **39** Colin Graham, '"... maybe that's just Blarney": Irish culture and the persistence of authenticity', in Colin Graham and Richard Kirkland (eds), *Ireland and cultural theory: the mechanics of authenticity* (New York: St Martin's, 1999), pp 7–16.   **40** Letter from Evelyn Gleeson, 9 Nov. 1904, EGP, Trinity College, Dublin.

The cathedral was a showpiece of Irish Revival arts and crafts and involved many craftspeople, including glassworkers Sarah Purser and A.E. Child.[41] The Loughrea banners were made of silk and wool embroidered on linen. Lily Yeats worked the main figures and most of the designs were by her brother, Jack Yeats, and his wife, Mary Cottenham Yeats, who designed the female saints depicted on the banners. The simplified design, rich colouring, and bold outlines of the figures, incorporated as a design feature, created a new approach to Irish applied art.

In addition to this major commission, the Guild exhibited works at the 1904 World's Fair in St Louis, Missouri. Triumphs of planning and coordination, the world fairs were occasions for agenda setting and identity formation. Fair villages, like the one exhibiting Dun Emer works, successfully merchandized Irish products and demonstrated the central role of craft revivals in awakening nationalist energies.[42] Dun Emer prominently displayed *The Orchard* and *The Meadow*, two needlework pictures executed by Lily Yeats, at the Irish pavilion of the St Louis World's Fair. Both pieces were presented as 'landscape embroideries' using silk threads embroidered on linen. Similar works were exhibited by the Guild with the Arts and Crafts Society of Ireland. With a distinctive embroidery technique that used unusually long stitches, the 'Irish' colouring of greens and purples of the local landscape, and innovative designs, these works helped originate the style of the Irish Revival.

When these works were first exhibited in 1904, the Anglo-Irish hold on the land in Ireland had been decisively and legislatively loosened.[43] The separation of the landed class from the traditional source of its authority is significant when looking at representations of the Irish landscape as imagined by middle-class Irish Protestant women. According to art historian Tricia Cusack, national imaginings of the land in Ireland generated two kinds of representations of the 'rural idyll': one based on the English ideal of estate and village, the other on an uncultivated wildness that was meant to signify non-anglicized Gaelic Ireland.[44] The Dun Emer landscape embroideries do not fit easily into either representational category. Rather, they perform a kind of balancing act between the two rural idylls. In *The Meadow* (1904) the viewer must look through the untamed wildflowers climbing up and across the foreground in order to see the trees of the

41 Purser was a stained glass worker and portrait painter most noted for establishing An Túr Gloine (Tower of Glass) stained glass workshop in Dublin. Child was a stained glass worker originally with Christopher Whall in England and then Purser's studio in Ireland. (See Cumming and Bowe, *The arts and crafts movements.*) **42** Neil Harris, 'Selling national culture: Ireland at the World's Columbian Exposition', in T.J. Edelstein (ed.), *Imagining an Irish past: the Celtic Revival, 1840–1940* (Chicago: David and Alfred Smart Museum of Art, 1992), pp 82–105. **43** A generation of land war and land legislation (in particular the Wyndham Act of 1903) brought about the break-up of the large estates and the creation of a multiplicity of small, independent farms (F.S.L. Lyons, *Culture and anarchy in Ireland, 1890–1939* (Oxford: Clarendon, 1979), p. 71). **44** Tricia Cusack, 'Migrant travellers and touristic idylls: The paintings of Jack B. Yeats and post-colonial identities', *Art History*, 21:2 (June 1998), p. 203.

background. The large expanse in the middle ground is specifically identified as a meadow and contrasted to the cultivated fields in the distance. The focus of this image, visually and in the title, is the uncultivated land of the meadow.[45] In *A Garden* (*c.*1905), an often-reproduced design for needlework pictures, this contrast is made by the title rather than in the picture itself.[46] This garden is reminiscent of Irish gardener William Robinson's 'wild gardening' style where native plants (foxglove, daisies, tulips, marigolds) were incorporated as though growing wild to signal national pride.[47] Set in the context of the land legislation and the break-up of the large, mainly Anglo-Irish estates in Ireland, these pictures can be read as a search for a sense of place, a fundamental part of territorial identity, by the middle-class Irish Protestant women who designed them. In these examples, the nationalism implied in the 'wildness' of the Irish landscape is 'tamed' by references to the ordered, settled and cultivated structure of the English-style 'rural idyll'.

This shifting and ambivalent representation of cultural identity characterizes the Guild as a whole. In the handmade journal produced by the Guild during its first three years, an ad reads: 'Decorate your home with Dun Emer tufted rugs, embroidered portières and sofa backs, put Dun Emer tapestries on your walls and Dun Emer books in your bookcases. This is the duty of an Irish woman.'[48] While the Dun Emer Guild was committed to a public role for art in the negotiation of Irish identity, the fact that not all Irish women could afford to decorate their homes with Dun Emer products appears to be overlooked. Irish identity, as it applied to the women involved in the Guild, was mediated by the class positions and experiences of both the founders and the workers. Though not part of the landlord class in Ireland, Gleeson and the Yeats sisters were part of an educated bourgeoisie while most of their workers were rural working-class women.[49] Still, the Dun Emer Guild can be read as a site of cross-

---

45 In another version of this design, the cultivated fields have been removed altogether, strengthening the emphasis on the meadow itself. 46 The first mention I have found of this design is in the handmade Dun Emer journal where it is listed as one of three embroidered panels sent to Liberty & Company on 3 July 1905 (the other two were *The Meadow* and *The Orchard*). (Cuala Press Archive, Early Printed Books, Trinity College, Dublin). 47 Born in Co. Down in 1838, William Robinson delivered one of the most pernicious attacks on the Victorian manner of gardening in his book *The wild garden* (1870), launching a campaign to reinstate indigenous shrubs, bulbs and perennials. He encouraged gardeners to study the wild flowers of meadows and follow nature's lead when creating a garden. (Wendy Hitchmough, *Arts and crafts gardens* (London: Pavilion, 1997), pp 54–69. 48 Dun Emer Journal, 1903–1905, Cuala Press Archive, Early Printed Books, Trinity College, Dublin. 49 Not all of the women working at Dun Emer were from working-class families, some even came from well-known artistic families: Beatrice Cassidy, the daughter of an official at Dundrum Asylum, came to work at the Press on 23 Feb. 1903. Her sister Frances was later employed in the embroidery section of the industry. Eileen Colum, sister of the poet Padraic Colum also joined the press. (Cuala Press Archive, Early Printed Books, Trinity College, Dublin).

class cultural exchange, where meaning and purpose were constantly shifting as workers were given more authority in the design and production of the works, paid higher wages according to merit, and became involved in the daily operation of the industry.

Ultimately, the Dun Emer Guild's involvement in the Irish Revival can be viewed as more closely linked with the progress of the arts than with political upheaval. The Guild promised economic revival through craft production and advertised the survival of artistic skills and common ideals to demonstrate its support for Revivalist politics. This home art industry sought to culturally validate the ambitions of the Irish Revival by appealing to 'local patriotism' rather than resorting to political radicalism. As one newspaper suggested in 1908: '[Evelyn Gleeson] is a good Home Ruler, but pending the attainment of her country's legislative independence, she wants to keep as many of the young people in their own country as she can, by giving them remunerative employment.'[50] This for Gleeson was her life's work, her cause. Clearly, she and the Yeats sisters preferred to assist in the economic and political growth of Ireland in a practical and tangible way. A marked concern for the living and working conditions of the local women and a desire to instil pride in a national heritage are evident in this Irish art industry. Drawing on the social ideals proposed by the home arts movement, Gleeson and the Yeats sisters sought to produce and market beautiful objects, while creating a viable industry that would supply employment and training to Irish women.

Although they attempted to foster a communal culture and heritage among all the women at Dun Emer, the relationships between Evelyn Gleeson, Lily Yeats, Elizabeth Yeats and their craftworkers were inevitably negotiated along class lines. The economic disparity between the three women and their workers was also occasionally political. In a letter to an American papermaker, Elizabeth Yeats writes that two of her printing assistants were arrested because the women 'belonged to Cumann na mBan – the woman's Republican Society – we are finished the book in spite of this upset'.[51] In running this art industry, the three middle-class women gained a greater understanding of the economic, social and political realities of the local women. It was this knowledge that drove them to politicize their philanthropic concerns and strive to improve the situation of these women.

Nationalist and feminist ideals were woven together in the Dun Emer Guild. The unmistakably Irish character of the Guild's work locates it within the Irish Revival, while awards won by exhibiting this work meant greater financial independence and professional exposure for the women involved. Challenging restrictive social codes, the Guild positioned these women within the public realm of industry and paid work.[52]

50 Newspaper clipping book, EGP, Trinity College, Dublin. **51** As quoted in Miller, *The Dun Emer Press*, p. 83. **52** The Guild exhibited at the 1904 Home Arts and Industries

The significance of the Dun Emer Guild's artistic contribution to the Irish Revival situates this industry within a historical moment marked by complex and changing power relations. At a time when key conflicts, negotiations and resolutions occurred along and between class and gender lines, these three entrepreneurial women remained dedicated to the education, artistic training, remunerative employment, and professional development of rural Irish women. This commitment highlights the extent to which Evelyn Gleeson, Lily Yeats and Elizabeth Yeats broadened their political horizons and impact through social activism and the belief that art is an instrument of social change rather than its result.

Exhibition at the Albert Hall in London, where Dun Emer embroidery won five stars, two of which were gold. One award from the Art Industries Exhibition of the Royal Dublin Society was worth £2. By 1905, the Guild was supplying embroidered panels to the London Arts & Crafts dealer, Liberty & Co, two of which also won awards at the Dublin Horse Show that year. At this same show, the tapestry, weaving and rugs exhibited by Dun Emer 'had the prizes' (Cuala Press Archive, Early Printed Books, Trinity College, Dublin; and the Dublin Horse Show, Special Issue of the *Irish Homestead*, 5 June 1905).

Explaining *Uladh*: cultural nationalism in Ulster[1]

MARNIE HAY

At the beginning of the twentieth century, a group of young people from Belfast banded together in an attempt to bring the province of Ulster into the Irish Literary Revival. They began in 1902 with the foundation of an amateur drama company that later became known as the Ulster Literary Theatre (ULT). Then they expanded into print with *Uladh*, a literary and critical magazine that appeared four times between November 1904 and September 1905. Although *Uladh* was modelled on W.B. Yeats' theatre journals *Beltaine* and *Samhain*, it differed from its models in two ways: it focused on Ulster, and it covered a far wider range of cultural topics than theatre. The magazine, however, was caught between a dismissive unionism and a southern Irish nationalism that disregarded Ulster's special circumstances. At the time of its inception, some critics misunderstood it because of its blatant regionalism. Due to its cultural nationalism, a wider Ulster audience in 1904–5, as well as Northern Irish literary critics during the so-called regional revival of the 1940s and 1950s, dismissed the magazine.

In the past, researchers have used *Uladh* as a tool to assist in the study of the ULT. This article is the first to examine the magazine as a subject in its own right. An idealistic exercise in constructive criticism and cultural propaganda, *Uladh* urged the people of Ulster to set aside bigotry and to value both economic *and* cultural pursuits, in order to take their rightful place in an Ireland that embraced its regional differences. Designed to advance the Ulster branch of the Irish Literary Revival in particular and the cause of cultural nationalism in general, *Uladh* attempted to explain Ulster to its own people and to the rest of Ireland. In doing so, the magazine helped to promote a sense of regional identity in Ulster. *Uladh* also helped to instigate the twentieth-century debate on Northern Ireland's separate regional literary and cultural status.

The Dublin-based Irish Literary Revival sparked a similar cultural nationalist movement in the North. 'Ardrigh', the Antrim Road home of Protestant

1 This paper is based on my 1999 MA thesis, 'Explaining *Uladh*: the promotion of nationalism and Regionalism in Ulster', which was completed at the Institute of Irish Studies, Queen's University Belfast. I would like to thank Ms Ophelia Byrne and Mr John Fairleigh for their assistance with my thesis research, as well as Dr Michael Laffan, Dr Charles Ivar McGrath, and participants in the UCD Open Postgraduate History Seminar, held on 21 Feb. 2002, for their comments on this paper.

Belfast solicitor Francis Joseph Bigger, served as the headquarters for a group of people interested in the revival of Irish culture. Frequent visitors included poet Alice Milligan and future martyr to the republican cause Roger Casement.

Alice Milligan, a Tyrone-born Protestant, was the driving force of the revival in Ulster in the early years. Along with poet Ethna Carbery, she started a publication entitled the *Shan Van Vocht* in 1896. The paper, which lasted three years, greatly influenced Milligan's young neighbour Bulmer Hobson, who subscribed to it while he was a student at the Friends' School in Lisburn. Although the subscription marked him out as an eccentric at this Quaker school, Hobson did not mind because the paper put him 'for the first time in touch with the forces that were beginning to stir in Ireland'.[2]

Recognising the propagandist potential of drama, Hobson and his friend David Parkhill organised the first production by the Ulster Branch of the Irish Literary Theatre, the forerunner of the ULT, in November 1902. Shortly afterwards, in early 1903, they established a propagandist organisation called the Protestant National Society, which provided a formal structure for their efforts to recruit young Ulster Protestants to the nationalist movement.[3] Members of the Society participated in the next recorded production of the fledgling theatre company, which was probably held in March of 1904.[4] Thus, although the Society 'had a brief and unimportant life', it attracted a group of young people who fostered the ULT, 'a body which exercised some influence on the cultural development of the North of Ireland'.[5]

As Ireland's first regional theatre company, the ULT was the most important theatre group of its day based outside Dublin.[6] Among the first plays to be staged by the ULT, then calling itself the Ulster Branch of the Irish Literary Theatre, were W.B. Yeats' *Cathleen Ni Houlihan* and George Russell's *Deirdre*. In 1904, the Irish National Theatre Society complained that the Belfast-based company had no right to use its former name and demanded royalties for the use of its scripts.[7] In response, the company changed its name to the Ulster Literary Theatre and began writing its own plays. In December 1904, in keeping with its new mandate, the ULT staged the work of two Ulster playwrights: *The Reformers* by Lewis Purcell (David Parkhill's pseudonym) and *Brian of Banba* by Hobson. In the previous month, the ULT had launched *Uladh* as a quarterly publication.

---

2 Bulmer Hobson, *Ireland yesterday and tomorrow* (Tralee: Anvil, 1968), p. 2. **3** Sam Hanna Bell, in *The theatre in Ulster* (Dublin: Gill and Macmillan, 1972), asserts that the Protestant National Society organized the theatre company's first production (pp 2–3). This Society, however, was actually established *after* the first production, as a response to an article by Seumas MacManus advocating the formation of a Young Protestant National Party, published in the United Irishman in Jan. 1903. **4** Bell, *Theatre*, p. 3. **5** Hobson, *Ireland*, p. 4. **6** Mark Phelam, 'The rise and fall of the Ulster literary theatre' (unpublished MPhil thesis, Trinity College Dublin, 1998), p. 54; Robert Hogan and James Kilroy, *The modern Irish drama*, vol. 2 (Dublin: Dolmen, 1976), p. 121. **7** Phelam, 'Rise and Fall', p. 4.

Hobson recalled that the magazine's 'working capital consisted of five pounds' subscribed by architect Parkhill, journalist James Winder Good, artist John Campbell, music critic W.B. Reynolds, and Hobson himself: 'We were the committee in charge with Reynolds as editor and Campbell as manager.'[8] In announcing the advent of *Uladh*, however, *The United Irishman* listed both Reynolds and poet Joseph Campbell as editors.[9] The magazine's title, 'Uladh', is the genitive case of 'Ulaidh', meaning Ulster in Irish. As its title suggests, *Uladh*'s focus was meant to be on the nine northern counties of Ireland, but its content betrayed a definite Belfast bias with occasional forays into counties Antrim and Donegal. The magazine featured a vibrant mix of essays, poetry, artwork, and drama, contributed by journalists, political activists, writers, artists, composers, and poets. It ran on the proverbial shoestring; contributors were not paid,[10] and only a few hundred copies of each issue were published.[11] Each copy cost sixpence, but, as the first editorial pretentiously declared, 'we do not aim at being sixpence-worth; we aim at being priceless, for honesty and good purpose are priceless'.[12] Despite an increasingly positive response from critics, *Uladh* folded after a year. The reasons for the magazine's demise remain in question.

In keeping with its commitment to cultural nationalism, *Uladh* provided a forum for artists, composers and poets, as well as essayists. The magazine's illustrators included several members of the Ulster Arts Club, which began in November 1902, as part of 'the same cultural quickening' that inspired the ULT, and shared many of the same members.[13] Illustrator and designer John Campbell, whose work displayed a distinctive Celtic style, contributed a number of images to *Uladh*. He continued to use his artistic talents to political ends by producing a postcard for the nationalist Dungannon Clubs, which Hobson co-founded in March 1905, and contributing artwork to Hobson's separatist newspaper the *Republic*, which ran from December 1906 to May 1907.[14]

Three of the eight Morrow brothers, the sons of Protestant Belfast painter and decorator George Morrow, contributed artwork to *Uladh*, while another brother, Harry, contributed an essay. The clubs to which they belonged and the publications to which they submitted work reflect their nationalist sympathies. Cartoonists and illustrators Edwin, George (the future art editor of *Punch*), and Norman Morrow belonged to a literary club in London, which also included *Daily News* reporter Robert Lynd amongst its membership. Edwin and Norman also joined a London Dungannon Club founded by composer Herbert Hughes.

8 Qtd. in Margaret McHenry, 'The Ulster theatre in Ireland' (unpublished PhD thesis, University of Pennsylvania, 1931), p. 83. 9 *United Irishman*, 15 Oct. 1904, p. 5. There is some confusion about the editorship of *Uladh*, possibly due to the existence of an editorial council. See Hay, 'The Promotion of nationalism and regionalism in Ulster', pp 10–11. 10 Forrest Reid, *Private road* (London: Faber and Faber, 1940), p. 39. 11 McHenry, 'Ulster Theatre', p. 7. 12 *Uladh* 1 (Nov. 1904), p. 2. 13 John Hewitt, *Art in Ulster: 1* (Belfast: Blackstaff, 1977), p. 68. 14 Theo Snoddy, *Dictionary of Irish artists: 20th century* (Dublin: Wolfhound, 1996), p. 50.

Like Campbell, the brothers used their artwork for political purposes. Edwin, George, and Norman illustrated Dungannon Club postcards while George, Norman, and another brother, Jack, contributed cartoons to the *Republic*.¹⁵ *Uladh's* artwork garnered critical praise throughout the magazine's existence.¹⁶

Uladh featured a number of contributions from composers, including Herbert Hughes, who achieved fame through his arrangements of traditional Irish folk songs, Carl Hardebeck, who later became professor of Music at University College Cork,¹⁷ and Reynolds, who was known for his musical compositions. Their essays examined Irish music within the wider context of European classical and folk music.

Uladh attracted poetry from several well-known poets of the day, such as Joseph Campbell, Alice Milligan (one of only two women who wrote for *Uladh*), Æ, and Padraic Colum, as well as individuals who were better known for other activities, such as Hobson and Good. The poetry tends to derive from Celtic mythology, as in Hobson's poem 'The Deluge', which featured Manannan Mac Lir,¹⁸ or follow what Terence Brown has called 'the rural, pastoral mode of poetry which the Irish national movement and its related literary revival confirmed as Irish aesthetic orthodoxy'.¹⁹ For instance, in a poem entitled 'At the End', Good recalled 'the blue of all the summers, the green of all the springs / And the white apple orchards where, thro' the silver rain / How sweet the blackbird sings!'²⁰ The magazine's poetry is indicative of its time and has not aged well.

Overall, however, the magazine's cast of contributors, who also included Bigger, Casement, and Gaelic League activist P.T. McGinley, was impressive. As such, *Uladh* represented one of the few times in Ulster history that a movement 'attracted such a galaxy of talent and in which men and women of such diverse creeds and political views were united in a common purpose'.²¹

Politically, the people who established the ULT and *Uladh* were an anomaly in Belfast, which the industrial revolution had turned into a 'sprawling manufacturing centre' with a large Protestant middle class who looked to England for cultural, political, and economic sustenance.²² The 'well-meaning band of young idealists' who produced *Uladh* naively believed that the problem of sectarianism in Ulster could be conquered by 'reason and enlightened humanism'. They originated 'mostly in a Presbyterian dissenting background, with a strong political allegiance stretching back to the ideals of the United Irishmen'.²³ A few Anglicans, Methodists, and Catholics also participated in these two ventures.²⁴

15 Ibid., pp 330–3. 16 F.M. Atkinson, 'A literary causerie', *Dana* 8 (Dec. 1904), p. 253; 'Uladh New Belfast Magazine', *Irish News*, 7 Nov. 1904, p. 4. 17 McHenry, 'Ulster theatre', p. 8. 18 *Uladh* 1, p. 13. 19 Terence Brown, *Northern voices: poets from Ulster* (Dublin: Gill and Macmillan, 1975), p. 2. 20 *Uladh* 1, p. 18. 21 David Kennedy, 'The drama in Ulster', in Sam Hanna Bell (ed.), *The arts in Ulster* (London: George G. Harrap, 1951), p. 57. 22 Peter K. McIvor, 'Regionalism in Ulster: an historical perspective', *Irish University Review* 13.2 (Autumn 1983), p. 184. 23 Hagal Mengel, 'A lost heritage', *Theatre Ireland* 1 (Sept.–Dec. 1982), p. 19. 24 Dorothy

As Stephen Gwynn, a contemporary writer and future Irish Parliamentary Party MP, pointed out, this band of idealists 'illustrated the truth that Belfast is not all of one orange colour'.[25]

Although some members of this group supported a cultural nationalism that promoted Irish language, literature, music, and sport as an end in itself, others saw cultural nationalism as a step toward the ultimate political goal of an independent Irish state. All those involved with *Uladh* would have agreed with the sentiments expressed in late 1905, when Hobson's republican friend Patrick McCartan informed Joe McGarrity, a Clan na Gael organizer in America, that *Uladh*'s 'present circulation is confined to wealthy protestants', and that the object of Hobson's colleagues 'will be to bring them along gradually to nationalism'.[26] Some, however, saw this nationalism as merely cultural, while others, such as Hobson and Joseph Campbell, saw it as political.

As their families and employers did not always agree with their political views, some members of the group submitted their work under pseudonyms. 'They had been gaily treading the path to perdition for several years before even their parents knew who [they] were,' noted Dorothy Macardle in the *Irish Press*.[27] The situation was best exemplified in the pages of *Uladh* itself by Lynd. Using the pseudonym Riobárd Ua Fhloinn, he stated in an essay entitled 'Ancestor-Worship in Ulster' that 'the unpardonable sin in the eyes of an Ulster father is that his son should hold a different opinion from his own', adding that this sin could affect one's employment prospects.[28] In light of this situation, it is not surprising that *Northern Whig* reporter James Winder Good wrote for *Uladh* under the initials J.W. to conceal his identity from his loyalist employer.

The editorial in the first issue of *Uladh* stressed that the magazine would be non-sectarian and non-political, and described its contributors as 'mostly young men, of all sects and all grades of political opinion'.[29] The magazine's focus was on cultural rather than political nationalism, despite the fact that many of its contributors were, as playwright Rutherford Mayne put it, 'flaming nationalist[s]' who advocated an independent Ireland.[30] The editorial also noted that the magazine would be 'run on broad propagandist lines', in order to tap into 'a strong undercurrent of culture in the North'. It concluded: 'if it is in our power to awaken the heroes to activity and the people to sympathy and life, surely our existence will be justified'.[31]

For novelist Forrest Reid, the pages of *Uladh* reflected 'the bravery of revolt – revolt against the tyranny of commercial materialism which weighed upon

Macardle, 'The Ulster Players', *Irish Press*, 10 Dec. 1931, p. 6. **25** Stephen Gwynn, *Irish literature and drama in the English language* (London: Thomas Nelson and Sons, 1936), p. 205. **26** National Library of Ireland (NLI), Joseph McGarrity Papers, MS 17,457(2). **27** Macardle, 'Ulster players', p. 6. **28** *Uladh* 3 (May 1905), pp 10–11. **29** *Uladh* 1, p. 3. **30** Qtd. in Sr Assumpta Saunders and A.A. Kelly, *Joseph Campbell: poet and nationalist* (Dublin: Wolfhound, 1988), p. 30. **31** *Uladh* 1, p. 3.

our native city and in the shadow of which we have all been brought up'.[32] Reynolds approached Reid about contributing to *Uladh* in December 1904, showering him with the first issue of the magazine, a list of eminent upcoming contributors, and a crash course on the 'Ulster Renaissance'. Despite Reynolds' enthusiasm, Reid remained unconvinced. Writing in 1940, he explained: 'Although Irish, I had never been interested in politics … had never distinguished in my mind between north from south, and the Ulster propaganda did not particularly appeal to me.'[33] Reid went on to point out that this 'Ulster propaganda', in contrast to the Northern Irish regionalism of the 1940s, was nationalist and 'merely insisted that Ulster should play its part in the Irish Revival'.[34]

The Ulster propaganda of *Uladh* differed from that of Northern Irish regionalism, best exemplified by the writings of poet John Hewitt, in that it embraced Ulster regionalism *and* Irish nationalism. *Uladh's* propaganda 'sought not so much to assert the independence of Ulster, as to define its distinctive character within "the generous circle of nationality"'.[35] *Uladh* explored the 'relationship of center to periphery' and aimed 'to foster a specifically Ultonian artistic spirit'.[36] The magazine's Ulster focus was initially problematic for southern critics. They feared that the magazine was encouraging the development of 'a separate culture from the rest of Ireland'.[37] *Uladh's* emphasis on an Ulster identity, however, was not endorsing some sort of cultural separatism but proposing that 'a nation is made up not only of similarities but also of regional differences'.[38]

At the same time, *Uladh's* creators realized that it was more difficult for the literary revival to take root in Ulster because of the predominance in the region of protestantism, unionism, and rampant industrialism.[39] They recognized that Ulster's differences would require a separate brand of propaganda in order to raise interest in cultural nationalism. *Uladh's* Ulster focus, coupled with its critical coverage of a wide variety of cultural activities, provided this separate brand of propaganda.

Each issue of *Uladh* was named after the traditional Celtic festival celebrated in the season in which the magazine appeared. Thus, the first issue, which came out in November 1904, was known as the Samhain number. Its editorial announced that 'this Ulster has its own way of things … still keeping on Irish lands', and that the Ulster way was what the new magazine wanted to discuss, influence, direct, and inform.[40] It predicted that *Uladh* would offer its readers a

32 Forrest Reid, 'Eighteen years work: the Ulster Players', *The Times*, Northern Ireland Supplement, 5 Dec. 1922, p. xviii. **33** Reid, *Private road*, p. 35. **34** Ibid. See Chapter Six of Gillian McIntosh, *The force of culture* (Cork: Cork UP, 1999) for a discussion of cultural regionalism in Northern Ireland. **35** Phelam, 'Rise and fall', p. 45. **36** Laura Elizabeth Lyons, 'Writing in trouble: Protest, literature and the cultural politics of Irish nationalism' (unpublished PhD thesis, University of Texas at Austin, 1993), p. 40. **37** Atkinson, *Dana* 8, p. 253. **38** Lyons, 'Writing in trouble', p. 37. **39** McIvor, 'Regionalism in Ulster', p. 184. **40** *Uladh* 1, p. 1.

far wider range of cultural topics than just theatre: 'as the Theatre is the most essential of all art activities, and the surest test of a people's emotional and intellectual vitality, *Uladh* starts out as an organ of the Theatre, the Ulster Literary Theatre, but proposes to be as irrelevant to that movement and its topics as is deemed necessary'.[41] In an effort to reawaken and foster Irish culture in the North, the magazine was to cover everything from Irish mythology to middle-class architecture. This variety sets the Ulster magazine apart from Yeats' contemporary theatre publications, which tended to concentrate on 'literary and aesthetical problems' associated with drama,[42] and thereby challenges Ernest A. Boyd's assertion that *Uladh* merely 'served … the same purpose as *Beltaine* and *Samhain*'.[43]

In a review of the first issue of *Uladh* in the December 1904 issue of *Dana*, a short-lived monthly magazine, literary critic F.M. Atkinson pronounced the venture 'very interesting and highly suggestive'. He had reservations, however, about the magazine's Ulster focus. 'It is sad to find it positively declaring that Ulster means to foster a separate culture from the rest of Ireland,' he wrote, noting that the island had always been cursed by 'its divisions and factions'.[44] Atkinson appears to have missed the point that the magazine would look at the Ulster way, while 'still keeping on Irish lands'.

Critics with the Belfast-based *Irish News* and Dublin-based *An Claidheamh Soluis* had a better grip on what *Uladh* was trying to achieve. The *Irish News* critic asserted: '*Uladh* merits the hearty support of all who profess to have an interest in the intellectual life of Ireland', adding that the magazine had 'a special claim upon the North'. This critic recognized that the magazine would examine Ulster within a broader Irish framework and saw the debate over *Uladh*'s regionalism as 'a moot question'.[45] Similarly, the review published in *An Claidheamh Soluis* hailed the first issue of *Uladh* as 'a new and beautiful periodical' illustrating 'that in the so-called "Black North" there are young Irish intellects in close communion with Ireland, thinking and writing and singing of and for Ireland'.[46]

The Ulster branch of the literary revival differed from the Dublin movement in that it looked to the region's own history, not just 'the peasant culture of the West', in order to uncover its cultural roots.[47] Thus, throughout *Uladh*'s history its contributors seem to have been engaged in a search 'for the identity of the province on the basis of a common notion of its social history and traditions'.[48] A number of contributions to the first issue illustrate this.

For instance, an essay on 'The Spinning Wheels of Ulster' by engineer and spinning wheel collector John Horner offered readers a lesson in the social his-

41 Ibid. **42** Hagal Mengel, *Sam Thompson and modern drama in Ulster* (Frankfurt am Main: Peter Lang, 1986), p. 23. **43** Ernest A. Boyd, *Ireland's Literary Renaissance* (Dublin: Maunsel, 1916), p. 364; *Contemporary drama of Ireland* (Dublin: Talbot, 1918), p. 72. **44** Atkinson, *Dana* 8, pp 252–3. **45** *Irish News,* 7 Nov. 1904, p. 4. **46** *An Claidheamh Soluis,* 26 Nov. 1904, p. 8. **47** McIvor, 'Regionalism in Ulster', p. 184. **48** Mengel, *Ulster drama*, p. 24.

tory of the linen industry. An *aisling*-inspired essay entitled 'The Sleepers of Aileach' by Joseph Campbell was rooted in mythological tradition. It urged Caitlín Ní hUallacháin, a symbol of Ireland used by Yeats in his play of the same (anglicized) name, to rouse the sleeping heroes of ancient Ulster.[49] The essay, which the *Irish News* called 'a propagandist parable', parallels *Uladh*'s own goal to rouse Ulster into action for the cause of Irish cultural nationalism.[50] With an essay on 'Art and Culture in Old Belfast', Bigger tapped into a contemporary view that the introduction of industry into Belfast 'was associated … not only with the loss of a more gracious way of life, but also with the loss of cultural identity and, by extension, with the loss of nationality itself'.[51] Bigger compared Belfast's current state of artistic and cultural decay with its vibrant state prior to the Industrial Revolution. He expressed hope that Belfast could regain its position as the 'Northern Athens': 'We see glimmerings of salvation in the present Gaelic revival and in the art and technical instruction at present being imparted in the city.'[52]

In the pages of *Uladh*, Ulster unionists were regularly criticized for allowing their political views to cloud their cultural vision. For instance, 'Literature and Politics', an essay in the first issue that was recently identified as the work of Belfast-bred Seamus Connolly, the secretary of the Dublin-based Theatre of Ireland,[53] lamented the Ulster unionists' lack of interest in native Irish literature: 'Their unionism was a narrow and barren creed, which would exclude all native beauty in art and literature, because it was native.' This attitude, he conceded, was due to 'a current of nationalism … in the literary output of Ireland of to-day'. He suggested that things were beginning to change, noting that 'without fear of compromising their political opinions, nationalist and unionist are preparing to co-operate in many things, and not least in literature, for the honour of Éire'. In conclusion, Connolly urged unionists and nationalists to work together 'in earnestness and fervour' to promote cultural nationalism.[54]

The second issue of *Uladh*, which appeared in February 1905, had more of an all-Irish feel with the inclusion of poetry by Padraic Colum and an essay by Stephen Gwynn. In 'The Northern Gael', Gwynn criticized economic boom-town Belfast for thinking itself in advance of Dublin, which he suggested was politically and culturally superior. Belfast had recently (and transiently) over-taken Dublin to become the largest city in Ireland. Despite this, Gwynn described Belfast as 'a provincial town of little interest, except for those who desire to study almost extinct types of religious bigotry'. He encouraged the so-called Northern Gael, a traditional leader in Ireland, to overcome bigotry in order to accept, rather than reject, his Irishness, and to join in the Irish cause: 'If Ulster, or even Belfast, is finally divorced in spirit from Ireland, it is a pity of pities; for Ireland,

49 *Uladh* 1, p. 6.   **50** *Irish News,* 7 Nov. 1904, p. 4.   **51** McIvor, 'Regionalism in Ulster', p. 185.   **52** *Uladh* 1, p. 12.   **53** Phelam, 'Rise and fall', p. 2.   **54** *Uladh* 1, pp 17–18.

wanting the hand of the North, will go maimed; but Belfast divorced from Ireland will be squalid, undignified, and contemptible.'[55]

The third issue of *Uladh*, which appeared in May 1905, included an essay entitled 'The Theatre and the People' in which Good defended the new cultural movement, which had been criticized for attacking the qualities that contributed to the success of Ulster. He explained the movement was not attacking these qualities, which 'are good in themselves', but was attacking 'that caricature of them that is so complacently accepted as the real thing in Ulster today'. Good urged the people of Ulster to value success in artistic endeavours, as well as success in industry: 'Energy, tenacity, and thrift are considerable qualities in the making of a people. But when thrift verges on meanness, when tenacity becomes obstinacy, and energy finds its only outlet in a frantic struggle for wealth, it is time for those who care for life and the beauty and graciousness of life to protest.' Good asserted that the ULT was staging this protest.

Ulster's connection to Scotland was acknowledged in the first three issues of *Uladh*. Reynolds discussed the impact of Ulster's Scottish and English heritage on acting in a ULT review in the first issue, while in the second Bigger highlighted the popularity of Robert Burns' poetry among members of an eighteenth-century Templepatrick lending library. The third issue promoted the Scots connection through the publication of an Irish-language translation of a Joseph Campbell poem about the MacCruimins, the hereditary pipers to the MacLeods of Skye. An illustration of a bagpiper by John Campbell accompanied the poem. The magazine made no mention of the Ulster Scots dialect, though the language of *The Enthusiast*, a Lewis Purcell play published in the third issue, is rich with Ulster colloquialisms.

The fourth and final issue of *Uladh*, which appeared in September 1905, included a nostalgic prose poem about 1798 by Bigger that sought to assert 'a sense of continuity of nationalist culture' in Ulster,[56] as well as an essay by Lynd entitled 'A Plea for Extremists'. Lynd encouraged people to adopt a 'magnificent and broad-minded bigotry' against English culture, recommending that moderation be countered by an extreme passion for culture 'in a really Irish vein', even if it was only 'middling'. In his view, nationality should come before art in order to prepare 'the soil in which a great and distinct national literature may flourish many years hence'.[57]

As can be seen from the preceding examples, certain themes typically ran through the pages of *Uladh*. These included: the celebration and criticism of things that made Ulster a unique part of Ireland; a nostalgia for Ulster's past; the value of cultural pursuits, especially those with an Irish accent; and the need for Protestants and Catholics, no matter their political hue, to come together.

55 *Uladh* 2 (Feb. 1905), pp 11–12. **56** McIvor, 'Regionalism in Ulster', p. 186. **57** *Uladh* 4 (Sept. 1905), pp 14–16.

The editorial in the final issue of *Uladh* gave no indication of its imminent demise: 'This number of *Uladh* ends our first year of publication. We can now stand on the four-cornered tower of our year's building and note the outlook, retrospective and future.'[58] Clearly, the editors expected the magazine to continue. A letter from Patrick McCartan to Joe McGarrity, dated 23 December 1905, indicates that there were plans to turn *Uladh* into a monthly publication.[59] On the same date, a poet signing herself Una (probably Alberta Victoria Montgomery) wrote to Milligan that *Uladh* had accepted her poem about the Strangford Lough for the first issue of 1906.[60] Her next letter, of 11 January 1906, expressed surprise that this issue was not out yet. It never appeared.

Margaret McHenry has noted that the magazine 'died an early death due to lack of financial sustenance';[61] Laura Elizabeth Lyons has concurred.[62] Neither researcher, however, cited the source of this information. The absence of advertising in the final issue supports their view.

In his autobiography, Reid painted a slightly different picture of the magazine's demise. In late 1905 Reid was invited to edit *Uladh*, but 'was too busy to undertake the proposed task, and *Uladh* expired, having run as long a course as such ventures usually do'. He later suspected that the magazine 'perished largely for lack of copy' because most of its contributors, including Reynolds, Good, Parkhill and Joseph Campbell, were busy writing plays. As Reid himself surmised, 'A magazine cannot be run on plays alone, and I don't think anybody except me was interested in other literary forms.'[63] By late 1905 Hobson was probably too busy with Dungannon Club activities to provide regular copy or editorial leadership. The fact that the shortest issue of *Uladh*, which contained only 27 pages of material, was to be its final issue may support Reid's view.

A revival of *Uladh* was contemplated in 1907. This was first announced in the *Republic*, Hobson's weekly newspaper, on 14 February 1907. Correspondence from Casement to Hobson suggests that an attempt to revive the magazine was made in the autumn of 1907.[64] In early August, Casement even submitted an essay to *Uladh* on the need for an Irish Olympic team.[65] A letter dated 24 October 1907 indicated that a new issue of *Uladh* was no longer in the works. Whether from lack of funds, lack of copy, or lack of an editor, *Uladh* was dead.

From the preceding analysis of *Uladh*, it can be seen that this short-lived but important magazine was the creation of a group of relatively young, idealistic, middle-class Ulstermen from mainly (but not exclusively) protestant backgrounds. Inspired by the ideals of Wolfe Tone and the United Irishmen, the members of this group shared a commitment to the Irish cause that varied from sup-

---

58 Ibid., p. 1. **59** NLI, McGarrity Papers, MS 17,457(2). **60** NLI, Alice Milligan Papers, MS 5048. **61** McHenry, 'Ulster theatre', p. 7. **62** Lyons, 'Writing in trouble', p. 50. **63** Reid, *Private road*, pp 39–40. **64** NLI, Bulmer Hobson Papers, MS 13,158. **65** NLI, Hobson Papers, MS 13,159.

port for cultural nationalism, to home rule, to outright independence. As Hobson optimistically noted, 'Protestant Ireland is awakening to the fact that its grand-fathers dreamed a dream, and its fathers tried to forget it – but the call of it is in their ears.'[66] This group, like the United Irishmen and the Young Irelanders before them, advocated the fusion of the Irish people – Catholic and Protestant, native and newcomer – into one nation. Unlike their forerunners, however, whose main concern was Irish identity, they addressed Ulster's regional identi-ty within the broader Irish context.

This group's concern for cultural nationalism, coupled with the overtly nationalist politics of some of its members, marked them out as rebels in Ulster. Enthusiastic and articulate, they used *Uladh* as a vehicle for constructive criti-cism and cultural propaganda, encouraging the people of Ulster to set aside reli-gious bigotry and to value both economic *and* cultural pursuits, in order to take their rightful place in an Ireland that embraced its regional differences.

By promoting this message in the form of an artistic quarterly, however, the magazine's creators limited its appeal to a small middle-class elite.[67] In addition, the magazine's inability to attract a wider Protestant audience may have been affected by the unfortunate timing of its publication during the devolution crisis of 1904–5. The nationalist bias of some of the publications that reviewed *Uladh*, such as the *Irish News* and the *United Irishman*, indicate that the magazine was preaching to the converted. *Uladh*'s small circulation and minority viewpoint ensured that ultimately it failed to change popular opinion in Ulster. Yet, in rec-ognizing Ulster's unique heritage within a wider Irish nationality, the magazine did succeed in promoting a regional identity that sparked a debate on 'the lit-erary status of Ulster ... which continues to this day'.[68]

Ironically, the Irish Literary Revival initially provoked a contemplation of Ulster's distinct literary and cultural position.[69] The founders of the ULT and *Uladh* realized that it was more difficult for the literary revival to take root in Ulster because of the region's Protestantism, unionism, and industrialism.[70] In order to raise interest in the revival, they developed, through their dramatic and journalistic activities, a separate brand of propaganda that took Ulster's differ-ences into consideration. Hobson, along with several *Uladh* contributors (most notably Good and Lynd), continued an overtly political form of this propagan-da through the activities of the separatist Dungannon Clubs and the *Republic* newspaper.

Uladh was a key part of this reconsideration of Ulster's literary and cultural status. It 'helped to articulate a distinctively Ulster voice, which was dedicated

66 Bulmer Hobson, 'The new Ulster', *Nationist,* 30 Nov. 1905, p. 169. 67 David Kennedy, 'Ulster unionism and the new nationalism', in Kevin B. Nowlan (ed.), *The making of 1916* (Dublin: Stationery Office, 1969), p. 75. 68 Phelam, 'Rise and fall', p. 45. 69 McIvor, 'Regionalism in Ulster', p. 180. 70 Ibid., p. 184.

to interpreting the North to the rest of Ireland, and Ulster to itself.'[71] Both *Uladh* and the ULT raised awareness about those aspects of Ulster culture that differentiated it from the other Irish provinces.[72] In praising Ireland for its regional diversity and criticising the cultural factors that prevented Ulster from supporting the Irish cultural nationalist movement, *Uladh* served as a vehicle to promote regionalism *and* nationalism.

Unfortunately, the ULT and *Uladh* 'have not always been recognized ... as the instigators of the debate on the North's regional literary status'.[73] For instance, editors of Ulster literary magazines that fostered the so-called regional revival of the 1940s and 1950s largely ignored its efforts. *Lagan* editor John Boyd wrote that his forum for Ulster writing, which ran from 1943 to 1947, was 'the first of its kind to appear in Ulster'.[74] Roy McFadden and Barbara Hunter, the editors of *Rann*, a quarterly magazine with a liberal and regional slant that appeared between 1948 and 1953, included *Uladh* in their list of Ulster publications.[75] They failed to mention, however, the magazine's significance in helping instigate the debate on Ulster's literary and cultural status.

In the first issue of *Threshold*, a publication of Belfast's Lyric Players, Mary O'Malley alluded to magazines like *Uladh* but did not mention any by name: 'Despite high literary standards and imaginative presentation of general topics few [Irish periodicals] have survived ... No one, however, would deny the value of their contribution of creative writing and objective criticism.'[76] *Uladh* contributed in both of these areas.

Although none of these three publications acknowledge *Uladh*, they all reflect its legacy. *Lagan* and *Rann* shared its sense of regional identity and combination of literary and critical content, while *Threshold* shared the latter element as well as its theatrical roots. The only real difference between these publications and *Uladh* is that they did not share its nationalism. *Uladh*'s overt cultural nationalism may be part of the reason why its contribution to regionalism in Ulster is not always acknowledged. Ironically, it was *Uladh*'s regionalism, not its nationalism, which initially disturbed the magazine's critics.

As noted at the outset, *Uladh* helped to instigate the debate on Ulster's literary and cultural status. This debate questions whether Ulster literature and culture are part of a broader British tradition, part of an Irish tradition, or, as Boyd and Hewitt asserted, a separate Ulster tradition.[77] More recently, literary critic Edna Longley has suggested that Ulster, or more precisely Northern Ireland, is a cultural corridor with one end open to Ireland and the other open to Britain.[78]

71 Phelam, 'Rise and fall', p. 49. 72 Lyons, 'Writing in trouble', p. 78. 73 Phelam, 'Rise and fall', p. 55. 74 John Boyd, 'Introduction', *Lagan* 1.1 (1943), p. 5. 75 Barbara Hunter and Roy McFadden (eds), 'Ulster books and authors', *Rann* 20 (June 1953), p. 72. 76 Mary O'Malley, 'Foreword', *Threshold* 1.1 (Feb. 1957), p. 5. 77 McIvor, 'Regionalism in Ulster', p. 186. 78 Qtd. in Maurna Crozier (ed.), *Cultural traditions in Northern Ireland* (Belfast: Institute of Irish Studies, 1989), pp 35, 97.

For the creators of *Uladh*, Ulster's literature and culture represented a unique regional tradition within a broader Irish tradition.

As manifestations of the Ulster branch of the Irish Literary Revival, the ULT and *Uladh* were designed to promote Irish cultural nationalism in Ulster. In responding to the unique challenges of promoting nationalism in the North, both the theatre company and the magazine advanced a sense of regional identity in Ulster. As the ULT's work grew in commercial popularity, 'the original nationalist impulse grew weaker', and the company 'developed a rich vein of comedy which helped to sweeten relations between unionist and nationalist in a period of bitter political strife'.[79] Had *Uladh* survived beyond its first year of publication, it might have gone the same route and abandoned its cultural nationalism in favour of a stronger emphasis on regionalism.

A regional bias has been evident in Ulster's literary output, dating back at least to the plantations of the early seventeenth century.[80] The friction between a particularly large influx of Protestant newcomers and the Catholic native population contributed to Ulster's unique heritage within Ireland. The Irish Literary Revival sparked a reconsideration of this regional bias by the Ulster branch of the revival. As a manifestation of this revival, *Uladh* promoted a sense of regional identity by explaining Ulster to itself and to the rest of Ireland. In doing so, it fanned the flames of a debate on Ulster's literary and cultural status that still continues.

79 Kennedy, 'Ulster unionism', pp 74–5. **80** McIvor, 'Regionalism in Ulster', p. 180.

Revivalist belligerence: three controversies

LUCY MC DIARMID

Two-and-a-half years before Francis Sheehy Skeffington was shot by a British officer in the name of the empire, he was nearly killed by an Irish mob in the name of 'faith and fatherland'. Believing that he was turning Catholic children over to Protestant proselytizers involved in the 'Save the Dublin Kiddies' campaign, a mob composed primarily of members of the Ancient Order of Hibernians attacked Sheehy Skeffington as he entered Kingsbridge station on 25 October with two sons of a locked-out worker. He was 'seized from behind, knocked down, and buffeted out of the station. He was bruised on the head and body.' The crowd shouted, '[K]ill him.' When he went back for his bicycle, the crowd 'kicked and struck him'.[1] William Orpen, who saw Sheehy Skeffington return that day to Liberty Hall, wrote, 'He had nothing on except a blanket wrapped around him.'[2]

Sheehy Skeffington had not gone to the station naively: he put his body on the line deliberately and provocatively to make visible the violence of those allegedly acting in the name of Irishness and Catholicism. Although not all controversies in the years before the Rising involved threats to life and limb, they often involved a similar belligerence expressed in the name of the national cause. If they had simply pitted the colonized Irish against the English colonials, revivalist controversies would lack drama for the scholar: the high moral ground would be obvious, the participants' roles predictable, and the stories unambiguous, reflecting the large-scale antagonisms of the great national narrative. But many cultural contests of this period show the way different subcultures within Ireland fought to control sites whose symbolic power associated them, by synecdoche, with the entire nation. The drama in the railway station did not, as its instigators insisted, pit Catholics against Protestants or Irish against English: fundamentalist Catholics fought labourite leftists over control of the bodies of poor children. The overriding cultural question, even before independence, was not Irish Ireland or English Ireland, but *whose* Irish Ireland?

Yeats referred to the Ireland of the early 1920s, the new Free State, as 'plastic', ready to be formed and molded. But Yeats himself, along with all the cultural leaders of the years before 1916, had been 'inventing' Ireland, in Declan Kiberd's phrase, for several decades already. That invention took place in large

1 *Freeman's Journal*, 6 Nov. 1913. 2 William Orpen, *Stories of old Ireland and myself* (London: Williams and Norgate, 1924), pp 85–6.

part through controversy. The colonial condition of Ireland provided the paradigm for these controversies, but each side – any side – could claim to be the 'Irish' side, thereby constructing the other as English. All power struggles replicated the master struggle. Invocation of the idea of 'Ireland' functioned as an automatic guarantee of high-mindedness and legitimized the free expression of animosity, however personal, however excessive. It gave license to the kind of public anger that nearly killed Sheehy Skeffington in October 1913 and signaled to all interested an invitation to attack.

Three controversies that began between 1908 and 1913, the period of high cultural nationalism, indicate with particular aptness the way any kind of nationalist discourse was always sufficient to license adversarial speech. This essay will show how the high-minded, belligerent use of Irishness functioned in the O'Hickey controversy of 1908–9, the Lane controversy of 1913, and the 'Save the Dublin Kiddies' controversy of 1913.

The O'Hickey controversy offers the clearest example of the license of controversy: a high-minded nationalist discourse gave the Revd Dr Michael O'Hickey freedom to express personal hostility as patriotism through his involvement in the 'essential Irish' campaign.[3] In August 1908, the parliamentary bill establishing the National University of Ireland was signed, and in the autumn the Gaelic League mounted a campaign to make the Irish language compulsory (or 'essential', in the language of 1908) for matriculation in the university. Everyone knew from the start that the issue would be decided by the vote of the thirty-six senators of the university, so the League aimed to rouse the public to pressure the senate.

Feelings among the clergy on this issue were mixed, because they were more concerned that the university be distinctively Catholic than that it be distinctively Irish; they wanted it marked as their turf, not as nationalists' turf. At a meeting of the Gaelic Society of University College Dublin on 27 November 1908, the president, William Delany, SJ, mentioned his opposition to 'essential Irish' because, among other reasons, he believed that non-Irish-speaking Catholics would end up going to Trinity College.[4] In order to have a senior cleric speak in opposition to Delany's view, Fr O'Hickey was invited to address a Gaelic League meeting at the Rotunda on 7 December. He seemed the perfect choice, because he was professor of Irish at St Patrick's College, Maynooth, and he had been vice-president of the Gaelic League between 1899 and 1903. O'Hickey accepted but rather than appearing in person, he sent a letter that was read aloud to great applause. That letter and all of his subsequent writings on the subject

---

3 For a more detailed analysis of the O'Hickey controversy, see Lucy McDiarmid, 'The Man who died for the language: the Revd Dr O'Hickey and the "essential Irish" controversy of 1909,' *Éire-Ireland* 35:1–2 (2000), pp 188–218.   4 *Freeman's Journal*, 28 Nov. 1909. For a description of the entire occasion, see Thomas J. Morrissey, *Towards a new national university: William Delany S.J. (1835–1924)* (Dublin: Wolfhound, 1983), pp 322 ff.

echo with a rage directed explicitly at the five clerical senators of the university (among them Delany himself, Archbishop Walsh of Dublin, and President
Mannix of St Patrick's College, Maynooth, his employer); it was their vote that
particularly excited him. He was already angry with Mannix for weakening the
Irish requirements for seminarians at Maynooth, and the controversy gave him
the opportunity to attack.[5] O'Hickey was taking the hostility from an internal
academic argument and expressing it in the public sphere.

Naturally, the Church hierarchy were not pleased to be attacked in public,
especially by a priest at their own seminary; so they sent O'Hickey a letter
through Bishop Sheehan of Waterford and Lismore (O'Hickey's own bishop) to
convey the request of the episcopal standing committee that he cease partic-
ipating in the campaign.[6] O'Hickey wrote back acquiescing, but throughout the
winter and spring of 1909, he continued publishing pamphlets and anonymous
letters on the subject. His 'silencing' became a matter of general knowledge and
discussion, especially in the pages of nationalist newspapers. In June, he was asked
to resign his chair. He refused, and on 29 July, he was dismissed. A testimonial
dinner was organized for him and funds collected, and in 1910 he went to Rome
to get the papal Rota to overturn his dismissal. O'Hickey remained in Rome
six years, but because of a technicality his case was never heard, and in August
1916 he returned to Waterford, dying there only a few months later. Meanwhile,
in June 1910, the senators of the university voted 21–12 to support the language
requirement, so the cause went on without O'Hickey.

The O'Hickey controversy was itself provoked by his allegedly high-minded
nationalist discourse, which was provoked, that is, by his aggressive and hostile
use of metaphors and allusions that troped this internal Irish cultural debate as
an actual military rebellion against British colonial rule. In fact, his rhetoric
seemed almost to go beyond figures of speech in identifying the opponents of
the Irish language requirement with the opponents of Ireland. His metaphors
were insults, and the people insulted were his employers, the bishops of Ireland.
It was not absolutely necessary to attack people while trying to save the language; Hyde, as the archbishop of Armagh, Cardinal Logue, pointed out to
O'Hickey, had used 'the language of a gentleman' in his Gaelic League speeches.[7] But O'Hickey's rhetoric was implicitly asking for trouble: he used the pre-
existing debate as an opportunity to enact his own rebellion against the author-

5 See Micheal Briody, 'From Carrickbeg to Rome – the story of Fr Michael O'Hickey,' *Decies*
57 (2001), pp 154–6. 6 Writing on behalf of the Episcopal Standing Committee, O'Hickey's
own bishop, Richard Sheehan of Waterford and Lismore, noted that the bishops 'take exception to the language' in his letters as 'wanting in reserve and moderation.' R.A. Sheehan to
M. O'Hickey, 29 Jan. 1909; O'Hickey papers 7/4(4), 9; Russell Library, St Patrick's College,
Maynooth. 7 Michael O'Hickey, *Statement concerning the dismissal of Dr O'Hickey from the Irish
chair of St Patrick's College, Maynooth*, printed as appendix in Padraig Mac Fhinn, *An tAthair
Micheál Ó hIceadha* (Baile Atha Cliath: Sairseal agus Dill, 1974), p. 181.

itarian structure of the church. For instance, he blamed the resistance to the Irish language on 'the class to which I belong, the Irish clergy,' and added, '[t]o be opposed by the colonists is a thing we are accustomed to; to be opposed by a section of our own, no matter how worthless and degenerate, is not to be endured.'[8]

O'Hickey's most notorious attack came at the end of a talk he gave to a group of Maynooth seminarians in mid-December 1908. The following week, the talk was published in Sinn Féin. At the end of the talk he said:

> Even in the Clerical Senators as a body I can repose little or no trust; although I cannot possibly imagine how any body of responsible Irish ecclesiastics could embark on a more foolish or reckless course than to take sides in this instance with the enemies of Ireland. The treachery of those who show themselves false to Ireland at this juncture must never be forgotten whilst a solitary fragment of the historic Irish Nation remains. Sir Jonah Barrington has preserved for us a Black-list of those who voted for the infamous Union passed
>> ... by perjury and fraud,
>> By slaves who sold their land for gold,
>> As Judas sold his God.
>
> A similar Black-list of the recreant Nationalist Senators must be preserved that, in after times, all men may know who were the false and vile, in a supreme crisis of Ireland's fortunes, and who the leal and true.[9]

Here O'Hickey is just one simile away from saying that the clerical senators betrayed God or might be about to betray God, or at least Ireland, if they vote against essential Irish. Of course all the revivalists used agonistic metaphors, quite often to attack Irish opponents, but O'Hickey is here attacking only five people, the clerical senators.

In two private letters written about his engagement in the Irish campaign, O'Hickey clearly sees himself as an Irish rebel taking on the colonial enemy. Defending his published words to Bishop Sheehan, O'Hickey wrote:

> Restraint and moderation of language are relative things. Language which in one case and set of circumstances might be quite unjustifiable, in different circumstances might well be not only warranted, but actually called for. That the language I have used was in no way too strong for the occasion that called it forth, I am convinced ... By the part I have taken in this controversy, it is my profound conviction that I have done the College and the Catholic Faith as well as the cause of Irish nationality a service.[10]

8 Michael O'Hickey, *An Irish university, or else –* (Dublin and Waterford: M.H. Gill, 1909), p. 132.
9 Ibid., p. 158. 10 M. O'Hickey to R. Sheehan, 31 Jan. 1909. O'Hickey Papers 7/4(4), 11.

Here O'Hickey explains what I have called the license of controversy: his unre-
strained and immoderate language was actually 'called forth' and required by the
situation. He then invokes the lofty values legitimizing his speech (college, faith,
Irish). His phrasing implies that he ought to be seen as a champion of those
values. In a letter written to Liam Bulfin after his dismissal, O'Hickey explicitly writes himself as the rebel hero against the West Briton bishops: 'when they
tackled the grandson of a United Irishman, who was not unacquainted with the
interior of a British dungeon, and the son of a Young Irelander and a Fenian –
well, they were, as the Yankees say, "up against a very serious proposition", were
they not?'[11] To be against O'Hickey was to be against Ireland.

    The framing of his controversy as a rebellion, and his own role as a heroic
one, led to an inevitable moment: O'Hickey gave a speech from the dock. It had
to go that way; if he had turned his employers, the bishops, into the British, then
he himself was on the way to martyrdom. When the trustees of St. Patrick's
College (Cardinal Logue and various bishops) summoned O'Hickey to the board
room and suggested that he apologize before he was 'deprived of his chair,'
O'Hickey refused and said, '[t]he writings complained of I published in the discharge of what I felt to be a duty. For any sacrifice the discharge of that duty
may entail I am prepared. Whatever may befall me, I cannot play false to my
conscience nor to Ireland.'[12] The drama in the board room was driven – like
the whole controversy – by O'Hickey's use of the pre-existing campaign as a
stage for his own rebellion. The construction of O'Hickey as a martyr was continued by his biographer Pádraig Eric Mac Fhinn, who wrote:

> Ag uaigh Sheáin Uí Éigeartaigh, chuir Máirtín Ó Cadhain I gcomórtas
> leis an Dochtúir O hIceadha é. Chaon duine acu ar a bhealach féin,
> d'fhéadfá a radh go bhfuair sé bás ar son na Gaedhilge.[13]
>
> [At Sheáin Uí Éigeartaigh's graveside, Máirtín Ó Cadhain compared him
> with Dr Hickey. 'It might be said that each in his own way died for the
> cause of the Irish language.']

    The Hugh Lane controversy also follows a colonial paradigm: the national
struggle is at stake here too and is fought once more in a small site. Lane was not
an articulate or even an especially verbal man; he did his thinking through things.
The high-minded anger in this case was not expressed by Lane but provoked by
him. Although for Lane the Dublin Municipal Gallery of Modern Art, which he
founded in 1908, embodied Irish national grandeur and dignity, for others its mate-

11 Michael O'Hickey to Liam Bulfin, 8/7/1909. National Library of Ireland 13, 820.   12
O'Hickey, *Statement concerning the dismissal*, p. 188.   13 Pádraig Eric Mac Fhinn, *An tAthair
Micheál Ó hIceadha* (Baile atha Cliath: Sáirséal agus Dill, 1974), p. 11.

rial form and shape replicated the social structure that Irish nationalism was out to destroy. It seemed like a big house. The controversy was not over the paintings; it was the inconvenient and threatening scale of the building required to house them. However generously, however unconsciously, Lane established, for the public good, an institution that Dublin businessmen felt it in the public interest to attack.

Lane was Lady Gregory's nephew, and with no education and no money whatsoever he earned a fortune dealing in old masters' paintings, which he had the gift of discovering in unlikely places. After a visit to her house at Coole Park, Co. Galway, in 1901, where Yeats, Hyde and other Irish revival leaders were staying, Lane allied his aesthetic interests and collector's talents with the cause of Irish cultural nationalism. With the money earned in dealing, he bought modern (contemporary) paintings – but only to give away, not to sell. After some success in organizing exhibitions of pictures by Irish painters, he decided to establish a municipal gallery of contemporary paintings for Dublin. In the gallery's original catalogue, put together for its opening in 1908, Lane wrote patriotically: 'Till today Ireland was the only country in Europe that had no Gallery of Modern Art ... That reproach is now removed.'[14]

For Lane as for O'Hickey, the national and the personal were not simply identified; they were indistinguishable. For Lane, it was in objects that the national and the personal met and blended: the paintings were both gifts and private possessions, and the gallery was both municipal and 'home'. Unlike the great continental galleries such as the Uffizi or the Louvre, the Municipal Gallery did not originate as the private domain of a single aristocratic family. It was Lane's own space – to be chosen, approved, decorated by Lane – but given as benefaction to the city of Dublin. Lane preferred to give a painting away rather than sell it because, as he put it, 'if I sell it to some millionaire it is lost, I don't see it again, it may not give any very great pleasure to him and it is lost to everyone else. But if I give a picture to a gallery ... It is as much mine as ever, I still possess it, I can see it when I like and everyone else can see it too.'[15] When, in 1914, Lane was applying for the job of director of the National Gallery of Ireland, he promised to turn over his entire salary for the purchase of more paintings, saying, '[T]ell [them] I will make it my adopted child.'[16] Given Lane's peripatetic childhood, in a sense both the Municipal Gallery (and, later, the National Gallery) functioned as home for him, and through these institutions the bachelor Lane constructed a kinship with Dublin and hence with Ireland. The populace, the putative audience for the paintings, constituted his symbolic heirs.

This emotional relationship with his Irish family began propitiously. At the Municipal Gallery's opening in January 1908, the paintings making up the collection were housed at 17 Harcourt Street. Lane had great public support. Alderman

14 *Tribute to Sir Hugh Lane* (Cork: Cork UP, 1961), p. 35. **15** Lady Gregory, *Hugh Lane's life and achievement* (London: John Murray, 1921), p. 195. **16** Ibid., p. 200.

Tom Kelly was his champion, as was Lord Mayor Lorcan Sherlock, and *Sinn Féin* praised his generosity. In February he was given the freedom of the city. By 1912, Lane felt the need to nudge the city to provide a permanent gallery: on 5 November he wrote a letter to the Dublin city clerk, turning over to the Corporation one set of paintings, 'on the condition that they are always on view free to the public,' but stating that another group, the thirty-nine 'continental' paintings, would be removed at the end of January 1913, if no decision about the gallery's site were made.[17] In January the Dublin Corporation voted 20–2 to give £22,000 for the new gallery (the building, not the site). After visiting and rejecting many possible sites, Lane was taken with the suggestion of a bridge gallery spanning the Liffey, replacing the metal Ha'penny Bridge; and he commissioned a design from Sir Edwin Lutyens. By the time of the January deadline, no other acceptable location had been discovered; by April, Lane's preference for the bridge gallery had become a stipulation. Without that design by that architect in that place, he would take back the conditional gift of the thirty-nine paintings (leaving, of course, the many other paintings he had already given or had promised unconditionally). Lane was stubborn and impatient; and even in private space Lane's 'taste' was virtually a religion. Walking into a friend's drawing room once, he strode to the window and pulled down the curtains, saying, '[Y]ou really must not have these in your house.'[18] Dublin was simply a larger space to decorate.

Given the scale and the grandiosity of the Lutyens design, as well as Lane's close alliance with Gregory and Yeats, the gallery became associated with the big house. There seemed to be a seigneurial quality in someone who insisted on tearing down a bridge and inflicting a building on the city; and clearly Lane's notion of a gallery was large, expensive, and grand. It was one thing to give a painting away and 'still possess it,' but Dublin was not Lane's demesne. This understanding of the gallery, emphasizing not the kinship but the class differences between benefactor and beneficiaries, was troublingly evident in all of Yeats's poems on the subject. It was also evident in Beerbohm's drawing of 'Sir Hugh Lane Producing Masterpieces for Dublin, 1909'.[19] Four years before the 1913 controversy, Beerbohm expressed visually the great distance between Lane and his public, to whom he appears as a magician on a stage pulling paintings of his top hat. To those not privy to Lane's acquisition of wealth year by year, deal by deal, painting by painting, his gifts did indeed seem like magic.

The ensuing public argument focussed on the control of urban space. When Lane stipulated that without the bridge site and the Lutyens design, he would take back the conditional thirty-nine, *Sinn Féin* withdrew its support, writing, '[N]o visitor to Dublin could miss seeing that Gallery … a £40,000 monument

17 *Irish Times*, 2 Dec. 1912.   **18** Lady Gregory, *Hugh Lane's life and achievements, with some accounts of the Dublin galleries* (London: John Murray, 1921), p. 246.   **19** Rupert Hart-Davis (ed.), *A catalogue of the caricatures of Max Beerbohm* (London: Macmillan, 1972), p. 228.

to Sir Hugh Lane far more conspicuous than the memorials ... to Daniel O'Connell and Charles Stewart Parnell.'[20] The scale of his gift, earlier the index of his munificence, became the measure of his arrogance. In this context, Lutyens's half-Irish ethnicity became an insult. In a letter to the *Irish Times* written in August 1913, William Martin Murphy implied that Lane insisted on the bridge site in order to assert his own dominance over the city:

> He is to choose the only site in the city against which he knows there is intense public feeling ... he figuratively wipes his boots in the architectural profession of Ireland, and a committee of Irish gentlemen are so obsessed by Sir Hugh Lane and his handful of pictures that they meekly swallow all his conditions, and are prepared if they can succeed in doing so to place all the citizens under his feet. It is a case of 'no Irish need apply' for any job besides digging the foundations in the Liffey mud.[21]

Two groups emerged to assert the rights of the business interests of Dublin – both their names reflecting the concern with space: the Central Highways Committee and the River Liffey Protection Association (never heard of before or since). To James Walker of the latter group, the Gallery was indeed a 'palace'. He said to the members of the Dublin Chamber of Commerce (of which Murphy was president):

> ... they had lost sight of the fact that there were 20,000 families living in one room each, and living under conditions which were a disgrace to the City of Dublin. Like any other 'white elephant', the collection in question might be described as being worth £10,000, and they were asked to provide for them a magnificent palace and a great retinue of servants to take care of them. He could not help but regard such a proposition as a scandalous waste of money.[22]

In Walker's attack, as in Murphy's, the gallery was not positioned as a threat to Dublin commercial interests but to the poor: the poor, living in one room, digging the foundations in the Liffey mud, offered the high moral ground on which the businessmen stood to attack the gallery. Richard Jones of the RLPA voiced concern that the gallery would injure the health of the poor:

> It would be an outrage on art and on common sense to adopt such a plan. It would obstruct a view painted by God Almighty, which no artist could imitate. It would be one of the most unsightly bridges ever erected in a large city, and [would] obstruct the diurnal passage of the sea air,

20 'Sir Hugh Lane and the Pictures', *Sinn Fein* (9 Aug. 1913), p. 5.   **21** *Irish Times*, 11 Aug. 1913.   **22** *Irish Times*, 12 Aug. 1913.   **23** Ibid.

which daily prevented the outbreak of disease in many filthy alleys.[23] Anti-religious, neo-colonial, aesthetically offensive, and a potential cause of epidemics, the bridge-gallery by its very size constituted a threat to all the best interests of the city.

When, after the Corporation's 19 September vote against the bridge site, Lane revised his will to leave the thirty-nine paintings of the 'conditional gift' to the National Gallery in London, his decision seemed to show that he deserved everything that had been said about him. But three developments conspired to destigmatize him. Firstly, he died suddenly and relatively young in tragic circumstances, drowning when the *Lusitania* was torpedoed by the Germans on 7 May 1915. Secondly, his will contained a recent codicil leaving the thirty-nine paintings to Dublin if a permanent gallery for them was built within five years of his death. Finally, in 1926 the British government, at the recommendation of a parliamentary committee of inquiry, officially refused to return the collection because the signature on the codicil was unwitnessed. What the Germans began with their torpedoes, the British completed with their committee: they made Lane and his paintings Irish. The Dublin Corporation commissioned a bust of Lane from the Irish sculptor Albert Power: in 1933, when the gallery was resituated in Charlemont House, the bust was stationed in solitary splendour in the final room, making Lane into a tutelary deity of this small bit of Dublin space. In 1959, the first of several agreements for sharing the paintings between Dublin and London was negotiated. But until then, the thoroughly hibernicized Lane stood on guard in his empty room, a patriotic reminder of unfinished national business.

Only six weeks after the final negative vote on the bridge site, the 'Save the Dublin Kiddies' controversy erupted on 22 October 1913. This controversy did not simmer and brew like the O'Hickey and Lane controversies: it erupted violently in the streets of Dublin. It was short and intense, its most dramatic conflict over in less than a week. Yet here, too, offended, outraged Irishness licensed public adversarial behaviours. In this case, the idea that any kind of aggression was licensed operated not only in the rhetorical but in the somatic realm: punitive physical violence was exercised in purportedly high-minded ways to defend Irishness.

In late August, the great strike of the Irish Transport and General Workers Union began; it did not end until February 1914, when the last of the 25,000 striking and locked-out workers returned to their jobs. In September and October, British unions began sending food and provisions to the workers' families, whose situation was desperate. The 'kiddies' controversy originated in a humanitarian plan suggested by the British socialist/suffragist Dora Montefiore to board the striking Dublin workers' children with socialist families in England and Scotland for the duration of the strike; the name 'Save the Dublin Kiddies' was her creation.[24] With labour leader Jim Larkin's blessing, she publicized her

24 Dora Montefiore, *Our fight to save the kiddies: smouldering fires of the Inquisition* (London: Utopia, n.d.), p. 2.

campaign through the socialist paper the *Daily herald*. By the time she arrived in Dublin she had offers of room for 300 children.[25] When the plan was put into effect on the 22 October, the ensuing hysteria took Montefiore and her helpers completely by surprise. Over a period of several days, outraged priests and angry mobs recruited by the Ancient Order of Hibernians grabbed many of the children from the hands of the social workers washing them at the Tara Street baths; pulled others off boats at the North Wall of the Liffey or off trains at Kingsbridge station; attacked anyone attempting to leave Dublin with a child; and marched triumphantly along the quays singing 'Faith of Our Fathers' after each day's successful 'rescues'. Although eighteen children made it to Liverpool and remained there until February, plans for getting more out of Dublin were given up. Montefiore and her principal helper, the American Lucilla Rand, were arrested and charged with kidnapping; they were released on bail and the charges were dropped when it was clear they had stopped saving Dublin kiddies.

A letter written by Archbishop Walsh and published in several newspapers on 21 October provoked the controversy that encouraged aggression by its high-minded outrage. Walsh's discourse evoked the sectarian rescue battles between rival Catholic and Protestant charities common in nineteenth-century Dublin, London, New York, and other cities:

> A movement is on foot … to induce the wives of the working men who are now unemployed by reason of the present deplorable industrial deadlock in Dublin, to hand over their children to be cared for in England by persons of whom they … can have no knowledge whatsoever. The Dublin women now subjected to this cruel temptation to part with their helpless offspring are, in the majority of cases, Catholics. Have they abandoned their faith? Surely not. Well, if they have not, they should need no words of mine to remind them of the plain duty of every Catholic mother in such a case. I can only put it to them that they can be no longer held worthy of the name of Catholic mothers if they so far forget that duty as to send away their little children to be cared for in a strange land, without security of any kind that those to whom the poor children are to be handed over are Catholics, or indeed are persons of any faith at all.[26]

Although Walsh received private assurances from Montefiore herself as well as from Catholics in Liverpool that the children sent there were going to Mass regularly, and although the private letter he sent to her suggested he knew that the children were not being proselytized, his public comments nevertheless referred to a sectarian plot.[27] His speech several days later to the St Vincent de Paul Society spoke of the plan to 'deport our Catholic children to England' and rein-

25 Ibid., p. 5. **26** *Freeman's Journal,* 21 Oct. 1913. **27** Archbishop Walsh to Mrs Montefiore, 22 Oct. 1913. Corrected typescript, carbon copy. Dublin Diocesan Archives 377 / 3. **28** *The*

forced the license for the violent gestures on behalf of 'faith and fatherland'.[28]

To a large extent, Archbishop Walsh and Dora Montefiore were in the same business, supplying welfare before the existence of a welfare state. The Catholic Church in Ireland dominated a huge network of social service institutions – orphanages, hospitals, asylums, schools, as well as the parish churches and convents that fed and cared for the local poor. The provision of housing, nourishment, medical care and education – all 'maternalist' enterprises – was the area of greatest concern to English women reformers, and it was of course the aim of socialists to make these services permanent state functions.[29] The Dublin workers' children represented an overlapping of two symbolic domains, that of the Irish Catholic Church and that of socialist women. The symbolic conflict over the children – a physical custody that signified an ideological power – was expressed gesturally, in the direct force applied by the priests against the women who were carrying off the children. The logic was geopolitical: to let a child leave the city was to lose control of the family and to let Protestant win over Catholic and English over Irish. Philip O'Leary has written about the metaphor of the 'wall around Ireland' that recurs in the writings of Irish language revivalists, that is, a linguistic wall 'against the onslaught of the enemies of our nationality and our civilisation,' as Pearse put it.[30] Although in the 'Kiddies' controversy anxiety was focused on the leaking out or loss of the national culture, Tom Garvin's analysis of 'fear of cultural change coming from outside and destabilizing the rather fragile social entity of Catholic Ireland' is also relevant.[31] The mobs opposing 'Save the Dublin Kiddies' used their own bodies to create that wall so the national culture could not leak out, child by child.

As the first 'kiddies' were being washed at the Tara Street baths on 22 October, Montefiore arrived on the scene to witness an adversarial encounter on a large scale:

> I went down to the baths and found an indescribable scene going on in the street, a surging crowd, some with us, some against us, beat up against the steps of the baths and was again and again pushed back by two red-faced, brutal-looking constables. Right inside the girls' side of the baths, where he had no business to be, stood a priest, who asked me what I was doing there. I told him I had come to help Mrs Rand with the children. He replied we should not have the children, and that he was there to prevent their going.

Dublin Children's Distress Fund, the Society of St Vincent de Paul: the archbishop's statements, pamphlet ([no publisher given], 27 October 1913, p. 1, in Walsh Papers, DDA. **29** For a discussion and analysis of maternalism in this period, see Seth Koven and Sonya Michelle, 'Introduction: mother worlds,' *Mothers of a new world: maternalist politics and the origin of welfare states* (New York: Routledge, 1993), pp 1–142. **30** Philip O'Leary, *The prose literature of the Gaelic Revival, 1881–1921: ideology and innovation* (University Park, PA: Pennsylvania State UP, 1994), p. 26. **31** Tom Garvin, 'Priests and patriots: Irish separatism and fear of the modern, 1890–1914', *Irish Historical Studies* 25:97 (1886), p. 76.

> When I met Mrs Rand I found he had already threatened and hustled her, and she had to warn him not to touch her again. The priests were shouting and ordering the children about in the passage-way ... some of the women were 'answering back' to the priests and reminding them [that] they had been refused bread by the Church and that now they had a chance of getting their children properly cared for; other women, worked on by the violent speeches of the priests, were wailing and calling on the saints to forgive them ... When we found we could do nothing more for the children we drove back to Liberty Hall through a crowd that threw mud at us and raised cries of 'Throw them into the Liffey.'[32]

The affronted sense of territoriality on both sides is evident even in Montefiore's openly partial narrative: the women feel the priest should not be anywhere near the room where the *girls* are being bathed; and the priest feels that the women should not be touching the *Catholic* children. The parties involved operate under conflicting taxonomies. The women respond to the priests as *men*: they feel 'threatened' and 'hustled' and resent being touched. The priests treat the women not as women but as *English Protestant* kidnappers who are endangering the children. In fact, Montefiore was the non-religious widow of an Australian Jew and Rand was an American Catholic.

The priests' violent intervention was legitimized by the religious and national values invoked in the archbishop's letter. When Fr William Landers and Fr Thomas McNevin, curates from nearby St Andrew's parish on Westland Row, interviewed the boys, 'almost without exception the little fellows sturdily asserted that they didn't want to go to England. Many of the lads shouted, "We won't be English children," and a few of the eldest said that they didn't want to renounce their Faith ... [when Fr Landers announced he was 'strenuously opposed' to the plan, he was] accorded an ovation by the gathering.'[33] The *Freeman's Journal* noted a crowd of '200 or 250' outside the baths who gave Fr Landers 'a very hearty cheer.'[34] To this crowd Landers read Archbishop Walsh's letter and gave a rousing speech, reminding his listeners 'that the Irish people knew what poverty was for a long time, but they were never reduced to the extremity of denying their Faith ... the Irish people would rather their children perish by the ditches than that they should be exposed to the risk of being perverted in their religion.'[35]

Over the next few days, 23–25 October, 'Catholic Vigilance' was at work along the quays and in the train station, ensuring that no child left Dublin. 'FATHERS & MOTHERS OF CATHOLIC DUBLIN,' read a handbill, 'Are you content to abandon your children to strangers, who give no guarantee to have them placed in Catholic or Irish homes? You may never see them again.' In the name of these same principles, adults were attacked also. Later that day

32 Montefiore, *Our fight*, p. 6. **33** *Freeman's Journal*, 23 Oct. 1913. **34** Ibid. **35** Ibid.

Montefiore was assaulted by one of the priests as she attempted to board the train for the Kingstown steamer: 'a priest thrust me rudely aside and held me by the shoulder'. Once she was aboard, another priest closed the door against her, 'hurting me considerably, and making me feel faint'. On the train, the priests 'started a systematic bullying' of the boys. As Montefiore 'sat passive and contemptuous in the corner', the priests told her they 'did not want any of our English charity'.[36]

And so it was in the midst of this fray that Frank Sheehy Skeffington went to Kingsbridge railway station 'as a journalist' to see, as he said later, if the previous days' scenes 'would be repeated' and to help get the children out of Dublin. There he saw a crowd of A.O.H. members and priests who shouted '[H]ere they are!' when he appeared with the children. Sheehy Skeffington's 'persistency roused the anger of the crowd,' said the *Freeman's Journal*, and it 'forcibly ejected him from the station premises. There were marks on his forehead, and his hat got lost in the rush.' Sheehy Skeffington's own description in police court the following week was more detailed, describing the kicks and beatings inflicted on him by the mob, and the shouts of '[K]ill him'. Sheehy Skeffington had no wish to press charges against the men who assaulted him most directly because, as he said in court, '[T]hey are merely the dupes of more astute persons in the background.' But his bruised body offered evidence of the hatred licensed by the archbishop in the name of the Irish Church.[37]

With the Rising, the War of Independence, and the Civil War, antagonisms were expressed in a different form of battle with different enemies, and cultural controversies temporarily receded from importance. Unlike wars, controversies do not usually cause change; they make it visible as it is in the process of occurring. In them large forces explode in small sites. Their conflicts are decided, if they are decided at all, by bluff and bravado, by improvisational flair and rhetoric rather than by any clear and consistent scoring system. Precisely because it is often irresolvable, a controversy registers with great clarity the tensions of a society at a particular moment. The controversies of the Irish Revival show the struggle to claim the discourse of Irishness, to insist on a role in the ideological apparatus of a state that did not yet exist.

ACKNOWLEDGEMENTS: For the use of archival materials, the author is grateful to the: National Library of Ireland; Russell Library, St Patrick's College, Maynooth; and the Dublin Diocesan Archives. Special thanks to the librarians at the National Library, to Penny Woods of Russell Library, and to David Sheehy of the Dublin Diocesan Archives.

---

36 Dora Montefiore, *From a Victorian to a modern* (London: Archer, 1927), pp 162–3. **37** F. Sheehy Skeffington, 'Wants priests in dock, Kingston Police Station', *Freeman's Journal*, November 1913.

Whoops from the peat-bog?:
Joseph Campbell and the London avant-garde

ALEX DAVIS

Thursday, 22 March 1923: Joseph Campbell, interned in a 'Tintown' at the Curragh, listened to Francis Stuart read his poems. 'Faint murmer of his voice à la Golding and Ezra Pound', Campbell recorded in his clandestine prison diary, adding parenthetically, '(Talked of Ezra's dressing-gown, beard, one gold earring in ear).'[1] This quiet recital and colloquy between the two prisoners faintly recalls a far more dramatic reading at the Poets' Club in London, nearly thirteen years previously, at which Campbell 'delivered [Pound's] "The Ballad of the Goodly Fere" in full sonorous grandeur clad in bardic robes'.[2] Campbell's flamboyant appearance on this December evening in 1910 was at one with his pre-war London image of kilted Irish bard.[3] In such apparel, as Walter Baumann observes,[4] Campbell more than matched his friend Pound's Kensington wardrobe of velvet jacket or grey overcoat with square buttons of lapis lazuli, purchased with the £5 Pound was paid by the *English Review* for his 'Ballad' and other poems.[5]

Such dressing up, of course, was the badge of many members of the London avant-garde. One of the foundational narratives of early modernism is by the *English Review*'s editor, Ford Maddox Ford, whose recollection of his initial meeting with Wyndham Lewis – proffering his 'Wild Body' narratives to Ford – pays

---

1 Eiléan Ní Chuilleanáin (ed.), '*As I was among the captives': Joseph Campbell's prison diary, 1922–1923*, (Cork: Cork UP, 2001), p. 57. The Republican sympathies of the Belfast-born poet and playwright Joseph Campbell (1879–1944), to which I return later in this essay, led to his arrest in the early stages of the Civil War, and his internment, initially in Mountjoy Jail, latterly at the Curragh. Shortly after his release at Christmas 1923, Campbell emigrated to the United States, where, in 1925, he established the School of Irish Studies in New York, the Irish Foundation in 1931, and the *Irish Review* in 1934. From 1927 to 1938 he lectured on Irish literature at Fordham University. He returned to Ireland in 1939, to spend the remainder of his life on a farmstead in Wicklow. For further biographical details, see Norah Saunders and A.A. Kelly, *Joseph Campbell: poet and nationalist, 1879–1944, a critical biography* (Dublin: Wolfhound, 1988); and the two theses of which Saunders and Kelly's book is largely a redaction: Norah Saunders, 'Joseph Campbell: the early years', MA diss., National University of Ireland, 1972; Norah Saunders, 'Joseph Campbell: struggle and exile (1911–1944)', PhD diss., National University of Ireland, 1977. **2** J.J. Wilhelm, *Ezra Pound in London and Paris, 1908–1925* (University Park: Pennsylvania State UP, 1990), p. 52. **3** See Saunders and Kelly, *Joseph Campbell*, p. 47. **4** Walter Baumann, *Roses from the steel dust: collected essays on Ezra Pound* (Orono: National Poetry Foundation, 2000), p. 211. **5** See Humphrey Carpenter, *A serious character: the life of Ezra Pound* (Boston: Houghton Mifflin, 1988), p. 129.

particular attention to Lewis's resemblance to a Russian anarchist, clad in black coat and cape and Latin-quarter hat.[6] Campbell's *outré* garb, however, would seem to differ from that of Pound and Lewis in that it acts as a mark of national identity: kilt and robes are clear indices of turn-of-the-century Irish cultural nationalism (with its 'cult of the kilt,' in Declan Kiberd's words),[7] whereas velveteen jackets and Russian-looking black capes would appear to signify a cosmopolitanism restless with the mores of Edwardian culture. The latter dress-sense would appear to function as a sartorial signifier of the pre-war avant-garde's internationalism, of an aesthetics that, for a writer like Pound, interrogated national as well as artistic boundaries.

Campbell's brief sojourn in London, from 1906 to 1911, coincides with the early stages of the avant-garde Imagist movement, which emerged in the wake of T.E. Hulme's self-styled 'secession'[8] from the Poet's Club in 1909. Early practitioners of and commentators on Imagism were keen to emphasize its cosmopolitan freedom from provincial and national traditions. In his 1913 article, 'Imagisme,' F.S. Flint stresses that the Imagists' 'only endeavour was to write in accordance with the best tradition, as they found it in the best writers of all time, – in Sappho, Catullus, Villon.'[9] In a related vein, Pound's preface to *Some Imagist Poets 1916* links Imagism to artistic movements on the European continent, wherein he tartly comments: 'It is small wonder that Imagist poetry should be incomprehensible to men whose sole touchstone for art is the literature of one country for a period of four centuries.'[10] Pound's remarks are of a piece with his 1917 assault, in the pages of the *New Age*, on 'Provincialism the Enemy,' among his targets 'the whole Irish business, and in particular the Ulster dog-in-the-manger'.[11]

From kilt to the Curragh, the Ulsterman Campbell remained committed to the 'Irish business' Pound airily denigrates. His presence, therefore, alongside other politicized Irish writers, including Padraic Colum, among the ranks of the cosmopolitan London avant-garde is of considerable interest in considering the complex relationship between the Irish literary revival and early modernism. Campbell's 'Irish Imagism' can be seen as a dimension to the vexed debate, within the revival, of whether the creation of a national culture was reinforced or diluted by internationalism, a discussion being conducted in the early years of the century between Yeats, D.P. Moran, T.W. Rolleston and John Eglinton, among others.[12] Furthermore, Campbell's commitment to Irish nationalism and, in his

6 See Paul O'Keefe, *Some sort of genius: a life of Wyndham Lewis* (London: Jonathan Cape, 2000), p. 93. 7 Declan Kiberd, *Inventing Ireland: the literature of the modern nation* (London: Jonathan Cape, 1995), p. 524. 8 See J.B. Harmer, *Victory in limbo: imagism, 1908–1917* (New York: St Martin's Press, 1975), p. 22. 9 F.S. Flint, 'Imagisme', *Poetry*, 1.6 (1913), p. 352. 10 Ezra Pound, preface to his: *Some imagist poets, 1916* (Boston and New York: Houghton Mifflin, 1916), p. x. 11 William Cookson (ed.), *Ezra Pound, selected prose 1909–1965* (New York: New Directions, 1973), p. 202. 12 For a judicious sampling of this fraught debate, see the texts selected by Luke Gibbons in Seamus Deane (gen. ed.), *The Field Day anthology of Irish writing* (Derry:

most achieved verse, avant-garde poetic devices, finds a corollary of sorts with the increasingly 'provincial' – in Pound's sense – cultural politics of the avant-garde in England, and on the continent, as the Great War broke over Europe.

Prior to coming to London, Campbell had been involved with the literary revival initially in Ulster, where the movement had prompted the creation of the Ulster Literary Theatre (1904) and the journal *Uladh* (1904), and subsequently in Dublin. By 1906, Campbell had published *Songs of Uladh* (1904) – a collaborative venture with the composer Herbert Hughes, for which Campbell provided English-language lyrics to Donegal folksongs collected by Hughes – and two volumes of poetry, *The Garden of the Bees* (1905) and *The Rushlight* (1906). On arriving in London in 1906, Campbell's literary activities were not confined to the Poets' Club and its offshoots; he assisted at the Irish Texts Society and also became secretary for the Irish Literary Society. Campbell would reside in London until 1911, when he returned to Ireland and to Irish revolutionary politics.

The London branch of the Irish Literary Society had considerable overlap with the embryonic London avant-garde. Hulme's 'Secession Club' from the Poets' Club first met at the Café Tour d'Eiffel, and present among the Irish contingent, according to Flint's 'History of Imagism', were Joseph Campbell and Florence Farr.[13] This 'forgotten school of 1909', as Pound later dubbed it,[14] also gathered at the Irish Literary Society, as Ronald Schuchard has discovered.[15] Schuchard has argued cogently that, through Farr, Yeats influenced the course of Imagist theory and practice, including the work of Campbell. Farr famously aided her friend and, briefly, lover Yeats in experiments in chanting his verse, experiments which culminated in the attempt to set the poetry to scores written for a psaltery made for Farr in 1901 by Arnold Dolmetsch. Yeats and Farr's determined dissemination of their ideas, through numerous lecture tours, found a responsive audience in many members of the Poets' Club, Campbell among them. According to Schuchard, Hulme's early theories, which argued for the necessary visuality of poetry, were formulated in reaction to the 'auditory poetics' of Yeats and Farr.[16] Hulme's lecture on modern poetry, probably delivered to the Poets' Club in 1908, contains an implicit counterstatement to Yeats and Farr's prosody in his confident assertion that, 'from this standpoint of extreme modernism', the 'new art' of poetry is 'read and not chanted': 'I quite admit that poetry intended to be recited must be written in regular metre, but I contend that this method of recording impressions by visual images does not require the old metric system.'[17] Schuchard's crucial observation is that, with Hulme's exchanging his literary for

Field Day, 1991), vol. 2, pp. 950–1020. **13** See F. S. Flint, 'The history of Imagism', *The Egoist*, (1 May 1915), p. 70. **14** Ezra Pound, Prefatory note to 'The complete poetical works of T.E. Hulme', in Lea Baechler and A. Walton Litz (eds), *Ezra Pound, personae: the shorter poems* (New York: New Directions, 1990), p. 266. **15** See Ronald Schuchard, '"As regarding rhythm": Yeats and the Imagists', *Yeats: An Annual of Critical and Textual Studies*, 2 (1984), p. 214. **16** Ibid., p. 210. **17** Karen Csengeri, (ed.), *The collected writings of T. E. Hulme* (Oxford: Oxford

philosophical interests in late 1909, Yeats and Farr's pressure on the development
of Imagism would entail the centrality of rhythm or cadence, though not metre,
to the movement's attempts at self-definition in the manifestoes of Flint and
Pound in 1913. But by that date, Campbell had removed to Dublin to marry and
passes out of the history of the London avant-garde.

Campbell takes back to Ireland a poetics that is moulded out of two contrary forces, which in England would shortly fuse in Imagism. On the one hand,
is the 'new art' of which Yeats writes in 'Speaking to the Psaltery',[18] a rhythmic
musical art; and, on the other, is that which, perhaps echoing Yeats, Hulme also
terms 'the new art',[19] a visual proto-Imagism.[20] Campbell's receptivity to both
currents of 'new art' parallels Pound's;[21] where Pound's desire to 'make it new'
differs from Campbell's in the nationalist dimension to the Irishman's project.
Pound had little time for Irish nationalism, as several comments in his articles
for the *New Age* make apparent. He would hold fast to his conception of Ireland
as an 'unspeakable and reactionary island'[22] throughout the war years and into
his unspeakable and reactionary commitment to Mussolini's fascism. In a 1916
review of Joyce's *A Portrait of the Artist as a Young Man*, Pound's antipathy towards
literature informed by nationalist sentiment can be gleaned from his comment
that, 'If more people had read *The Portrait* and certain stories in Mr Joyce's
Dubliners there might have been less recent trouble in Ireland. A clear diagno-
sis is never without its value.'[23] For Pound, in the same context, Joyce's novel
transcends nationality: it is a 'permanent part of English literature – written by
an Irishman in Trieste and first published in New York City.'[24] Pound's transna-
tional view of the *Portrait* is a cornerstone of the edifice of 'International
Modernism,' so-called, the erection of which would be completed as modernism
entered the canon in the middle of the century. Of the 'masterpieces of
International Modernism', opines one of the chief architects of this monolith-
ic edifice, Hugh Kenner, 'None of them, certainly not *Ulysses*, can be claimed
for the literature of its author's country: no, they define a tradition of their own.'[25]
Kenner's cultural internationalism has its roots in, among other soils, Wyndham
Lewis's political argument, in *Paleface* (1929), for the desirability of national 'mis-
cegenation' in the face of 'the artificial principle of european *separatism* (of all

UP, 1994), p. 54. **18** W. B. Yeats, *Essays and introductions* (London: Macmillan, 1961), p. 19. **19**
Hulme, *Collected writings*, p. 54. **20** At the secessionist group of 1909, remarks Schuchard,
'Hulme carried the imagist case to Joseph Campbell … and to Padraic Colum' (Schuchard,
'Yeats and the Imagists', p. 215). **21** See Schuchard, 'Yeats and the Imagists', p. 216: 'as an
imagist who would strongly come to believe that poetry should be read aloud, [Pound] became
a bridge between the two poetries.' **22** Ezra Pound, *Jefferson and/or Mussolini: l'Idea statale
fascism as I have seen it* (1935; New York: Liveright, 1970), p. 27. **23** Forrest Read, ed.,
Pound/Joyce: the letters of Ezra Pound to James Joyce with Pound's essays on Joyce (New York: New
Directions, 1967), p. 90. **24** Ibid. **25** Hugh Kenner, *A colder eye: the modern Irish writers* (New
York: Alfred A. Knopf, 1983), p. 15.

the Irelands, Ulsters, Catalonias, Polands, Czecho-Slovakias and the rest)'.[26] As an instance of the artificiality of the case for 'separatism', Lewis refers his reader to his deconstruction of Matthew Arnold's notion of the 'Celt' in *The Lion and the Fox* (1925), a racial concept that is, says Lewis, 'a complete myth ... staged [by Arnold] as an ironical drama for the John Bulls and Fenian Paddies of his time.'[27]

Campbell's belief in Irish 'separatism' from the British empire would seem to situate him as tangential to the course of modernism subsequent to his return to Ireland. However, the remarks by Pound and Lewis quoted above date from the time of the Great War and its aftermath and do not represent the cultural politics of the English avant-garde in the years immediately preceding the outbreak of hostilities. In 1914, Pound coined the term Vorticism for Lewis's emergent group of painters and sculptors, and increasingly identified himself as a fellow Vorticist, contributing to Lewis's short-lived journal *Blast*. In the same year, Imagism, as a movement, passed largely out of Pound's control, into the hands of Amy Lowell and crossed the Atlantic. While the fairly genteel cosmopolitanism of Imagism continued in 'Amygisme', Vorticism was aggressively chauvinistic. Lewis's movement constituted an English challenge to the nationalism of the Italian Futurists, who had burst noisily upon the London art scene with an exhibition in 1912. Marinetti's celebration of technology, war, speed etc. is indissolubly entwined with an advocacy of Italian imperialism; in the words of Paul Peppis, 'Marinetti publicly affiliated Futurism with the Young Nationalists' Pan-Italianist advocacy of war and imperial expansion.'[28] As Peppis demonstrates, Lewis's counter-*Blast*, despite its anarchist rhetoric of anti-statism and individualism, is itself contradictorily governed by imperialist and nationalist imperatives: the journal, a 'Review of the Great London Vortex', contests Marinetti's Italian jingoism through assertions of England's greater cultural, economic and military prowess.

Campbell was doubtless cognisant of this avant-gardist muscle flexing. Among the numerous literary gatherings he attended in Dublin was one held by UCD's newly appointed assistant lecturer in English, Thomas MacDonagh,[29] a poet and critic well aware of developments in contemporary poetry both at home and abroad. Campbell's and MacDonagh's shared political views would see both poets on the committee of the Irish Volunteers in 1913, and both cleaved to the minority group after the movement split in September 1914, opposing any support for Britain in the war against Germany. Concurrent with his political dissent from the United Kingdom, MacDonagh was developing the nationalist poetic theory of *Literature in Ireland: Studies Irish and Anglo-Irish* (1916): the idea that

26 Wyndham Lewis, *Paleface: the philosophy of the 'melting pot'* (London: Chatto & Windus, 1929), pp. 283, 282; Lewis's emphasis. **27** Ibid., p. 283. **28** Paul Peppis, *Literature, politics, and the English avant-garde: nation and empire, 1901–1918* (Cambridge: Cambridge UP, 2000), p. 82. **29** See Saunders and Kelly, *Joseph Campbell*, p. 53.

there exists an independent, quintessentially 'Irish Mode' of poetry, as distinct
from what he calls 'that vague and illogical Celtic Note'.[30] MacDonagh's thesis
can be interpreted, in an Irish literary context, as related to the shift in Irish
poetry early in the century from the 'Note' of the Celtic Twilight to more robust
folkloric verse-forms, as anthologized in George Russell's *New Songs* (1904).
However, MacDonagh is keen to connect his argument to poetic convulsions
elsewhere in Europe:

> I am not writing here of European literature in general, or of English lit-
> erature in particular. I am introducing a movement that is important to
> English literature, because it is in part a revolt from it – because it has
> gone its own way, independent of it, though using for its language English
> or a dialect of English. I am treating it as a separate thing; and all that I
> have said so far is said rather by way of comparison, to set it in its true
> light. It enters literature at a period which seems to us who are of it as a
> period of disturbance, of change. Its mode seems strange to the critics
> and to the prosodists of the old order. Its mode is not that of the Futurists
> or writers of *vers libres*; but still, coming with the work of these, it stands
> as another element of disturbance, of revolution; it is comparatively free
> from the old authority imposed by the Renaissance, while the other ele-
> ments in this disturbance are rebelling against that authority ... The poets
> of this mode have till now been ignorant of the parallel movement; they
> have taken little or no note of the new writers of free verse or of the
> futurists. Yet their work may appear one with the work of these. And
> indeed there is a near kinship. The freedom being sought now elsewhere
> has long been enjoyed here.[31]

The nationalist 'separatism' of this extraordinary exercise in literary history are
audible in MacDonagh's choice of diction: the Irish Mode's successful 'revolt'
from English literature has founded an 'independent' poetry, 'a separate thing.'
More intriguing is MacDonagh's claim that the Irish Mode's revolution from
'authority' finds analogues in early modernism and the avant-garde, in the *vers
libre* of the Imagists and the rebelliousness of the Futurists. In terms of *poetics*,
MacDonagh's analogy springs from the disruption of authoritative and/or conventional linguistic and/or generic conventions common to the Irish Mode and
the avant-garde. From a *political* perspective, it is noteworthy that the 'kinship'
between the two 'parallel movement[s]' extends to their intense nationalism, that
of Italian Futurism busily being aped, even as the Vorticists in London vigor-
ously debunk it. However, the nationalism of Futurism and Vorticism is that of

30 Thomas MacDonagh, *Literature in Ireland: studies Irish and Anglo-Irish* (1916; Relay: Tyrone,
Nenagh, 1996), p. 4. **31** Ibid., pp 5–6.

competing imperialisms, one emergent, the other established, albeit threatened. MacDonagh's further contention that the Irish Mode is a *precursor* to the avant-garde, in that it has attained a 'freedom' from 'the old authority' that the latter still seeks, thus inverts on the cultural level the unequal relationship between imperial centre and subjugated colony. This bold declaration grants the Irish Mode a freedom the Irish nation, as a whole, is still denied.

The Irish Mode is empirically identifiable, according to MacDonagh, through certain auditory qualities of Anglo-Irish literature that derive from the linguistic and literary history of the Irish language. For MacDonagh, many younger Irish poets, including himself, have produced examples of the Irish Mode, while the work of a few, Campbell among them, 'is constantly of this mode'.[32] MacDonagh thus hears a national poetic mode in the Irish poets of his generation most deeply involved with the pre-War London avant-garde. Campbell's occasional experiments in the cadences of free verse had, in his earliest work, stemmed from the examples of Whitman and the Bible, as J. B. Harmer notes:[33] witness the strophes of 'The Dark' (one of the new poems included in *The Mountainy Singer* [1909]):

> This is the dark.
> This is the dream that came of the dark.
> This is the dreamer who dreamed the dream that came of the dark.
> This is the look the dreamer looked who dreamed the dream that came of the dark.
> This is the love that followed the look the dreamer looked who dreamed the dream that came of the dark.[34]

The incremental repetition of this poem has a slightly laboured feel, as have the ejaculations and archaic pronouns of 'O beautiful dark woman', an earlier exercise in free verse (collected in *The Rushlight* [1906]):

> O beautiful dark woman, weep no more.
> Weep not for thy princes who have gone from thee: they shall come again.
> Cease thy crying and thy lamentation.
> Thou shall be raised up as a star-cluster.
> Thy hair shall shine as a river in the dusk, and thine eyes as the blue-bough when the summer is full.[35]

Though maintaining an interest in metrical verse-forms throughout his career, the *vers libre* Campbell composed subsequent to the debates surrounding Farr's

---

32 Ibid., p. 124. **33** Harmer, *Victory in Limbo*, p. 49. **34** Austin Clarke, (ed.), *Joseph Campbell, poems* (Dublin: Figgis, 1963), p. 83. **35** Ibid., p. 56.

theories on poetic performance brings to mind the Imagist injunction (as formulated by Pound), 'to compose in the sequence of the musical phrase, not in sequence of a metronome'.[36] Consider, for instance, the rhythm of 'By the brink of water', from Campbell's finest collection, *The Earth of Cualann:*

> Black bog-mould,
> The fledged green of young ferns,
> And water covered with brooklime.
>
> Water covered with brooklime –
> The cup-bearers of Conarí
> Thought that a drink
> Worthy of a High King.[37]

This short poem opens arrestingly with a line or 'phrase' of three stressed syllables, and thence modulates its cadence with two end-stopped lines containing four stresses each with an admixture of unstressed syllables. The absence of a metrical pattern does not mean the lines lack rhythm; rather, they possess a 'musical' quality that MacDonagh, in the course of a close reading of Yeats' 'The lake isle of Innisfree', describes as 'a recurrence in this verse, but it is not the recurrence of the foot'.[38] The near-repetition of the third line in the fourth signals a verbal motif, highlighting the phrase's thematic importance, which is expounded in the final three lines of the poem. The enjambment of the free verse at the close of the poem gives it that 'conversational tone, which disallows inversions, quaint words and turns of speech', that MacDonagh heard in poems in the Irish Mode.[39] Yet Campbell's Irish Mode is not only rhythmical (which is fundamental to MacDonagh's thesis), but visual. His imagistic practice clearly influenced by ideas imbibed from Hulme (his advocated 'method of recording impressions by visual images'). The opening lines of 'By the brink of water' are a case in point, as Campbell attempts that 'Direct treatment of the "thing"',[40] in a language shorn of 'superfluous' diction, on which the Imagists of 1912, after Hulme, insisted. Likewise, in 'The moon', also from *Earth of Cualaan,* Campbell conducts an Imagist rewriting of Sidney's sonnet, 'With what sad steps', foregoing the explicative commentary of the Renaissance poet in favour of a foregrounding of the literary devices of metaphor and simile:

> The moon climbs and climbs,
> Till it is no bigger
> Than a moon-penny.

36 Ezra Pound, *Literary essays of Ezra Pound,* ed. T.S. Eliot (London: Faber, 1954), p. 3. 37 Ibid., pp. 176–7. 38 MacDonagh, *Literature in Ireland,* pp. 49, 48. 39 Ibid., p. 51. 40 Pound, *Literary essays,* p. 3.

Darkness and the hills lie together
As in a bed,
Sleeping lovers.[41]

Campbell's fascinating symbolic 'designs' to *Earth of Cualann* are of a piece with such felicitous verbal images, by creating powerful exempla of 'the visible language of modernism,' in Jerome McGann's phrase, in this now sadly neglected collection.[42] Campbell's poetics, like MacDonagh's *Literature in Ireland*, illustrate the fertile cross-pollination between early modernism and Irish literature and literary theory. The militant nationalist politics embraced by MacDonagh and Campbell, which would lead to execution and internment, respectively, find a correspondence in the politics of the avant-garde, at a time MacDonagh saw as 'a period of disturbance, of change.'

In an enthusiastic review of *Earth of Cualann*, for the *Egoist*, T.S. Eliot tried to convey a sense of Campbell's cosmopolitan yet intensely nationalist poetry and his Imagistic procedures in a determinedly Irish Mode: 'Mr Campbell is one of the half-dozen or so writers who are responsible for their being any contemporary poetry. He has established his own style of *vers libre* ... The stuff is Irish, with a peculiar bitter flavour, a dourness, of Mr Campbell's own. He uses Gaelic names with effect, but none of the poems is simply a whoop from the peat-bog.'[43]

41 Campbell, *Poems*, p. 179. **42** See Jerome McGann, *Black riders: the visible language of modernism* (Princeton: Princeton UP, 1993). **43** [T. S. Eliot], 'Short reviews', *Egoist* (11 Dec. 1917), p. 172. The attribution of these unsigned reviews to Eliot is made in Donald Gallup, *T.S. Eliot: a bibliography*, 2nd ed. (New York: Harcourt, Brace, 1969), p. 200.

Thomas William Rolleston:
the forgotten man

MARIA O'BRIEN

Thomas William Rolleston was involved in the Irish Revival in its various guises from its inception in the mid 1880s till his own death in 1920. This essay will highlight Rolleston's involvement in the Irish Literary Revival, the Gaelic League and Plunkett's co-operative movement. Rolleston has hitherto been a shadowy figure passing through Irish history and culture. His involvement and commitment to Irish culture and economics was immense but not without some controversy.

Thomas William Rolleston (1857–1920) was an author, poet and journalist. He was a member of the minority landowning class, his family having arrived in Ireland as part of the plantations in 1610. In the tradition of his class, he was educated at St Columba's, Rathfarnham, and Trinity College, Dublin. Trinity was the bastion of unionism in Ireland, but in the last two decades of the nineteenth century it produced a number of graduates who reacted against their alma mater and began to explore the possibility that a new Ireland might be created where instead of cultural friction, cultural fusion might be created.[1] These graduates included Rolleston, Charles Hubert Oldham who was the driving force behind the Contemporary Club, the Irish Protestant Home Rule Association (hereafter IPHRA) and the *Dublin University Review*, and Douglas Hyde, a founder of the Gaelic League in 1893.

After a spell in Germany (for his wife's health), Rolleston returned to Ireland in 1884 and immediately became involved in the Young Ireland Society, the Contemporary Club and later the IPHRA. Rolleston, like many others of that period, was profoundly influenced by Standish O'Grady's bardic sagas of Ireland. John O'Leary, the old Fenian, also exerted a powerful influence on Rolleston. O'Leary was imprisoned and later exiled for twenty years for his part in Fenian plans for an uprising in the 1860s. His exile ended in 1885, and his return to Ireland coincided with Rolleston's return. Rolleston believed O'Leary was 'trying to instil a spirit of tolerance into the narrow and bitter patriotism of the National League'. During his exile, O'Leary's nationalism had developed a cultural aspect. Believing all literature was essential to the development of nationalism, O'Leary saw all literature as nationalist and all nationalism as literature. He followed in the tradition of the Young Irelander, Thomas Davis, arguing in favour of a cam-

---

1 F.S.L. Lyons 'Yeats and Victorian Ireland' in A. Norman Jeffares (ed.) *Yeats, Sligo and Ireland* (Gerrard's Cross: Colin Smythe, 1980) p.120.

paign to convert the Protestant gentry to Irish nationalism. He believed they had been bribed into becoming West Britons by corrupt patronage of Dublin Castle. His desire to win back Protestants to the national movement was reminiscent of Tone and indeed of O'Connell. By doing so, O'Leary believed it would remove one of the visible props of English conquest in Ireland.[2]

Consequently, it is not surprising that O'Leary cultivated the friendship of people like Rolleston, Charles Hubert Oldham and the young Yeats. All were members of the Protestant ascendancy and were just the recruits to the national movement O'Leary sought. Rolleston, Yeats and John Taylor, a barrister, were known as O'Leary's disciples. By 1885, Rolleston was regarded as the most devoted of these disciples.[3] Roy Foster has highlighted O'Leary's importance to people like Yeats and Rolleston, as O'Leary was an introduction not only to the acceptable face of the extremist Fenian tradition but also to a kind of free-thinking Catholic intelligentsia of whose existence Sligo unionists (and to this could be added King's County Protestants) were blissfully ignorant.[4] O'Leary indicated new ways in which both Yeats and Rolleston could 'belong' to the new Ireland – an Ireland where like-minded people of both religious traditions could share pride in an ancient culture rather than remember the conflicts and dispossessions of the past.[5]

In February 1885, a new journal, the *Dublin University Review* (hereafter *DUR*), was founded in the tradition of the *Dublin University Magazine*. A journal of literature, philosophy, poetry and politics, it was edited and contributed to mainly by members of the Contemporary Club, although Rolleston and Oldham did the vast majority of the work. Discussions at the Club were often incorporated into the contents of the Review.[6] Rolleston is often quoted as the person, who launched the Review, but William Crook suggested it, and a group consisting of Crook, W.F. Bailey, a barrister and later governor of the National Gallery, and C.H. Oldham among others collectively launched it.[7] The *DUR* was a product of Trinity College, Dublin, and Rolleston later described it as emanating from Trinity.[8] As early as 1880, Rolleston broached the idea to Walt Whitman, the American poet, of establishing 'a paper in which politics, literature etc would all be treated from the highest republican standpoint, it might do much'.[9]

---

2 Ibid., p. 165. **3** Kevin Alldrit, *W.B. Yeats: The man and the mask* (London: John Murray, 1997) p. 49. Also, see Mary Macken, 'W.B. Yeats, John O'Leary and the Contemporary Club' in *Studies*, 28 (Mar. 1939) p.138; and W.B. Yeats, *Autobiographies: memoirs and reflections* (London: Bracken, 1955) p.213. **4** Roy Foster, *W.B. Yeats: a life: I – the apprentice mage* (Oxford: Oxford UP, 1998) p.43. **5** Ibid. **6** Yug Mohit Chaudhry, *Yeats, the Irish Literary Revival and the politics of print* (Cork: Cork UP, 2001) p.47. **7** Horst Frenz (ed.) *Whitman and Rolleston: a correspondence* (New York: Kraus Reprint, 1969), p.7. Frenz mistakenly identifies Rolleston as the force behind *DUR*. See also P.S. O'Hegarty 'Whitman and Rolleston: 'A Review' in *Dublin Magazine*, 1 (Jan.–Mar. 1953), p. 53. O'Hegarty corrects Frenz's mistake. See also Padraig Yeates, *Dublin lockout, 1913* (Dublin: Gill and Macmillan, 2000) p. 352. He mistakely identifies Rolleston as the founder of the *DUR*. **8** Alldritt, *W.B. Yeats* (1997), p. 41; see also Frenz *Whitman and Rolleston* (1969), Rolleston to Whitman, 4 Aug. 1885, p. 102. **9** Ibid., p. 18; Rolleston to

The *DUR* was established to aid the direction and development of Irish opinion among the 'cultivated classes of the country'. Its proclaimed *raison d'être* was the rehabilitation of Protestants to the centre of Irish affairs. Yug Mohit Chaudhry argues that the *DUR* was a political enterprise from its very inception and drew its impulse from a political project, that is, home rule, and consequently it had a clear political agenda.[10] Foster disagrees with this assessment and regards the *DUR* as part of the attempt to create a national literary culture. It was an alternative to politics and was concerned with the aftermath of national autonomy.[11] Foster's argument is supported by the fact that political discussion was prohibited in the Review.

After six months, the embargo on political discussion was lifted. Around this time, Rolleston became editor of the Review (until this point Oldham was the nominal editor), and it is possibly to surmise that he was responsible for the change in editorial policy. He sent Whitman a copy of the magazine 'of which I have been made editor'.[12] Yeats later claimed responsibility for securing Rolleston the post.[13] Yeats told Lady Gregory how he and another convinced Oldham to make Rolleston editor. Oldham was the prospective editor of the *DUR* but according to Yeats, he knew nothing of literature. It was of some amusement to Yeats and his friends to suggest something to Oldham and make him believe the idea was his. Consequently, Yeats went to Oldham and 'suggested in that way that he should make Rolleston editor. So next time I went to see him he told me that he was not all pleased with the present editor. Now there is a man called Rolleston who lives twenty-five miles out of Dublin, I am going to make him editor'.[14]

The *DUR* remains significant because it was the first journal to publish Yeats. This occurred under Rolleston's editorship of the Review. It offered a broad intellectual range and cultural cosmopolitanism. It introduced Irish readers to translations of Heine and serialized Turgenev's recently translated *On the Eve*. Rolleston is in fact credited with introducing Turgenev to Irish readers.[15] It also published important articles such as Hyde's 'A Plea for the Irish language', which was an outline of his seminal address 'The Necessity for De–anglicising Ireland' that he later delivered in 1892. This plea fell on deaf ears at the Review as its coverage of Gaelic literature and interests amounted to twenty-five pages in twenty-three publications.[16] Its editors (Rolleston and Oldham) questioned the futility of the Irish language:

Whitman, 30 Oct. 1880. **10** Ibid., p. 55. **11** Foster, *Yeats apprentice mage*, p. 41. **12** Frenz, *Whitman and Rolleston*, p. 101; Rolleston to Whitman, 4 Aug. 1885. **13** James Pethica (ed.), *Lady Gregory's diaries* (Gerrard's Cross, Bucks.: Colin Smythe, 1999) p. 172; also see Denis Donoghue (ed.), *W.B. Yeats, memories: autobiographies – first draft journal* (London: Macmillan, 1972), pp 50–1. **14** Pethica, *Lady Gregory*, p. 172. **15** Alldritt, *W.B. Yeats*, p. 41. **16** Chaudhry, *Yeats Irish Literary Revival*, p. 63.

Do they wish to make Irish the language of our conversation and our newspapers? Impossible and wholly undesirable. Do they wish to make us a bi-lingual people in the sense that everybody should know two languages? But peasantry and artisans cannot be expected to know two languages except at the expense of both. Would they separate Ireland into an English speaking country and an Irish speaking country? But how seriously this would affect the free circulation of thought ... what is there left except to treat Irish as a classic, and leave it to the Universities?[17]

The Irish Literary Society in London evolved from the Southwark Irish Literary Club, which had been established in 1883.[18] The initial meeting to discuss the formation of the Irish Literary Society took place at Yeats's home in Bedford Park at the end of December 1891. Yeats, Rolleston, Dr John Todhunter, a doctor and poet, D.J. O'Donoghue, journalist, biographer and later president of the National Literary Society, William P. Ryan, a journalist, and J.G. O'Keefe, secretary of the old Southwark club, attended the meeting.[19] Before the meeting, Yeats and Ryan discussed Rolleston's role in the society.[20] Ryan states that Rolleston was well known for his work as a scholar, a critic and an editor, but it was Rolleston's Irish work for the *Dublin University Review* that appealed to them. After a number of meetings held throughout January (including some at Rolleston's house in Wimbledon), it was decided to form the Irish Literary Society on 13 January 1892, at the Clapham Reform Club. Rolleston was appointed provisional secretary and proved to be 'an enthusiast and a capable organizer'.[21] Yeats acknowledged Rolleston's contribution to the establishment of the society: 'it was because he had much tact, and a knowledge of the technical business of committees, that a society was founded which was joined by every London-Irish author and journalist'.[22] He described Rolleston as the true founder of the society although he retained some of the glory as the 'general idea was mine'.[23] C.H. Rolleston credited the foundation of the Irish Literary Society to the fact that his father, T.W. Rolleston, was living in London at the time. He mistakenly dated the foundation of the society in 1893 and claimed it evolved from an attempt to issue Irish books.[24] According to his son, Rolleston was the person to whom everyone turned for advice and guidance. His niche in the movement was his organizational skills as he was the practical man, the

17 Ibid.   **18** John Kelly and Eric Domville (eds), *The collected letters of W.B. Yeats, Vol. 1, 1865–1895* (Oxford: Clarendon, 1986) p. 495.   **19** William P. Ryan, *The Irish Literary Revival* (New York: Lemma, 1970) p. 52; also see Kelly, *Yeats Collected Letters*, vol. 1, p. 495; and Foster, *Yeats apprentice mage*, p. 118.   **20** Ryan, *Irish Literary Revival*, p. 52.   **21** Ibid., p. 56.   **22** Yeats, *Memories*, p. 199. Yeats and Rolleston are generally regarded as the main instigators of the Irish Literary Society; also see F.S.L. Lyons, *Culture and anarchy in Ireland* (Oxford: Oxford UP, 1982), p. 38.   **23** Yeats, *Memories*, p. 51.   **24** C.H. Rolleston, *Portrait of an Irishman – a biographical sketch of T.W. Rolleston* (London: Methuen, 1939), p. 10.

man who thought things out and directed the human factors that had fallen naturally under his influence. He told each member to what end his particular talents might best be directed in order to achieve a more glorious future for the
Ireland they loved.[25] Discounting the unconscious bias and hyperbole, Rolleston
was regarded by others as the moving spirit behind the Irish Literary Society in
London. *United Ireland* identified Rolleston as the prime mover behind the society: 'a few more words about the Irish Literary Society in London, Rolleston,
Yeats, O'Keefe and Foley are the prime movers. Rolleston, most of all, very ener-
getic, suave and enthusiastic'.[26]

   The political upheavals of 1891, the death of Parnell and the split within the
Irish Parliamentary Party gave Yeats the opportunity to push a national literary
movement. If Yeats intended to present the cultural revival as politics continued
by other methods, then it was doomed as he and his associates were destined to
disagree over the question of politicizing literature.[27] This 'disagreement' became
apparent with the new 'Library of Ireland' scheme in 1892.[28] The publication and
circulation of popular Irish books was an important objective of both literary
societies in Dublin and London. To a certain extent, the argument was concerned
with control over the series but essentially it was ideological. That is, it addressed
the different conceptions of what a 'national' literature should be. Charles Gavan
Duffy, a Young Irelander of the 1840s and an associate of Davis, advocated Davis'
definition of literature as a propagandist arm of cultural nationalism; while Yeats
desired popular and imaginative literature inspired by Irish themes but not written with a political objective.[29] Yeats believed that Duffy was attempting to complete the Young Ireland movement, to finish what had been left undone because
of the Famine, Davis's death and Duffy's own emigration.[30] The dispute was complicated by the prevailing animosity between Parnellites and anti-Parnellites, of
whom many were members of the National Literary Society.[31]

   In *Memoirs*, Yeats claimed that Gavan Duffy had suggested a similar scheme,
and it was decided to amalgamate the schemes and organize the sales of the
books through the Irish Literary Society in London and the National Literary
Society in Dublin.[32] But in *Autobiographies*, Yeats stated that 'the always benevolent friend (Rolleston) to whom I had explained in confidence, when asking
his support, my arrangements with my publisher, went to Charles Gavan Duffy
and suggested they should together offer Mr Fisher Unwin a series of Irish
books. Gavan Duffy knew nothing of my plans, and so was guiltless, and my
friend (Rolleston) had heard me discuss many things that evening.'[33] Throughout

---

25 Ibid., p. 24. 26 *United Ireland*, 16 Apr. 1892. 27 Foster, *Yeats apprentice mage*, p. 115. 28
This scheme was a revival of the Young Ireland scheme of the 1840s, which was produced by
Charles Gavan Duffy. 29 Kelly, *Yeats Collected letters*, vol. 1, p. 501. 30 Yeats, *Autobiographies*
(1955), p. 206. 31 Ibid., p. 204. 32 Yeats, *Memories* (1972), p. 51; also see Kelly, *Yeats Collected
letters*, vol. 1, p. 500. 33 Yeats, *Autobiographies*, p. 227.

1892, working with the publisher Edmund Downey, Rolleston and Duffy worked tirelessly to get their scheme off the ground, but their attempts proved futile when they failed to raise the necessary capital for the venture. In October 1892, Rolleston approached Edward Garnett, a reader at Fisher Unwin, to take over the scheme without Yeats' knowledge. At this point, he divulged details of Yeats' earlier negotiations with Unwin to Duffy. Yeats objected to Duffy's editorship of the series, as he believed that Duffy had been absent from Ireland for too long and was no longer in touch with the mood of the country. For months, the dispute oscillated between London and Dublin with claims and counter-claims. Yeats believed that Rolleston was entirely under the influence of Duffy and had no control over his own actions. Concurrently, Rolleston believed that Yeats was attempting to make himself the leader of a small clique of 'advanced' men in Dublin. By early 1893, the two societies in London and Dublin reached a limited compromise. Duffy was editor of the series, with Hyde, representing Dublin, and Rolleston, representing London, the assistant editors.

Rolleston is remembered as a minor poet; indeed, he is forgotten, albeit for one poem 'The Dead at Clonmacnoise'. But his poems were included in several important anthologies: *Poems and Ballads of Young Ireland* (1888) and two anthologies of the Rhymers' Club (1892 and 1894), which Rolleston help found with Yeats and Ernest Rhys. He was included in Yeats' anthology *A Book of Irish Verse*, although Yeats omitted any mention of Rolleston in the second edition. Rolleston with his father-in-law published an anthology *A Treasury of Irish Poetry in the English Tongue* (1900). It was considered one of the most important anthologies published at the time; however, it met extreme hostility from Irish Ireland quarters, particularly from D.P. Moran and Arthur Griffith. Both denied that Irish literature or poetry written in the English language was Irish. Moran called it 'mongrel'; it was neither Irish nor English.

Rolleston expressed some scepticism over the possible restoration of the Irish language as the national language of Ireland. In early 1896, this scepticism was still apparent in a speech he delivered to the Dublin Press Club, during which he suggested that the Irish language was not suitable as an instrument for the expression of modern and scientific thought. He added that the Irish language as a medium for social intercourse had disappeared save for some places along the western seaboard.[34] Rolleston's comments resulted in a flurry of letters to the *Irish Daily Independent* that censured his comments. Michael Cusack, founder of the Gaelic Athletic Association, professed amazement 'at his recklessness of assertion. I was indignant that he had not a tear to shed in memory of the departed soul of Irish National life.'[35] Another asserted that whilst Rolleston's comments were true 'it affords a reason for cultivating a literary revival of the Irish

---

34 *Irish Daily Independent,* 20 Jan. 1896.   35 Michael Cusack to the *Irish Daily Independent,* 31 Jan. 1896.

language rather than a reason to why it should be left to rust'.[36] Rolleston suggested a 'scientific test'. He proposed to give two representative pieces of modern English prose to Hyde who would translate them into Irish. Hyde would then return them to Rolleston who in turn would give them to another Gaelic scholar to translate back into English and then publish the results in the *Gaelic Journal*. Rolleston promised: 'if the result shall show that I was wrong in my assertion I will only too gladly admit it, and one of the most remarkable facts in the history of language will have been brought to light'.[37] It was decided to hold the proposed test privately between Rolleston, Hyde and MacNeill. The pieces chosen were from the *Life of Goethe* by George Henry Lewes and the *Grammar of Science* by Karl Pearson. The yearbook for the Gaelic League remarked that the result surprised Rolleston and showed him that Irish possessed powers of word formation of which he had not dreamt.[38]

But in 1900, Rolleston returned to familiar territory when he claimed that the Irish people were solely responsible for the decline of the Irish language. The Irish language, 'our great National Treasure' was lost and its vicissitudes was the responsibility of the Irish people:

> Not the Sassenach! Have not our whole people, with their social and political leaders, for the last sixty years, co-operated eagerly with the National Board of Education in digging the grave of the ancient tongue?'[39]

England had offered no opposition to the Gaelic revival, Rolleston declared; the chief secretary was in favour of Gaelic League policy. It was the Irish who were the willing partners in the anglicization of their own country. It was the height of pro-Boer feeling in Ireland; anti-Imperial sentiment reinvigorated Ireland and Irish nationalism, particularly physical force nationalism. Earlier that year, Rolleston dismissed the pro-Boer feeling as a matter of tradition and inheritance, by insisting such feelings were shallow and led to exhibitions that were both silly and harmful.[40] Within Gaelic League circles, Yeats reported to Lady Gregory that Rolleston received a frosty reception at a lecture given by Hyde at which Rolleston spoke.[41] Despite these differences of opinion, Rolleston was an active and enthusiastic member of the Gaelic League. In September 1900 he offered £50 as a prize for the best modernization of an ancient Irish tale.[42] He was a member of a committee established by the National Literary Society to

36 Joseph McKenna to the *Irish Daily Independent,* 27 Jan. 1896. **37** TWR to the *Irish Daily Independent,* 29 Jan. 1896. **38** Gaelic League Yearbook of 1896 (MS 10900 MacNeill Papers) p. 16. **39** TWR, 'Æ and Fiona MacLeod' in *All Ireland Review,* 25 Aug 1900, p. 1. **40** *Echo,* 4 Oct. 1899. **41** Yeats to Lady Gregory 13 Oct. 1900 cited in: Warwick Gould, John Kelly and Deirdre Toomey (eds), *The collected letters of W.B. Yeats,* vol. 2, *1896–1900* (Oxford: Clarendon, 1997) p. 576; also see *Irish Daily Independent,* 12 Oct. 1900 for a report on the meeting and the *Leader,* 20 Oct. 1900. **42** *An Claidheamh Soluis,* 22 Sept. 1900.

inquire into the provisions of Irish classes for members of the society.[43] He was president of the Five Branches of the Provinces in Dublin, and the Glenealy committee invited him to become president of their Gaelic League branch.

The Gaelic League professed itself to be non-sectarian and non-political, but by the early 1900s, it was becoming more identified with nascent Catholicism and Gaelicism. D.P. Moran's newspaper, the *Leader*, regarded Irishness intrinsic with Catholicism, 'In the main non-Catholic Ireland looks upon itself as British and as Anglo-Irish, and if non-Catholics sought to throw their lot in with the Irish nation, it was imperative that they must recognize that the Irish nation is *de facto* a Catholic nation'.[44] Pamphlets by Fr Forde and Fr O'Leary published under the auspices of the League indicated the easy association of Catholicism with the Irish language. In his pamphlet 'The Irish Language Movement – Its Philosophy', O'Leary claimed that Irishness was tied with Catholicism and that the Irish language was infused with religious life.[45] The pamphlet incensed Rolleston and in a letter to Hyde, he warned that Protestants would defect from the Gaelic League if what he described as the 'sectarian and intolerant party' continued to retain the upper hand in the League. He further stated that it would be easy to form a strong party with Castletown as its head who would take up the Celtic Association and make a Gaelic organization for Protestants who were interested in Gaelic matters and Catholics who disliked the introduction of sectarianism in the Gaelic League. Lord Castletown was the leader of the Pan Celts in Ireland and had served in the Boer war. Rolleston insisted this was a serious possibility:

> I am going to thrash the matter out with Lord C. (Castletown) and others, but at the same time I think it is a great pity that it should be so. There are only a million Protestants in Ireland, they cannot be driven out nor can they, like Catholics in England, be regarded as a more or less negligible quantity.[46]

In conclusion, he urged Hyde to redirect the Gaelic League back on its original non-sectarian course.

Whilst Rolleston expressed concern about the Catholic Church becoming dominant in the League, he was also concerned about the Church of Ireland's lack of interest in the League. He outlined in an article 'Irish Protestantism and the Gaelic Movement' the consequences of the Church of Ireland's antipathy to the Irish language.[47] He berated Church of Ireland clergymen for their blind-

43 See Minute Book of the National Literary Society, 9 and 16 Oct. 1899 (NLI MSS 645–6).
44 Georg Grote, *Torn between politics and culture: the Gaelic League, 1893–1993*(New York: Waxmann Munster, 1994) p. 80. 45 Revd Peter Forde, *The Irish language movement: its philosophy*, Gaelic League pamphlet, No. 21 (Dublin, 1899) p. 27. 46 Ibid. 47 TWR 'Irish Protestantism and the Gaelic movement' in the *Church of Ireland Gazette*, 17 Nov. 1905.

ness to the vital point that a national church would have to be Irish above all things. He believed that the Church of Ireland had demonstrated a reluctance to all things Irish in the last three centuries and consequently it found itself 'an alien minority, it has cut itself off from all development and all national influence, it lives, one may say, on an island within an island, insulated from all vital contact with the people and keeping up this insulation through all the education institutions in which its influence is strong'.[48] Rolleston asserted that the Gaelic League now presented the Church of Ireland an opportunity to redeem itself in a movement that promoted national feeling. It was non-political, and involvement would not compromise them religiously or politically. Despite his faith in the Gaelic League as a non-political organization, Rolleston worried about the increasing influence of the clergy within the League. He warned the Revd James Hannay that the influence of the clergy would have to be monitored if the League was to preserve its independence. Like Rolleston, Hannay was an advocate of the Gaelic League, but he had first-hand experience of the power of the Catholic clergy. In 1906, John Dillon unmasked Hannay as the author George A. Birmingham. Under this pseudonym, Hannay published two novels, *The Seething Pot* and *Hyacinth*. The theme of both books dealt with the increasing isolation of the Anglo-Irish ascendancy in Ireland. The unmasking of Hannay led to a series of controversies. In these, what Birmingham wrote was inextricably mixed up with whom (Hannay, the Church of Ireland rector) wrote it. Hannay was censured for his alleged attacks on the institutions and religious faith of Catholics in Ireland. The initial controversy was a local affair, but it reached national level following a meeting of the Gaelic League in Claremorris in late 1906. Hannay was a member of the Coisde Gnotha (Executive Committee) of the League. The parish priest of Tuam, Canon Macken, objected to Hannay's presence on a committee because of Hannay's portrayal of Irish Catholics in his books. Macken's action breached the constitution of the League, and when this was pointed out to him, he replied he was bound to a higher constitution. The incident sent shockwaves throughout the Gaelic League, but Hannay diffused the situation with his resignation from the Coisde Gnotha. In the wake of such incidents, Rolleston clung to the belief that:

> Politics is fact have now been, like everything else, absorbed into the Church, everything but *one* (Rolleston's emphasis) thing, and that one thing is the Gaelic League. The League represents the last effort of the Irish spirit for nationality and a personal independence. The Church began by opposing it; it's now, as usual, doing its utmost to absorb it, when it will become the mere tame cat like the political party and cease to have any vital existence for the future of Ireland. Whether the League can resist

48 Ibid.

the Church any better than the politicians did is very doubtful, but we must fight the matter out as best we can – and qui vivra verra.[49]

By 1907, he regarded the non-sectarian constitution of the League as a joke and was unable to give a lecture on the non-sectarianism of the League, 'knowing what I do, to preside at a meeting devoted to a discussion of the non political character of the Gaelic League. I cannot champion it without saying what I know to be untrue'.[50] In 1907, the threat of a Protestant secession from the Gaelic League was resurrected. It arose from a number of meetings held under the auspices of the Branch of the Five Provinces, a branch of the League with a Protestant majority. Irish Protestant Gaelic Leaguers held a number of meetings throughout May to discuss ways and means of bringing the League to the notice of their fellow co-religionists and inducing them to take their part in the movement.[51] Rolleston denied vehemently that there was any discussion among Protestants to secede from the League. Certain Protestant Gaelic Leaguers used the rooms of the Five Provinces 'with a view to concerting measures for extending the principles of the League among their co-religionists'.[52] Rolleston asserted that Catholics predominated the membership at the Five Branches and Protestants would object to such a move. He declared, 'I should never have encountered any such body, much less held office in it'.

Rolleston saw the Gaelic League as a vehicle to bring Irish Protestants into Irish life. He was not concerned with the restoration of the Gaelic language *per se*; this was a chimera as far as he was concerned. He believed the Gaelic League had the potential to be a 'true' national movement on non-sectarian and non-political lines, but this 'potential' was threatened by the nascent Gaelicism of Moran's *Leader* and increasing clerical dominance within the League.

The 1890s saw the blossoming of the Irish literary revival but it was also a period of 'conciliation' in Irish politics. Redmond, the leader of the Parnellite section of the Irish Parliamentary Party, embraced this new direction in Irish politics. According to Paul Bew, Redmond sought to achieve home rule by affecting a shift in the English public and parliamentary opinion.[53] How was this 'shift' to be achieved? It was to be achieved by creating first a new and harmonious era of co-operation between the different creeds and classes in Ireland.[54] Redmond believed that tension between southern Irishmen gave many British voters a reason to defeat home rule.[55] Sir Horace Plunkett, a

49 TWR to Hannay, date unknown but early 1905 (Hannay Papers Trinity College Dublin MSS 3544). 50 TWR to Hannay, 11 Jan. 1907 (Hannay Papers Trinity College Dublin MSS 3544). 51 *An Claidheamh Soluis*, 18 May 1907; also see *Freeman's Journal*, 18 May 1907; and the *Leader*, 11 and 25 May 1907. 52 TWR to the *Freeman's Journal*, 28 May 1907; also see TWR to *An Claidheamh Soluis*, 28 May 1907. 53 Paul Bew, *Conflict and conciliation in Ireland 1890–1910: Parnellites and radical agrarians* (Oxford: Clarendon, 1987). 54 Ibid. 55 Ibid., p. 25

unionist, asserted that the root of Ireland's problems was economic rather than political. He believed it was necessary to wean the Irish people from their obsession with politics to concentrate on their economic plight. In the late 1880s, Plunkett established the first co-operative creamery in Limerick. In 1894, he presided over the establishment of the Irish Agricultural Organisation Society (hereafter IAOS).

It is not known when or how or even why Rolleston became interested in the co-operative movement. In 1900, Rolleston published an article in which he outlined his vision of the role of organizations such as the Gaelic League, the IAOS, the Irish Industries Association (hereinafter IIA) and the Literary Society. He regarded these organizations as the embodiments of the true national spirit; they were practically the 'sole fosterers and guardians of the national idea'.[56] Rolleston pointed out that these movements ran counter to the trend of political nationalism, which he believed opposed any co-operation between home rulers and unionists; this was something 'to be denounced and smitten down. The nationalism of the spirit and the nationalism of contemporary party politics refuse to coalesce and harmonize.'[57] Rolleston's involvement was not initially with Plunkett's movement. In 1893, he was appointed managing director and secretary of the IIA. Lady Aberdeen, whose husband served as lord lieutenant of Ireland on two separate occasions, founded the IIA in 1886. The IIA was primarily concerned with handicrafts industry in Ireland – lace making and the manufacture of homespuns. Rolleston's position within IIA required him to spend much of his time travelling around Ireland, lecturing and encouraging the organization of industries suitable to each locality.[58]

In 1899, the Department of Agriculture and Technical Instruction Act established a new department, which came into existence in 1900. But by then, the air of conciliation that had been palatable in Irish politics slowly dissipated, although it continued until the landlord conference in 1902, which resulted in the Wyndham Land Act of 1903. Four separate events – the 1798 Centenary celebrations, the Boer war, the formation of O'Brien's United Irish League and the re-unification of the Irish Parliamentary Party – revitalized Irish nationalism. A more hostile and suspicious approach in the manner of John Dillon replaced Redmond's conciliationist approach. Dillon was inimical to Plunkett's efforts, as he believed it was just another means of killing home rule by kindness. Rolleston was appointed Organiser of Lectures at the new department. His remit was similar to his position at the IIA. He organized lectures on various subjects relating to technical instruction throughout Ireland. His major contribution to the Department of Agriculture and Technical Instruction (hereafter DATI) was the organization of the Irish Historic Loan to the St Louis World Fair in 1904.

---

56 C.H. Rolleston, *T.W. Rolleston* (1939), p. 60. 57 Ibid. 58 Ibid., p. 58.

In 1908, Rolleston unwittingly played into the Irish Parliamentary Party's hands. In 1906, the Liberals were returned to office, and the Irish Parliamentary Party was determined to have Plunkett removed from the headship of the DATI. Plunkett eventually handed over office to T.W. Russell. In 1907, Plunkett resumed the presidency of the IAOS but relations remained strained between the two groups. Later that year, he gave a wide-ranging speech on the role of the IAOS and asked Rolleston to send copies of the speech to friends in America to solicit funds. Rolleston sent copies of the speech with a covering letter. As noted earlier, Rolleston had very little enthusiasm for the Irish Parliamentary Party. In 1890, he described them as 'this damnable gang of swindlers and murderers'. In his letter, Rolleston described Plunkett's speech as an attempt to organize Irish farmers to shake off the grip of the country publican and the gombeen man, who hitherto controlled the parliamentary representation of the country.[59] The letter found its way into the possession of John Redmond who published it in the *Freeman's Journal*. As far as Redmond was concerned, the letter was proof of a plot by the co-operative movement to usurp the position of the Irish Parliamentary Party. Rolleston accepted responsibility for the letter and the opinions expressed in it, claiming they were his and were not representative of the IAOS However, his letter ended any hope of reconciliation between the DATI and the IAOS It gave the DATI a reason to withdraw funds from the IAOS, which was now forced to rely entirely on its own resources.[60]

In 1909, Rolleston moved to London to take up a position as a reviewer of German literature for the *Times Literary Supplement*. He continued to take an interest in Ireland, but it was from a position of observation rather than participation.

For a variety of reasons, Rolleston has been ignored, but he was one of the very few who managed to engage in the revival in its different manifestations. He has been neglected for a variety of reasons. His imperialistic vision of Ireland in an 'Anglo-Celtic' empire did not sit easily with his earlier devotion to John O'Leary. Arthur Griffith, the founder of Sinn Féin, repeatedly criticized Rolleston's conversion from nationalism to imperialism. In one article, Griffith wrote: 'I do most heartily congratulate him on his exit from Irish nationalism.'[61] Even Yeats dismissed Rolleston's nationalism as child's play: 'his nationalist convictions had never been more than the toys of a child and were put away when the bell rang for meals'.[62] In the aftermath of Parnell's death and the split in the Irish Parliamentary Party, Rolleston appealed to organizations like the National Literary Society, the Gaelic League, the IIA and the IAOS to fulfil the role of the Irish Parliamentary Party. He desired for these organizations to create harmony and co-operation between nationalists and unionists.

59 Trevor West, *Horace Plunkett: co-operation and politics – an Irish biography* (Gerrard's Cross: Colin Smythe, 1986), p. 84.   **60** West, *Plunkett* (1986), pp 83–4.   **61** *United Irishman*, 24 Mar. 1900; also see *United Irishman*, 12 May, 9 June, 1 Sept. and 20 Oct. 1900, 19 Jan., 2 and 23 Feb. 1901 and 21 Jan. 1905 for further attacks on Rolleston.   **62** Alldrit, *W.B.Yeats* (1997), p. 49.

As he saw it, they represented 'the true, genuine, and practical nationalism of the country'.[63] But the events of Easter week 1916 and the subsequent War of Independence meant that the contribution and role of figures such as Rolleston came to be neglected.

63 C.H. Rolleston, *T.W. Rolleston* (1939), p. 60.

Robert Lynd, paradox and the Irish Revival: 'acting out' or 'working through'?

G.K. PEATLING

Modes of representation of Irishness consistent in part or in whole with negative stereotyping of Ireland and 'the Irish' have long outlasted nationalist Ireland's formal political domination by the English/British. One particular critical commentary on the Irish Revival depicts it as a parallel mode of acceptance, or 'acting out', of aspects of a stereotype of 'the Irish' previously created by the British, or at least limited by a discursive space framed by British sources. As David Cairns and Sean Richards suggest:

> Although conventionally referred to as the Irish literary revival or Renaissance, it was, in essence, a decisive engagement with an agenda whose items had been inscribed in the course of the nineteenth-century 'war of position' as English and Anglo-Irish intellectuals attempted to avert 'The coming crisis'.[1]

There is, in other words, a suggested dimension of the Irish Revival that involved reifying the stereotypical otherworldliness of the Celt and pursuing it as a political and cultural objective, through essentialist drives to purge Ireland of crass modernity, impurity and British materialism.[2] To summarize crudely, while British stereotypes suggested that the Irish lacked the practical hard-headedness to succeed in the commercial and capitalist spheres, revivalists are sometimes depicted as responding: 'Yes, that's true: but it's the best way to be.' This essay will explore some of the obstacles to avoiding the 'acting out' of such stereotypes in critical commentary on the Irish Revival, and the locations from which such crude pre-defined ethnic compartments and stereotypes may be 'worked through' or escaped. In particular, the work of the essayist Robert Wilson Lynd (1879–1949), whose career and prominence was cognate to the Revival,[3] is scrutinized, firstly, for the

---

1 David Cairns and Sean Richards, *Writing Ireland: colonialism, nationalism and culture* (Manchester: Manchester UP, 1988), pp 50, 57. 2 J.V. Kelleher, 'Matthew Arnold and the Celtic revival', in Harry Levin (ed.), *Perspectives of criticism* (Cambridge Mass.: Harvard UP, 1950), p. 205; Tom Garvin, 'Priests and patriots: Irish separatism and the fear of the modern, 1890–1914', *Irish Historical Studies*, 25 (1986–7), pp 67–86; Tom Garvin, *Nationalist revolutionaries in Ireland, 1858–1928* (Oxford: Clarendon Press, 1988), pp 57–77; John Hutchinson, *The dynamics of cultural nationalism: the Gaelic Revival and the creation of the Irish nation state* (London: Allen & Unwin, 1987). 3 Sean McMahon 'Robert Lynd: an introduction', in Robert Lynd,

presence of 'acting-out' and 'working-through', and, secondly, to suggest that Lynd's work and personal narrative offer some insights for Irish and non-Irish commentators and readers alike into the possibilities of 'working-through'.

An important theoretical perspective on the issue of 'acting-out' and 'working-through' can be gleaned from Dominick LaCapra's essay, 'Writing history, writing trauma'.[4] For LaCapra, the possibilities in historical writing about certain 'limit-events'[5] parallel, and may even facilitate, modes of identification based on such events. LaCapra argues that an individual (or group) traumatized by an experience – especially in the extreme mode of repetition compulsion – is clearly not in a desired state, either for themselves or others.[6] LaCapra, however, suggests that to 'work through' traumatic experiences, or to base processes of identification on experiences *other* than a past trauma, may be problematic: certain 'limit events' are in fact so troubling that to 'work through' them in the sense of regarding the events as 'closed' would be deeply inappropriate.[7] Similarly, individuals in a position to attempt to 'work through' may be held back by a sense that it would constitute a desertion of other, or particular, victims.[8] LaCapra's application of an overtly psychological meaning of 'acting-out' and 'working-through' to collective as well as individual traumatic experiences has a resonance in the present context on account of the links in Irish history and culture between stereotyping, processes of identification, and experiences perceived (albeit often retrospectively) as traumatic, experiences by no means limited to obvious candidates such as the famine. In such a context, 'acting-out' can constitute marking oneself as Irish by conforming to a pattern of behaviour bequeathed by a historical trauma. The misrecognition of such behaviour as ethnically determined in institutions, conventions or markets indeed can make it difficult to contest stereotypes and can inspire fears that a personal attempt to subvert a stereotype would leave isolated those subjected to the fullest objectifying force of such representations.

Traces of such possibilities of 'acting-out' and 'working-through' can be located in the work of Robert Lynd. Lynd is to be associated with the Irish Revival for a number of reasons. Both Lynd and close associates such as James Winder Good contributed prominently to the revivalist Ulster-based periodical *Uladh* in the early twentieth century.[9] He reflected on the Revival's themes, personalities and literature, by his own confession idolizing George Bernard Shaw.[10] Most importantly, Lynd's work, in important ways, can be represented as cohering

Galway of the races: selected essays, ed. Sean McMahon (Dublin: Lilliput, 1990), pp 1–44. **4** Dominick LaCapra, *Writing history, writing trauma* (Baltimore: Johns Hopkins UP, 2001). Also see Dominick LaCapra, *History and memory after Auschwitz* (Ithaca, NY: Cornell UP, 1998), pp 180–210. **5** LaCapra has the Jewish Holocaust in mind. **6** LaCapra, *Writing history, writing trauma,* p. 28. **7** Ibid., pp 41–2, 14. **8** Ibid., p. 22. **9** See Marnie Hay, 'Explaining *Uladh*: the promotion of nationalism and regionalism in Ulster', in this collection. **10** Lynd, *Galway of the races,* pp 54–7, 101–29.

with concerns commonly identified as Irish: in addition to a large output concerned with Irish politics, culture and society, Lynd's prose and journalism arguably encapsulated an approach that to many contemporaries fitted an assumed typology of 'literary Irishness'.

There are many reasons for praising Lynd. Although a Presbyterian from Belfast and the son of a unionist, Lynd became a nationalist, and his books and columns in English publications (principally the *Nation*, the *New Statesman* and the *Daily News*) made a sustained contribution to putting forward the case for Irish independence (though unable to prevent a partition he passionately opposed).[11] Unlike some products of the Revival, however, Lynd was by no means narrowly obsessed by insular political causes.[12] He was at times a brilliant writer. His 1916 *New Statesman* essay 'If the Germans conquered England' particularly worthy of mention for its debunking of self-congratulatory narratives of English history and subtle advancement of Sinn Féin's aspiration to an independent Ireland, while still fulfilling the conventions of British war-time propaganda.[13] He also reported on other grave events such as the economic depression in the north of Britain in 1923.[14] On less serious issues, he was idiosyncratic and often amusing, wih his prose being punctuated by his obsessions with birdsong,[15] horse-racing,[16] and tobacco (Lynd smoked a hundred cigarettes a day),[17] and by irritation with such features of life as customs barriers.[18] Modest self-deprecation throughout his work did not prevent him from making occasional points of real weight, and his readers had many reasons to regard his prose with affection. Lynd wrote in the British press for over four decades, with his own conquest of the commanding heights of British journalism mirroring the prominence of Shaw, Yeats, O'Casey and a striking number of other contemporary Irish writers and journalists, and thus the achievements of the Revival itself. As Lynd's half-Irish wife Sylvia, a poet and critic worthy of attention in her own right, wrote in 1923: 'The Irish novel indeed is not a lovely maiden in need of a rescuer; but a dragon that is devouring the novels of both England and America … Irish literature has never been more alive than it is at present.'[19]

In the present context, however, it can be suggested that three aspects of Lynd's writing and literary persona involved 'acting out' certain modes of Irish

11 Robert Lynd, *Home life in Ireland* (1909; London: Mills & Boon, 1910); Lynd, *Ireland a nation* (London: Grant Richards, 1919). **12** [Lynd], 'The old mistake about patriotism', *New Statesman*, 15:365 (10 Apr. 1920), pp 8–9. **13** Lynd, *If the Germans conquered England, and other essays* (Dublin, 1917), pp 1–8, first published anonymously in the *New Statesman*, 6:156 (1 Apr. 1916), pp 612–4. **14** Lynd, 'Cotton clouds', *Daily News* (hereafter *DN*), 15 Oct. 1923, pp 1a, 3d–e. **15** Lynd, 'Nightingale music', *DN*, 14 May 1923, pp 1g, 3a–b; Lynd, 'Into the birds' Mecca', *DN*, 15 June 1926, p 5b–c. **16** Lynd, 'Galway of the races', in *Galway of the races*, pp 58–87; [Lynd], 'The intellectual side of horse racing', *New Statesman*, 15:374 (12 June 1920), pp 274–5. **17** McMahon, 'Robert Lynd', p.39; Lynd 'Complete change', *DN*, 15 Aug. 1923, p. 4d; Lynd, 'Doctor's orders. The brighter medicine of to-day', *DN*, 23 July 1924, p. 4e. **18** Lynd, 'Why I hate the customs', *DN*, 1 Aug. 1923, p. 4e. **19** Sylvia Lynd, 'Genius and humour', *DN*, 9 Oct. 1923, p.7d.

stereotype. These are, firstly, moments in Lynd's depiction of Irish society, secondly, Lynd's suspicion of science and of modern technology, and thirdly, Lynd's predilections for paradox and levity, which occasionally reduce his prose to little more than flippancy. In each case, the fact that the prose of a subtle writer such as Lynd moves in the direction of 'acting-out' demonstrates the inherent difficulty of avoiding such a process in Irish writing, especially in this period. However, in important particulars, Lynd ultimately tackles this difficulty more successfully than many authors, including more recent writers.

In describing rural Ireland in his 1909 book *Home Life in Ireland*, Lynd remarked on the poor quality of home maintenance in many parts of Ireland:

> ... if a window is broken or a spout injured, some hopelessly inefficient steps will often be taken to stave off the critical day when a new window must be put in or the spout properly seen to. People who do not examine into the causes of things look upon this untidiness of the country-side as a deep-seated Irish characteristic, born of Irish blood rather than of Irish conditions. There could not be a shallower thought. The Irish farmer originally became untidy in self-defence. He knew that, if his house looked beautiful and his hedges trim, the quick eye of the land-agent would soon size him up as a prosperous man, and raise his rent accordingly.[20]

At first sight, this appears to be an essentialist vision of Irishness consistent with discourses of the Revival and of subsequent formations: the inefficiency of an archetypal 'Irish farmer'[21] is not queried, merely depicted as 'functional'. What redeems Lynd's passage, however, is the greater subsequent flagging of counterinstances.[22] In particular, he evinces a sense of how such a national reputation had been overstated by both maligners of, *and* those identifying with, Ireland:

> Pro-Irish politicians, wishing to make a pitiable and sympathy-winning show of the country, have dragged forward the dirtiest and most dismantled mud hovels as demonstrations of the wretched condition of the people. Anti-Irish politicians, on the other hand, have called up these same dirty and dismantled hovels as witnesses to the fact that the Irish are a half-savage and worthless people, less fit than any other in Europe to be trusted with the government of their own land ... All sides have agreed to judge Ireland by its worst, and have held up as the typical Irish home not anything like the average Irish home, but the most tumbledown and ill-kept Irish home they could find.[23]

A second trait in Lynd's prose that can be seen as 'acting out' an Irish stereotype is his self-consciously anti-scientific or -technological disposition:[24] the fact that,

---

20 Lynd, *Home life in Ireland*, p. 14. **21** Lynd later criticized just such abstractions: Lynd, 'Invented people', *DN*, 16 Jan. 1924, p. 4e. **22** Lynd, *Home life in Ireland*, pp 14–5. **23** Ibid., p. 16. **24**

in his own words, 'I usually find it rather difficult to believe what the men of science say.'[25] Scientific explanations for inclement weather (a frequent topic in his prose) failed to satisfy him.[26] Lynd also had misgivings about what he called 'The triumph of the machine'.[27] He heard of the development of what was being termed 'radiovision' with 'a pang of regret': 'Let us, then, pass a law forbidding any further inventions, except in food and medicine, for a thousand years. We have invented enough: let us begin to enjoy ourselves.'[28] Similarly, when reporting on the economic depression of 1923 for the *Daily News*, Lynd's attitude to the technological aspects of the Lancashire cotton industry was almost superstitious: machines were 'the good fairy of the modern world' or perhaps 'demons ... pressed into service by the good fairy. I found them, on the whole, frightening.'[29] All this would appear to connect with anti-modernist aspects of revival Ireland. There are two mitigating circumstances, however, to this feature of Lynd's prose and character. Firstly, while an aversion to industry in an Irish nationalist might be said to fulfill some political stereotypes, such an aversion in a Belfast Protestant hardly fulfilled an *ethnic* stereotype. Indeed, Lynd elsewhere challenged images of Ulster as a barren industrial landscape, especially in a suggestively titled essay 'Beautiful Ulster'.[30] Secondly, while Lynd may have failed to come to grips with technology, his grasp of economic argument was lucid, and in his depression pieces he articulated a rudimentary version of a Keynesian multiplier.[31]

Another possible defence of Lynd's writings on science is that these were deliberately and obviously tongue-in-cheek. But this is suggestive of a third possible mode of 'acting-out' in Lynd's work, by the articulation of arguments which were, or made their author seem, foolish, nonsensical or in jest. These traits are encapsulated in Lynd's fascination with paradox, in the sense of statements which are seemingly contradictory or opposed to common sense but which contain or hint at truth. In Lynd's view, 'life' was 'full of such paradoxes'[32] as 'how odious is violence and yet how charming it can be to the imagination',[33] and 'stupidity is not such a bad thing as is generally supposed'.[34] In short, Lynd suggested, 'most of the good things in life are the result of the bad things of life'.[35]

On the antipathy to science and modernity of aspects of Catholic and nationalist Irish culture at this time see Gordon L. Herries Davies, 'Irish thought in Science', in Richard Kearney (ed.), *The Irish mind: exploring intellectual traditions* (Dublin: Wolfhound Press, 1985), pp 294–310, especially p. 310; Greta Jones, 'Catholicism, nationalism and science', *Irish Review*, 20 (Winter/Spring 1997), pp 47–61. **25** Lynd, 'Shaped like a pear', *DN*, 10 Jan. 1923, p. 4d. **26** Y.Y. [Lynd], 'The weather: an explanation', *New Statesman*, 1:13 (new series), (23 May 1931), p. 457. 'Y.Y.' was a pseudonym Lynd commonly used in his *New Statesman* pieces. **27** Lynd, 'The triumph of the machine', *DN*, 16 July 1924, p. 6d. **28** Lynd, 'Too many inventions', *DN*, 9 Jan 1924, p. 6d. **29** Lynd, 'The romance of cotton', *DN*, 23 Oct. 1923, p. 6d–e. **30** Lynd, 'Beautiful Ulster', *DN*, 23 July 1914, p. 4d. **31** Lynd, 'How Leeds faces the winter', *DN*, 12 Nov. 1923, p. 5c–d. **32** Lynd, 'Making room', *DN*, 9 May 1923, p. 4d. **33** Y.Y., 'Paradox', *New Statesman and Nation*, 22:545 (2 Aug. 1941), p. 109. **34** This was because 'stupid people at least save us from the dangers of being ruled by clever people': see Y.Y., 'In praise of stupidity', *New Statesman and Nation*, 18:451 (14 Oct. 1939), p. 517. **35** Lynd, 'The good of bad weather', *DN*, 14 Jan. 1925, p. 6d.

Sometimes Lynd's love of deploying paradoxes could lead to observations of penetrating or even prophetic pertinence. Lynd, for instance, insightfully used comments by Lord Reith, director-general of the BBC, in 1930 to observe that 'if you set out to give the public what it wants, you will probably end by giving it less and worse than it wants'.[36] Another clever essay was inspired by a suggestion that the pattern of near-universal motor-car ownership in the United States was worthy of emulation since it had proved an effective antidote to Communism. If everyone owned a car, Lynd suggested, 'half of us would be unable to get to our offices before lunch owing to the block in the traffic ... [O]n Saturdays and Sundays the south of England would resemble nothing so much as a huge garage.'[37] But the insistent articulation of the paradoxical was also a technique which could misfire and produce misreadings. Lynd often pondered whether the writers of letters to newspapers 'intended to be ironical or serious',[38] and an article by Lynd himself late in his career endeavouring to demonstrate the heavily intellectual nature of English culture evoked similar reactions. Lynd reported that a critic had responded '"on first reading the article, I had grave doubts as to this point, as to whether or not it was supposed to be a satire"'. Lynd stated that this had not been the intention, but admitted, 'I have unfortunately little comprehension of logic': 'I ... find it extremely difficult to perceive the flaw in one of my own arguments.'[39]

While Lynd's difficulties in ratiocination perhaps did not constitute a revolt against the despotism of fact, the prominence of the paradoxical in Lynd's prose can make its levels of seriousness, irony and levity hard to disentangle. Combined with Lynd's Irish background, his jokey weekly essays on the lighter side of life could surely have been read by contemporaries as a variant of the 'stage Irish' performance. Such an image could not but undermine the effect of Lynd's more sober pieces, since the consequence of finding a paradoxical good in life's injustices was to depict the world, in Lynd's phrase, as 'a delightful playroom'.[40] Negative attributes such as laziness become in Lynd's columns an 'excellent thing', since 'civilisation is simply an expression of man's desire to make things as easy as possible for himself'.[41] Dyspepsia gave 'a man a new interest in life'.[42] He even appeared to show an exaggerated respect for activities of which he heartily disapproved, such as discarding litter.[43] According to one editor regularly to publish Lynd's work, it was not in his literary persona alone that Lynd found it hard to regard any entity as irredeemably bad: 'I do not believe he really hates the Devil: I doubt if he [even] hates Lord Carson.'[44]

36 Y.Y., 'What the public wants', *New Statesman*, 34:876 (8 Feb. 1930), pp 563–5. **37** Lynd, 'Motor-cars and Bolshevism', *DN*, 6 Nov. 1924, p. 6e. **38** Y.Y., 'Only kind to be cruel', *New Statesman*, 9:221, (18 May 1935), p. 710. **39** Y.Y., 'A Letter', *New Statesman and Nation*, 25:623 (30 Jan 1943), p. 75. **40** Lynd, 'Looking into a shop-window', *DN*, 24 Sept. 1924, p. 6e. **41** Lynd, 'The lassitude of spring', *DN*, 12 Mar. 1924, p. 6d. **42** Lynd, 'In defence of indigestion', *DN*, 16 May 1923, p. 4e. **43** Lynd, 'The art of throwing litter', *DN*, 22 July 1925, p. 6f–g. **44**

Apart from entertainment value, and more than occasional flashes of brilliant prose, there are several reasons why Lynd even at his most indulgent to the
paradoxical should not be condemned for 'acting out' a stereotype. Firstly, it can
be argued that paradox is a defence mechanism for one who associates himself,
as Lynd did, with the Irish experience of disadvantage. The counterintuitive
nature of paradox means that, in skilled hands, it enables one to hint at the superior intelligence, competence and self-possession of those who appear to be
stupid, incompetent or wild. Lynd was certainly keenly aware of stereotypes of
the Irish in Britain which incorporated the latter characteristics.

In 1941, recalling his earlier arrival in England, he wrote:

> I had scarcely set foot on English soil when an Englishman … looked at
> me affectionately and, shaking his head, said: 'Wild Irishman. You're all
> the same. Always ready for a scrap.' … Sometimes I have tried to disillu-
> sion them; but sometimes the pleasure of being mistaken for a man who
> loved nothing better than a scrap [has] been too much for me, and I have
> accepted the compliment with a fraudulent smile.[45]

One of the passages in Lynd's work most often quoted,[46] written in 1908, had
also reflected on such early encounters with the English:

> What I especially like about Englishmen is that, after they have called you
> a thief and a liar and have patted you on the back for being so charming
> in spite of it, they look honestly depressed if you fail to see that they have
> been paying you a handsome compliment.[47]

It is suggestive, too, that Lynd so admired Bernard Shaw, the writer at this time
of the most famous inversion of the binary opposition between stereotypes of
the Irish and the English/British.

A second and more important defence of Lynd, however, is that ethnicity,
and therefore the 'acting out' of ethnic stereotypes, did not play as large a part
in his life or writings as might be thought. Notwithstanding the difficulties hinted
at in Lynd's description of his encounters with the English soon after arriving
in the country, Lynd's personal narrative in Britain was largely one of integration, which certainly entailed 'working through' any atavistic sense of Anglo-
phobia. After almost two decades of working in England, even during the opening phases of the war of independence, Lynd could describe himself as 'an almost
fanatical pro-Englishman'.[48] The conclusion of that war seems to have increased

Stuart Hodgson, 'Mr. Lynd's essays', *DN*, 29 Nov. 1924, p. 8g. **45** Y.Y., 'Paradox', p. 109. **46**
Sean McMahon (ed.), *A book of Irish quotations* (Dublin: O'Brien Press, 1984), p. 90. **47** Lynd,
Irish and English: portraits and impressions (London: Griffiths, 1908), p. viii. **48** Lynd, *Ireland a
nation*, pp 235–6.

Lynd's sense of having a stake in England. After the Second World War, Lynd even defended 'England' from insular critics:

> Now that England has ceased to be the boastful country of the end of the last century there is room for … a reaction against those who are inclined to see only the virtues of foreign nations and the crimes and faults of their own … After all, English history, with all its black pages, is the most remarkable that the world has seen since Rome perished.[49]

Lynd's admiration of contemporary Irish writing was not inimical to veneration of many aspects of English literature: his favourites included such English worthies as Byron,[50] Samuel Johnson,[51] and, of course, Shakespeare, whom he paid the following striking compliment: 'It is, I believe, impossible to prove that Shakespeare smoked, but if he did not smoke, how could he have written his plays?'[52] It would have been hard for Lynd to avoid cherishing many aspects of English culture since so much of his career was given up to the appreciation of literature in the English language, notwithstanding his own fluency in the Irish language (a key revivalist objective which Lynd, predictably, pursued while in London).[53] Lynd was never an assimilated member of an imagined English nation and continued to reference his Irish background and Irish concerns; but he had succeeded in 'working through' any visceral antagonism to English culture.

Larry Morrow was another member of the large group of Irish journalists prominent in London, and occasionally filled in for Lynd in his weekly jovial essay slot in the *Daily News*.[54] Morrow told English readers in 1925, with reference to the reputation of Ireland:

> The blame, I'm afraid, must lie with us in Ireland, although on your side you Englishmen have done your best for the legend through Geraldus Cambrensis, Edmund Spenser and James Anthony Froude. We have let you talk and write nonsense about Ireland for almost 500 years, and we have written a good deal of it ourselves.[55]

Robert Lynd's writings demonstrate some of the difficulties for Irish individuals, at least in certain locations at certain times, of avoiding the writing of nonsense, and the cognate difficulty of avoiding 'acting-out'. Ultimately, however, Lynd deserves credit not only for his efforts to 'work through', but also for personally adding less to the stock of 'nonsense about Ireland' than many others.

49 Lynd, *Books and writers* (London: Dent, 1952), p. 306. 50 Lynd, 'Byron's bad press', *DN*, 16 Apr. 1924, p. 6c. 51 Lynd, 'Dr Johnson', *DN*, 4 July 1924, p.7b–c. 52 Lynd 'A word for tobacco', *DN*, 13 May 1925, p. 6d. 53 McMahon, 'Robert Lynd', pp 18–9. 54 H.L. Morrow, 'Advice to burglars', *DN*, 13 Aug. 1925, p. 4f–g. 55 H.L. Morrow, 'Ireland revisited', *DN*, 7 July 1925, p. 6d.

The Revival at local level: Katherine Frances Purdon's portrayal of rural Ireland

BRIAN GRIFFIN

Until relatively recently, most of the attention of scholars of the Irish literary revival has been focused on the writings of the 'leading lights' of the movement, especially those of Yeats and, to a lesser extent, Synge. Although Yeats and Synge still continue to attract their share of attention from academics, research into the literary revival and its political, cultural and social contexts has considerably widened in scope. One of the important areas that is still under-researched is that of the literary revival's impact at the regional and popular level, and the extent to which its representation of Irish life took distinctive regional forms. By exploring the work of the Meath author, Katherine Francis Purdon (1852–1920) – one of the numerous writers of minor rank who contributed to the work of the literary revival but whose publications are now largely over-looked – this essay demonstrates the potential that a focus on the regional dimen-sion of the revival offers to historians.

As stated above, Katherine Frances Purdon's writings are now largely ignored. Kevin C. Kearns, in his recent book on the oral history of the Dublin slums, contains a number of references to *Dinny of the Doorstep*, Purdon's only novel dealing with city life, but such glaring errors as mistakenly dating the novel to 1920 (it was published in 1918) and, more regrettably, using the masculine first person singular pronoun when referring to Purdon, merely serve to highlight the neglect accorded to her and her work.[1] Sadder still is the fact that no extracts from Purdon's work have been included in volumes four and five of the *Field Day Anthology of Irish Writing* devoted to women authors. This neglect of Purdon's work is even more surprising when one considers the popularity of her writ-ings in the early twentieth century, the critical acclaim she received, and the fact that she published in some of the leading Irish literary journals of the period. From January 1906, Purdon wrote the regular 'Gardening Notes' column for the *Irish Homestead*, the journal of the co-operative movement. Her gardening column frequently reflected the spirit of the Revival.[2] She contributed fairy tales and tales of rural life to the *Irish Homestead*'s popular 'Celtic Christmas' numbers

---

1 Kevin C. Kearns, *Dublin tenement life: an oral history* (Dublin: Gill and Macmillan, 1994), p.39.
2 There is a very fine example in the 28 Apr. 1906 issue.

from 1899 to 1910, as well as to *The Shanachie* in March 1907 and the *Irish Review* in August 1911. Another mark of her contemporary stature is the fact that many of her writings were illustrated by leading Irish artists. Jack B. Yeats illustrated four of her *Irish Homestead* stories,[3] and George William Russell (Æ) illustrated two.[4] While in 1914, Beatrice Elvery illustrated *Candle and Crib*, Purdon's reworking of the Christmas nativity story in an Irish rural setting.[5] Another famous contemporary British magazine illustrator, Arthur Rackham, illustrated Purdon's posthumously published fairy tale, 'Living or Dead', in 1927.[6] Purdon's most famous novel, *The Folk of Furry Farm*, proved to be so popular that it went through two editions in 1914 and was also republished after her death, in 1926. *Candle and Crib* was also reissued in December 1920, and Purdon's dramatized version of this novella was performed on the Abbey stage in the same month.[7]

The distinctive quality of Purdon's work was frequently commented on by contemporaries, and it is this distinctiveness which makes her contribution to the revival so worthwhile to historians of the movement. Canon James Owen Hannay (George Birmingham) was an enthusiastic admirer of Purdon's fiction, and in his introduction to *The Folk of Furry Farm* he summarized much of what was unique in her novel:

> Her distinction is that she has chosen a new part of the country to write about. I do not know exactly where the Furry Farm is, but I am inclined to place it somewhere in the western part of Leinster, in Meath or Kildare, on the great plain which fattens cattle for the market. Other Irish writers, whether they wanted humour, romance, or mysticism, have gone to the maritime counties for their material. Galway, Cork, and Wicklow provide scenes for most of the plays which are acted in the Abbey Theatre. Some poets write about Donegal, others prefer North-East Ulster, and a few brave spirits have ventured into the streets and suburbs of Dublin I cannot remember that any plays or poems of importance have been written about the people of the central plain. They are regarded, for some reason obscure to me, as unworthy of a place in literature. They have, one would gather, lost the virtues of Gaeldom without acquiring the sentimental regard for them which rescues Dublin from the reproaches of 'seoininism'. The accepted view of literary Ireland is that the people of

3 'Match-Making in Ardenoo', *Irish Homestead*, Dec. 1902, pp 12–15; 'A Settled Girl', *Irish Homestead*, 5 Dec. 1903, pp 1–5; 'An American visitor', *Irish Homestead*, 3 Dec. 1904, pp 1–6; 'The furry farm', *Irish Homestead*, 2 Dec. 1905, pp 1–5.   4 'Comrade children at the Furry Farm', *Irish Homestead*, Dec. 1907, pp 11–15; 'On the stray', *Irish Homestead*, Dec. 1908, pp 10–14.   5 For more on Beatrice Elvery, see her memoirs (written as Beatrice Lady Glenavy), *'Today we will only gossip'* (London: Constable, 1964).   6 'Living or dead', *Nash's and Pall Magazine*, 79, no. 407 (Apr. 1927), pp 14–17, 85–90.   7 *Abbey Plays 1899–1948, including the productions of the Irish Literary Theatre* (Dublin: Sign of the Three Candles, 1949), p. 44.

Meath are as uninteresting as the bullocks which they herd. Miss Purdon comes to us to prove the contrary.[8]

Purdon's fictional Ireland draws, for the most part, on her native Church of Ireland parish of Rathcore, in southern Meath. Purdon resided all of her life at Hotwell, the 'Big House' at Ballinakill, that is named after the natural hot spring in its grounds. She gives the name of Ardenoo or the Furry Hills to her native district, an area of generally flat land but with some gently rolling hills and one large hill, the Hill of Rathcore, which is about half a mile from Hotwell. Purdon's close friend, Susan L. Mitchell, pointed out that the Ardenoo of the novel and some of her short stories 'is less a townland of that name than an extension of her own rich personality into the lives and interests of the folk who live scattered in small houses on the roads of Meath'.[9] Purdon's sympathetic portrayal of her native area proved very attractive to her readers, and also provides an important social document to historians of this part of the country and an insight into how some of the main motifs and preoccupations of the more famous figures in the revival were recast and reworked in the unlikely fictional setting of southern Meath. Jack B. Yeats's illustrations of some of Purdon's Ardenoo short stories might at first glance seem incongruous, since they evoke images that are more suggestive of the West of Ireland than the Meath plain. One can argue, however, that Purdon's general portrayal of rural life has much in common with the romanticization that was a hallmark of many of the other revivalists' writings. From this perspective, Yeats's illustrations are not entirely inappropriate. As pictorial representations, they evoke the Revival's idealized landscapes of the West rather than the visually uninspiring Meath plains, but they nevertheless serve to capture the Arcadian quality of Purdon's rural world.

Purdon, like many other revivalist writers, was fascinated with the language of the peasantry. In her *Irish Homestead* pieces, she renders the narrative voice and the speech of the peasant characters phonetically. Many of these short stories were reworked and incorporated into *The Folk of Furry Farm*; however, the narrative voice of the novel is in standard English, with the distinctive Meath accent being reserved for the peasant characters. In the novel, Purdon included footnote explanations or translations of some of the distinctive words and phrases used by her peasant characters, many of which derive from the Irish language. Her Ardenoo fiction[10] is an important social document as her phonetic rendering of peasant speech gives an invaluable glimpse into the way in which people in southern Meath spoke in the early twentieth century, and indeed one can still

8 George Birmingham, 'Introduction', in K.F. Purdon, *The Folk of Furry Farm* (London: James Nisbet, 1914, 2nd edition), pp xiv–xv. **9** Susan L. Mitchell, 'Introduction', in K.F. Purdon, *The Folk of Furry Farm* (Dublin: Talbot, 1926), p.ix. **10** The name Ardenoo is probably derived from the townland of Ardenew, which is roughly midway between the villages of Rathcore and Rathmolyon.

hear strong echoes of her characters' voices in the Rathcore area today. Unlike Synge, who invented his own peasant speech after being inspired by reading Lady Gregory's 'Kiltartanese', Purdon may be seen as having portrayed the language of her peasant characters in a fairly accurate manner.

The accuracy of the peasant speech in Purdon's writings is vouchsafed for by a number of contemporaries, including her close friend and fellow *Irish Homestead* contributor, Susan L. Mitchell. Mitchell, who was familiar with Purdon's native area,[11] wrote of Purdon's language: 'Her dialect is genuine. It is a vivid and homely speech, the speech of midland Ireland. She wrote it as one who lived it …'[12] Æ was another admirer of Purdon's language:

> She has a feeling for words. She has listened to the dialect of her county until she knows it by heart … Painters often speak of the nice fat colour, at least those do who are in love with their materials. Miss Purdon is in love with nice fat phrases. It is not merely dialect which is revealed in them but imagination and humour.[13]

Purdon's 'nice fat phrases' reveal her to be a sympathetic observer of the peasant life around Hotwell, and they added to the appeal of her literary output.

The 'nice fat phrase' that particularly caught Æ's fancy was the following description by Dark Moll Reilly, an old woman who pretends to be blind, of the 'returned Yank', Patsy Ratigan, after she encounters him on one of the roads of Ardenoo:

> it's that bright boyo, Patsy Ratigan, as sure as God made little apples! And the great big size of him now! The broad red face of him! and he the full of his skin; instead of the way he was, so thin that there wasn't as much fat upon him as would grease a gimlet! And the thick back to his head! and [he] used to have a long neck upon him, like a distracted gander peeping down a pump-hole to look for poreens![14]

One can point to numerous further examples of Purdon's gift for employing simple but vivid imagery for the telling phrase or description. For instance, when Mickey Heffernan, the middle-aged bachelor, sees young Rosy Rafferty in her house, the following description of the impact of her beauty on him is given:

11 Hilary Pyle, *Red-headed rebel: Susan L. Mitchell, poet and mystic of the Irish cultural renaissance* (Dublin: Woodfield Press, 1998), p. 138.   **12** Mitchell, 'Introduction', p.x. For other reviewers' agreement on the accurate manner in which Purdon had depicted the Meath peasants' speech, see *Irish Independent*, 9 Mar. 1914; *Meath Chronicle*, 14 Mar. 1914; *Freeman's Journal*, 14 Mar. 1914.   **13** *Irish Homestead*, 14 Mar. 1914.   **14** Ibid.; Purdon, *Folk of Furry Farm* (2nd 1914 edition), p. 211.

> To Mickey Heffernan in especial, that had never before passed much
> remarks about any girl, it appeared something altogether strange and new,
> to see the bright little face of her, shining there in the dim, smoky cabin,
> like a lovely poppy among the weeds of a potato-patch.[15]

When Heffernan later discovers that he has been thwarted in his hopes of marrying Rosy, Purdon writes that he 'just gave one laugh out of him; like the cough
of a sick sheep it was …'[16] She writes of Hopping Hughie, the crafty, itinerant
man without permanent work who does various odd-jobs around Ardenoo, that
'He could build a nest in your ear, he was that cunning', while Dark Moll Reilly
'was that clever, she could knot eels, the people said'.[17] The most vivid physical
description of any of Purdon's characters is that of Peetcheen Caffrey, a lazy
labourer who rises in the world as the result of marrying Julia Heffernan, the
sister of the 'comfortable' farmer, Mickey Heffernan: 'and he wid a head upon
him that you'd think should fizz, if he put it into could water, it's that red! And
the mouth of him! the same as if it was made wid a blow of a shovel!'[18] Hopping
Hughie is the subject of another well-chosen observation: 'Gay and happy he
was after his supper, and soon fell asleep on the straw, with his ragged pockets
that empty, that the Divil could dance a hornpipe in them and not strike a copper
there.'[19] Purdon's other writings offer other examples. For instance, in *Candle and
Crib*, she describes Mrs Moloney's house-cleaning on Christmas Eve as resulting in the tables and chairs being 'scoured like the snow, and the big old pewter
plates and dishes upon the dresser polished till they're shining like a goat's eyes
from under a bed!' While in *Dinny of the Doorstep*, Purdon's account of the slum-
dwelling Doran orphans, a character remarks on their tenement room: 'Sure
there's not as much coal in the place as ud blind the eye of a bee!'[20]

Purdon brought similar astute powers of observation to the activities of the
peasantry. Indeed, according to one commentator, in *The Folk of Furry Farm*
Purdon 'altogether has succeeded in approximating to real life and with much
attractiveness'.[21] Fr Stephen Brown concurred with this positive estimation in
his description of the novel as 'depicting in the most intimate way the conversation, manners, humours, kindliness of the people'.[22] Purdon had already shown
in her first short story for the *Irish Homestead*, 'Her Christmas Cailey', that she
had an intimate acquaintance with farming homesteads, as is apparent in her
evocative description of the living room of the 'snug farmers', the Fogartys:

> She [Mrs Fogarty] had had visions of a new table-cover and curtains, and
> maybe even a sofa for 'the room', a somewhat desolate apartment open-

15 Purdon, *Folk of Furry Farm* (2nd 1914 edition), p. 13. 16 Ibid., p. 33. 17 Ibid., pp 38, 88.
18 Ibid., p. 76. 19 Ibid., p. 39. 20 Purdon, *Candle and Crib* (Dublin: Talbot Press, 1920), p.3;
Purdon, *Dinny of the Doorstep* (Dublin: Phoenix, 1918), p. 4. 21 *Freeman's Journal*, 14 Mar.
1914. 22 Stephen J. Brown, *Ireland in fiction* (Shannon, 1969 reprint of 1919 edition), p. 257.

ing off the big cheery kitchen, and which was devoted to the accom-
modation of an old brass-mounted bureau, battered and worm-eaten, a
tall clock 'that didn't lose more nor two hours in the week', some chairs
covered in hair-cloth, sacred pictures, and photographs of friends in
America. No one ever used this room from choice; still it was a certain
satisfaction to Mrs Fogarty to know that it was there, a kind of white ele-
phant, conferring dignity, but otherwise useless.[23]

Most of Purdon's fiction affords us glimpses into the homes and lives of the 'snug'
and especially the small farming classes – and, occasionally, the gentry – of her
part of southern Meath, although some of her fiction is also set in other parts
of Ireland. Her writings also feature a vivid array of people living on the margins of rural society, such as tramps, peripatetic matchmakers, 'tinkers' (who are
usually portrayed in an unsympathetic light) and people coming out of, or about
to enter, the workhouse. The main focus of her interest, however, is the daily
round of the settled, small farming community. Her tales are mostly simple and
gently humorous stories, affectionate portrayals in which failed and successful
attempts at matchmaking are central to the dynamics of the community. The
overwhelming impression is one of a neighbourly, harmonious, compassionate
community, whose people rarely exhibit unpleasant traits and whose equilibri-
um, although it might be occasionally upset, is invariably restored at the end of
each episode. Æ gave an effective summary of Purdon's fictional world:

> We have written ourselves hastily about Meath and its humanity, and as
> if to rebuke us a cloth has been let down from the heaven of the affec-
> tions filled with every manner of human thing that moves in Meath and
> we are challenged to say that there is anything vile in it. Miss Purdon
> knows her people as intimately as Mr Stephens knows his charwomen,
> his clerks, or his policemen, and we feel affection for them growing as
> we read her book … Miss Purdon's affection for her people gives her a
> vision of their nature and she finds the love inside them all which endears
> them to us. We will always think now of County Meath as a county with
> exceptionally nice people in it.[24]

Purdon's rural world is, then, in many ways, a Kickhamesque Arcadia, but without the melodramatic extremes of *Sally Kavanagh* or *Knocknagow* and with the
additional ingredient of what one reviewer referred to as 'the mysticism which
is inseparable from the Celt'.[25] It was an appealing mix to her contemporaries;

23 Purdon, 'Her Christmas cailey', *Irish Homestead*, Dec. 1899, p. 13. **24** *Irish Homestead*, 14
Mar. 1914. **25** *Irish Independent*, 9 Mar. 1914. It is telling that the same writer gives an extremely negative review of Patrick MacGill's *Children of the Dead End* as containing 'much that nau-
seates and revolts and very very little that either edifies or entertains'.

indeed, according to Susan L. Mitchell, the 'great literary success' that *The Folk of Furry Farm* had in the troubled year of 1914 rested to a large extent on the novel's rose-tinted portrayal of a stable society: 'At a time of extraordinary agitation in men's minds there were readers who seemed to cling to this book as to an anchor. There seems something prophetic in the reception it met with in those days when the old order was about to slip from under our feet.'[26]

Purdon's portrayal of relations between the various strata of settled rural society promotes a picture of a harmonious world. In particular, there is no sense of hostility between the peasantry and the people in the 'Big House', which might be a reflection of the Purdons' relations with the local farming community. Purdon's gentry are invariably depicted as living in good relations with their peasant neighbours. For instance, in her early short story 'Christmas in the Valley', which is set in the Wicklow mountains, Ould Mickey Byrne, a poor, small tenant farmer has a fond, almost feudal, regard for his landlord, named O'Byrne. The O'Byrnes used to reside in Grouse Lodge, and according to Ould Mickey: 'It was once very grand, but the O'Byrnes that owns it is very bet down now, and can't live there theirselves, only lets it for shootin', and fine sport there does be in it too.' Ould Mickey 'remembered to see great style kep' up there, the Lord knows how long ago, by an O'Byrne that was a grand soart of a man, at a time when the poor in Ireland wanted a protector'. He goes on to explain the reason why he holds the O'Byrnes in high esteem:

'Yiz may talk about Crumwell and all the rest,' he'd say, 'but any of them had humanity and nature in them, only Lord Norbury. Wasn't I one of twinty he sintinced in a batch on circumstance evidence? An' 'twas well for us that had the O'Byrne to spake up for us – a Justice ov Paice and Dain of the church he was. "Your Lordship," says he, "I know them boys well, and there's not a word agin wan ov them, barrin' the sup they might take an odd time. An' sure that's only human nature, and no man can alter that only God. An' you can't put an ould head on young shoulders." So he got us off, the Lord mark him to grace! An' the next fair day ov Ballinclash wasn't every hat off to him, and we drew him home in his carriage, till, says he: "For God's sake, boys, put to the horses agin before yiz are all stufficated!".'[27]

In 'The Marrying of Barney Maguire', set in the townland of Ballinamaddagh, about whose exact geographic location it is impossible to be certain, Mr O'Farrell, the landowner, is a benevolent landlord: 'Scarce a house in the whole countryside but was behoulden to him at one time or another, for the lind of

26 Mitchell, 'Introduction' (1926), p. xii. **27** Purdon, 'Christmas in the valley', *Irish Homestead*, Dec. 1900, p. 6.

money, or seed pitaties, or to do a bit a ploughin', an' a dacent tinant like Barney [Maguire] always got his time to pay'. Miss O'Farrell, the landlord's daughter, repeatedly gives presents of flowers and books to Maneen, a young girl who has been taken in by the Maguire household and cared for as one of their own, and Miss O'Farrell frequently 'pass[es] the time of day and take[s] a hait of the fire' in the Maguires' house. The Widdah Maguire repays Miss O'Farrell's kindness with presents of eggs or spring chickens, and an easy familiarity exists between the two women.[28] A similar state of cordial relations is evident in the Ardenoo story 'On the Stray', between Old Judy Scanlan 'who lived by herself in the tumble-down cabin a piece up Scanlan's boreen' and Miss Rosy, 'the only child at the Big House beyant'. Miss Rosy spends much of her time in Judy's company, and ensures that the indigent old woman is supplied with cartloads of her father's turf.[29] It is noteworthy that the deplorable state of Judy's cabin is not blamed on Scanlan, her landlord, who is described with sympathy by Judy as 'out of his health, God help him … livin' somewheres far – seven miles beyant France, some says.' She explains that 'It's Halligan, the steward, has a right to look after things; but he's as bad a baste as ever stood on two legs, as cross as a briar and as conthrary as an armful as cats!'[30] These warm relations between landlords and landholders are mirrored by the charity and friendliness shown by the small and 'comfortable' farmers towards itinerant and semi-itinerant members of the community, with the exception of 'villyans of tinkers'.[31] Indeed, the roguish Hopping Hughie, who was crippled in both legs 'ever since he had got implicated with some sort of mesheen he was striving to work', probably while under the influence of drink,[32] manages to make quite a comfortable living for himself by relying on the charity of his neighbours. The narrator of *The Folk of Furry Farm* tells us that 'His pockets would be like sideboards, the way he would have them stuck out with meat and eggs and so on, that he would be given along the road. Hughie was better fed than plenty that bestowed food upon him.'[33]

The charm of Purdon's fictional rural world was added to by the inclusion of details of peasant folk beliefs and superstitions, particularly relating to the fairies. Such aspects were almost a prerequisite for contemporary portrayals of life in the Irish countryside, and the frequency with which Purdon incorporates fairy lore into her work helps to firmly locate her as a revivalist writer. Purdon often slips these details into her narrative in an unobtrusive manner, helping to open a window into the peasant worldview rather than adding to the plot. A good example of this occurs in 'Christmas in the Valley', when Biddy lights her kitchen fire and 'the fire blazed up the minute she put her hand to it, and that put Biddy in great humour, for it's a sign whoever you're thinkin' of is thinkin'

28 Purdon, 'The marrying of Barney Maguire', *Irish Homestead*, Dec. 1901, p. 26. **29** Purdon, 'On the stray', pp 10, 12. **30** Ibid., p. 12. **31** Purdon, *Folk of Furry Farm* (2nd 1914 edition), p. 229. **32** Purdon, 'Christina divelly,' *Irish review*, i., no.6 (Aug. 1911), p. 287. **33** Purdon, *Folk of Furry Farm* (2nd 1914 edition), p. 40.

of you'.[34] References are also made to the belief that if young women looked into a well or a mirror on Halloween Eve they would see the image of their future lover reflected there,[35] and that if an unmarried woman accidentally burned her dress it was a sign that she would get married.[36] In 'Rosy at Furry Farm', one of the chapters of Purdon's most successful novel, we learn of the superstition against opening a grave on Tuesdays.[37] The hot spring at Purdon's home features as a holy well in *The Folk of Furry Farm*:

> The Holy Well lay in a corner, where the Big Pasture Field sloped down to a hollow. Many's the time Marg had seen it, of a Saint's Day, with the lone thorn that leans out over the water all dressed up with bits of ribbon, and even rags, that the people would tie there, when there would be a Pattern at the Holy Well.[38]

It is to the Holy Well that Marg Heffernan goes on Hallow Eve to collect some water to cure her husband's lame leg.[39] People also repair to the 'Fairy Doctor', a seventh son, who effects cures for various ailments, particularly toothache.[40]

As stated above, most of the references to folk belief concern the fairies. In 'Owny on the Turf', Purdon's interest in plants and fairy lore shows when she has the eponymous hero, a tramp just out of the work-house, discuss the rag-weed or 'boholauns' that are 'all about us here':

> 'I often heard tell, and so did you, maybe, how that at night them very boholauns will turn into little horses, saddled and bridled, and bells jig-glin' out of them, for the f— the Gentle People to go off on their pattheroles all over the whole of Ireland.'[41]

Many more characters in the region of the Furry Hills express or show their belief in the 'Gentle People'. One such example is 'The Daylight Ghost', a love story in which Christina Flanagan mysteriously disappears after realizing that the 'returned Yank', Jim Cassidy, loves her sister Nelly rather than herself. After Nelly and Jim get married, they always leave the door of their house open, and food ready at night, particularly on Hallow Eve, as they are convinced that Christina is not dead 'only "away" with the Good People in the old rath, at the top of the hill behind Greenan-more' and that she will return to Ardenoo.[42] The rath at Greenan-more is described as having 'a hollow, with a Lone Thorn grow-

34 Purdon, 'Christmas in the valley', p. 8. **35** Purdon, *Folk of Furry Farm* (2nd 1914 edition), p.223; idem, 'Rebels they were called', *Nash's and Pall Mall Magazine*, lxxviii, no.406 (Mar. 1927), p. 80. **36** Purdon, 'Treasure', *Irish Homestead*, 11 Dec. 1909, p. xi. **37** Purdon, *Folk of Furry Farm* (2nd 1914 edition), p. 258. **38** Ibid., p. 223. **39** Ibid., p. 221. **40** Ibid., p. 296. **41** Purdon, 'Owny on the turf', *The Shanachie* (Mar. 1907), p. 20. **42** Purdon, *Folk of Furry Farm* (2nd 1914 edition), pp 130–1.

ing in the middle of it, and nettles and stones. Lonely places, raths are! where
the Good People live, and their music can be heard, and they themselves be seen,
by them that are able to do so.'[43] The peasantry use various charms to remain
on good terms with their fairy neighbours:

> Marg was counted a very lucky hand over a dairy, and always had good
> yield from the milk. Near though she was to the Furry Hills, that were
> well known to be full of fairies, she never got any annoyance from them,
> such as the Good People to 'milk the tether' on her, or to take away the
> value of the milk from her. But, of course, that mightn't be luck, so much
> as that Marg knew what she was about. She was very particular not to
> give anything away to a stranger that might come borrowing from her
> on May Day; a mistake that has cost many a woman the loss of a fine cow.
> And she never forgot to throw a grain of salt into the churn, before she
> began to stir the dash. And as soon as ever she had the butter taken off
> the churn, she took care to stick the first bit against the wall, for the fairies.
> People can't be too careful in such things, especially if they live anyway
> near such a place as the Furry Hills.[44]

The ubiquity of the fairies in the area becomes apparent when the reader learns
that in one part of the Furry Hills there is a gap, like a cleft, 'and the old people
said, it had been made there by a fairy sword'; fairy music can be heard there, and
people never travel on the road through the cleft by themselves, or late at night.[45]

In addition to incorporating elements of fairy lore into her fiction, Purdon
also wrote two complete fairy tales, 'The Witchery Ladder' and 'Living or Dead',
that are set in Ardenoo. The former is a didactic tale cautioning against the evils
of drink, and has unmistakeable echoes of Dickens's *A Christmas Carol*. It relates
the story of drunken Dinny O'Dowd and his wife, the unnamed 'Vanithee' who
gives hospitality to a mysterious 'little Black Man' one night when Dinny is away
at a fair selling his wife's pig. In return for the kindness which Mrs O'Dowd
shows to him, the Black Man sets out to shock Dinny into changing his drunk-
en ways. He does this by transforming himself into a giant and forcing Dinny
to climb a magic ladder on which he and Dinny travel into the future; like
Ebeneezer Scrooge, Dinny gets to see what the inevitable consequences of his
unreformed behaviour will be. In this case, it means the break-up of his family,
with some of his children 'at sarvice' for poor pay and the others languishing in
the workhouse with his wife, while Dinny ends his drunken days contemplat-
ing suicide in a canal in an unnamed English town. This pathetic vision of the
future is enough to shock Dinny into reforming his ways.[46] 'Living or Dead' is

43 Ibid., p. 96. **44** Ibid., p. 214. **45** Ibid., p. 215. **46** Purdon, 'The Witchery Ladder', *Irish Homestead*, 17 Dec. 1910, pp 1043–7.

a more complicated story. Set on Geraghty's Island in Lough Bo-Finn, it tells the tale of how the old, eccentric, hunchbacked bachelor, the Butt Geraghty, befriends a 'Poor Scholar' who has had to abandon his studies due to poor health. The Poor Scholar loses his way in a bog in Ardenoo while making his way home, and the Butt saves his life. The taciturn and lonely Butt grows to relish the Poor Scholar's company, especially as he is a gifted fiddle player and reads stories to the Butt from his stock of ancient books. Their idyllic existence comes to an end, however, when the Poor Scholar digs under the lone 'sciog' or thorn bush on the island and unearths a store of treasure. He falls into a trance, in which he sees a group of 'wild and fierce' men in 'some old far-away forgotten days' bury-ing the treasure on the island. Their leader gets one of the group, a slave, 'to put his hand to his forehead and swear by all his heathen gods, that he would guard that treasure, living or dead, for ever'; after the slave has sworn this oath, the leader kills him by stabbing him through the heart with a spear, and the man falls into the hole in which the treasure has been hidden. This slave, the Poor Scholar recognizes with a shock, is the Butt Geraghty! The enraged Butt, true to his oath, attacks the Poor Scholar and we are told at the end of the story that 'That young stranger was never seen after, by any son of man'.

Purdon's fictional world was, then, both enchanted and enchanting, the world of the Celtic Twilight transported to the unlikely setting of Meath. As stated ear-lier, it proved to be tremendously popular with contemporary readers. One reviewer, probably Æ, was particularly entranced by Purdon's depiction of rural life: 'We suspect that though the hither side of Ardenoo may hug the homely earth, there is a far side of it that rolls up to the celestial mountains. Over there beyond the gentle Furry Hills people often meet their heart's desire and are no whit surprised at the familiar face it wears.'[47] It is instructive to note that Charles L. Graves included one chapter from *The Folk of Furry Farm* – 'The game leg' – in his 1915 anthology of representative tales of Irish humour, and he wrote of Purdon's fiction that 'the dominant impression left by its perusal is one of con-fidence in the essential kindliness of Irish nature'.[48] Purdon, however, did not entirely ignore some of the seamier sides of Irish life. For instance, the fear of ending in the workhouse torments several of the lonely old women in her writ-ings; the following description is one of several in which Purdon alludes to the fate of these vulnerable members of rural society:

> At last we got to the ward, and you'd wonder where all the old women came from, to fill it! It was as big as the chapel beyant …but as large as it was, it was small enough for all it had to hold. You could scarcely drop a pin between the beds. And some of the women were asleep and a few

---

47 *Irish Homestead*, 12 Dec. 1914.   **48** Charles L. Graves (ed.), *Humours of Irish life* (Dublin: Talbot, 1915), p. xxxviii.

lay there middling quiet. But the weight of them were sitting up, talking and laughing, or fighting with one another; and a few were crying to themselves. And most of them had little weeny tin boxes in their hands that they held out, begging you for a pinch of snuff. You'd have to pity them, they were so anxious for it![49]

Purdon also touches on the topic of crime in 'An American Visitor', a tale in which the 'returned Yank', Patsy Ratigan, supports his extravagant lifestyle by stealing cattle from his erstwhile neighbours and a substantial sum of money from Marg Heffernan. She also wrote a number of children's novels, didactic tales denouncing animal cruelty. These contain surprisingly graphic descriptions of cruelty towards animals, with drink being a common causal factor in the abuse suffered by pets and other animals. 'Tinkers' are common offenders in these novels, but so are members of the settled community, particularly the lower orders.[50] It should be noted, however, that there are no instances of cruelty towards animals in Purdon's Ardenoo stories.

While there are, then, some suggestions of a darker reality behind the idyllic southern Meath world portrayed by Purdon, it is, in the main, a comforting picture that emerges in her writings. Purdon obviously loved her local area, and succeeded in presenting a case, to echo George Birmingham, that the people of Meath had not lost the 'virtues of Gaeldom'. The last words should be left to Æ:

> Her peasant folk are real human beings, not like the criminals and lunatics who form so large a part of the population on the Abbey stage, and whose boast it is that they are realistically Irish. Miss Purdon is perhaps more akin to Padraic Col[u]m than to any other of our writers, not because there is any affinity of style, but because they both know and love country people as they really are. So many Irish writers insist on treating Irish people humorously or making them the vehicle for expressing ideas of their own, that we have few books to which we could point and say, 'Here are Irish country people as they really are.' Padraic Col[u]m wrote such a book in 'My Irish Year'. Miss Purdon has written such a book in 'The Folk of Furry Farm', with a wealth of humour and insight and affection, and over it all flits, like sunbeams over a field, the essential Irish spirituality.[51]

---

49 Purdon, *Folk of Furry Farm* (2nd 1914 edition), p. 269. **50** Purdon, *The Fortunes of Flot: A dog's story, mainly fact* (London, Thomas Nelson, 1910); idem, *Spanish Lily, or Only an ass* (Dublin: Educational Company of Ireland, 1920); idem, *Kevin and the cats* (London: Society for the Promoting of Christian Knowledge, 1921). **51** *Irish Homestead*, 14 Mar. 1914.

A currency crisis: modernist dialectics in *The Countess Cathleen*

MICHAEL MC ATEER

The Countess Cathleen is the first Yeats play to contain a dialogue between history and the imagination within its dramatic structure and to posit a conception of history particular to the dramatic form. The play dramatizes the story of
a noble lady who offers her soul to demons in exchange for their relinquishing
the souls of starving peasantry. In their desperation, members of the peasantry
offer their souls to the demons in exchange for gold. The play focuses on one
peasant family in particular, in which the father, Teigue, is keen to accept the
offer of gold made by the demons in exchange for their souls, though his wife
Mary resists. Their souls are saved through the final intervention of the Countess
Cathleen, though she, like Mary dies. The concluding image in the play is of an
angel who announces to the peasantry that, because of her heroic magnanimity, the countess's soul has been saved. Yeats claimed that he first encountered this
story in a newspaper article on Irish folklore and traced its source to *Les Matinées
de Timothé Trimm* in which Léo Lespès gave it as an Irish story. Yeats praised the
tale as 'the most impressive form of one of the supreme parables of the world'.[1]

From its first publication in 1892 through the many revisions of the play over
subsequent years, the play's historiographic structure would determine its
strengths and shortcomings as a dramatic piece. Consideration of the play offered
here aims to delineate the form of history intrinsic to the play's formal and thematic elements. In pursuit of this objective, the practice of situating the play's
development in relation to Yeats's involvement with Maud Gonne will not be
followed on the grounds that it risks reducing the play's historical complexity
to the ultimately indeterminable nuances of this relationship. In addition, I do
not identify the play's shortcomings with its symbolist obscurity and/or the
quaintness of its peasant dialogue and the archaism of its aristocratic speech
forms. On the contrary, it will be argued that the dichotomy of the play's speech
patterns as developed by Yeats throughout the revisions is one of its great
strengths. Its chief weakness, however, lies in the fact that Yeats, following his
predecessor Standish O'Grady, by harbouring a sentimental aspiration of reconciling peasant and aristocrat that had the effect of restraining the dramatic
conflict latent within the play.[2] Undoubtedly, this corresponded obliquely to

---

1 Russell K. Alspach (ed.), *The Variorum edition of the plays of W.B. Yeats* (London: Macmillan,
1966), p. 170. 2 Adrian Frazier writes of this in terms of 'transvaluation' in relation to the

Yeats's hopes for (and fear of) passionate intimacy with Gonne. However, even
if such hopes and fears lay at the root of his dramatic intentions, the play that
resulted carried a theatrical meaning extending far beyond this personal obsession, indeed, making of that obsession an economy of symbolism that linked the
play into a pattern of historical consciousness characteristic of much European
modernist drama in the early twentieth century.

Much reference has been made to the view that the play's genesis lay in Yeats's
first encounter with Gonne in 1889 in which "'the troubling of my life began'"[3]
Ronald Schuchard refers to the *The Countess Cathleen* as 'a play first written for
Maud Gonne,' following Michael J. Sidnell, who has made the case that the final
two scenes of the original play were written or substantially revised after Gonne's
refusal of Yeats's first offer of marriage on 3 August 1891.[4] Acknowledging the
fact that, in May 1889, Yeats told John O'Leary that he hoped Gonne would play
the leading role, and the seemingly conclusive evidence supplied by the dedication to Gonne in the 1892 printed version of the play, Peter Ure has nonetheless disputed the view that Gonne lay at the origin of the play's conception. He
offers the somewhat thin evidence of a statement made in a letter to O'Leary
on 1 February 1889 (two days after Yeats's first encounter with Gonne) in which
Yeats wrote that he had '"long been intending" to write a play founded on the
tale *Countess Kathleen O'Shea*'.[5] Ure is more convincing when he argues that
none of the versions of the play points directly to the figure of Gonne as a
woman whose purity of soul is disturbed by political fanaticism.[6] Indeed, Ure
argues that had it done so, the play would have been much more effective theatrically.[7]

This question of Gonne's influence can only be ignored at the cost of over-
looking the historical specificity of the play's origins. However, to place it at the
centre of an evaluation of *The Countess Cathleen* is to obscure the deeper shifts in
historical consciousness within the play that are directly relevant to assessing its
strengths and shortcomings as a work of drama. Observing these shifts enable us to
position the play in relation to the cultural and political movements that effectively shaped those cultural and political forms internal to the play's dramatic structure.

famine, of 'turning a Protestant moral catastrophe into a miracle of benevolence, and one of
the world's remarkable cases of a people's devotion to a faith into wholescale infidelity.' *Behind
the scenes: Yeats, Horniman, and the struggle for the Abbey Theatre* (Berkeley: University of California,
1990), p. 14. The difficulty here, however, is a reductionism that leads to the kind of dismissive claim Frazier makes regarding the play's modern relevance, that 'the play is now as insignificant a piece of drama as a press keeps in print.' *Behind the scenes*, p. 3. **3** R.F. Foster, *W.B.
Yeats: a life*, vol. 1, *The apprentice mage* (Oxford: Oxford UP, 1998), p. 87. **4** Ronald Schuchard,
'The Countess Cathleen and the revival of the bardic arts,' *South Carolina Review*, 32: 1 (1999),
p. 24. Michael J. Sidnell, 'Manuscript version of Yeats's *The Countess Cathleen*,' *Papers of the
Bibliographical Society of America*, 56 (1962), p. 102. **5** Peter Ure, *Yeats the playwright: a commentary on character and design in the major plays* (London: Routledge and Kegan Paul, 1963),
p. 17. **6** Ibid., p. 17. **7** Ibid., p.18.

It is significant in this regard that while the dedication to Gonne in the 1892 version of the play commands critical attention, little has been written about Yeats's location of the play in sixteenth-century Ireland in his 1892 version, a period reference he chose to replace with the vague 'old times' in subsequent versions. The significance of the period reference lies in the fact that it is the first occasion in which history is addressed explicitly in Yeats's dramatic writing, marking it off from the immature attempts at poetic drama that preceded it, including the first drafts of *The Shadowy Waters*. The sixteenth century was important to Yeats for many reasons, and carries particular significance for the cultural and economic questions that *The Countess Cathleen* addresses. He felt it was the last period in which European civilization achieved what he termed unity of being, an idea to which he returned with increasing frequency in his later years.[8] Of more pressing significance to the play's Irish context, however, is the fact that the century ended with the wars following the Spanish Armada of 1588. These wars provided the context within which the indigenous Gaelic order of tribal chieftains would finally collapse, receiving its deathblow in the defeat at Kinsale of 1601, thus paving the way for the major plantations of the beginning of the seventeenth century and the institution of a new civic polity replacing the old feudal system of *tuathaigh*. The events and characters of this period were captured vividly by Standish O'Grady, in works such as *The Bog of Stars*, *Red Hugh's Captivity* and O'Grady's edition of *Pacata Hibernia*, works exerted an enduring if understated influence on the young Yeats.[9]

The relevance of these events to the play resides in the fact that *The Countess Cathleen* deals with a clash between two orders and two value systems broadly corresponding to the native feudal order of tribal society led by such clan leaders as Red Hugh O'Donnell, and a modern regime of civic polity conducive to the acceleration of commercial activity founded on a profit motive. The play depicts a feudal aristocratic order on the one hand, and a modern order of commerce on the other; a value system based on communal loyalty and one based on individual self-preservation. The countess is presented in such a manner by Yeats that her representative character is deliberately left unclear in this regard – was she to be taken as an emblem of an old Gaelic order or the Anglo-Irish ascendancy that displaced them?[10] Part of Yeats's strategy in combining the ornate

---

8 W.B. Yeats, *Autobiographies* (London: Macmillan Press, 1955), p. 291. James Flannery identifies in the countess 'an image of that unity of being that Yeats strove to attain for himself and pass on to his countrymen as an image of unity of culture.' *W. B. Yeats and the idea of the theatre* (London: Macmillan Press, 1976), p. 144. 9 For a discussion of O'Grady's Elizabethan histories, see Michael McAteer *Standish O'Grady, Æ, Yeats: history, politcs, culture* (Dublin: Irish Academic, 2002), pp 81–4. 10 The point is rarely acknowledged that the figure of Cathleen could just as easily be read as a type of Maeve (drawn from O'Grady's *History of Ireland*), as that of a member of the Anglo-Irish gentry. Commentators have sometimes regarded her too quickly as an Anglo-Irish aristocrat without entertaining the possibility that her name might just as easily have referred to an Old Gaelic tribal leader.

speech of the aristocrat with the names and images of native Gaelic culture was
to plant in the minds of his audience the idea that a common set of cultural values
united the old Gaelic order of tribal chiefs and the Anglo-Irish gentry class that
replaced it; such an idea would help to mitigate, if not entirely obscure, the violence of the historical conflict between the two orders. Thus, on the one hand,
we are presented in the play with the setting of a great hall at the beginning of
scene two in the 1892 version, in which are hung tapestries representing 'the wars
and loves of the Fianna and Red-Branch warriors'.[11] On the other hand, the
speech of Cathleen and Oona (and in post-1892 versions, Aleel) is tinged with a
note of haughtiness that would sound uncomfortably affected to a nationalist-
minded audience, and point directly to the speech patterns of the Anglo-Irish
gentry. In this expression of Gaelic legendary content through Victorian gentil-
ities and archaisms, Yeats reveals the influence of O'Grady's *History of Ireland*, a
work that narrated the heroic saga of the *Táin Bó Cuailgne* in a decidedly archaic and ornate style. Like O'Grady, Yeats sought in this combination of anglicized
style and gaelicized content the means through which the values of decorum,
loyalty and magnanimity, common in their view to Gaelic and Anglo-Irish civilization, could be given cultural expression in order to obscure the historical dis-
placement of the former by the latter, and in order to identify a common enemy
against which both civilizations could be united – the bourgeoisie.

   History, therefore, is not exclusively a question of the play's content, but is,
in fact, written into its form. Indeed, the structural alterations effected by Yeats's
revisions to the play correspond to the shift from a late Victorian to a properly
modernist form of historical consciousness. Subsequent to the 1899 performance
of the play, Yeats's revisions were concerned less with a reconciliation of Gaelic
and Anglo-Irish and much more with developing a form of theatre that, in its
artifice and 'fascination with what's difficult', demanded a consciousness sensi-
tive to what he regarded as the violation of the human spirit at the heart of modernization processes.[12]

   It is significant in this regard that R.F. Foster reads the inclusion of Aleel in
the 1899 version of the play as 'a pointer towards the increasingly subjective
direction which the play would take'.[13] This repeats the assertion made years
earlier by Ure that the play grew into a portrait of the artist as the rejected lover
of Maud Gonne as it evolved through the revisions.[14] Ure sees in this the emer-

11 Alspach, *Variorum plays*, pp 42, 51.   12 This antipathy to modernization undoubtedly cul-
tivated fascist sentiments in Yeats towards the end of his life, despite arguments made by
Cullingford and Howes to the contrary. See, particularly, Yeats's concluding comments in 'A
general introduction to my work,' *Essays and introductions* (London: Macmillan, 1961), p. 526;
Elizabeth Butler Cullingford, *Yeats, Ireland and Fascism* (London: Macmillan, 1981); Marjorie
Howes, *Yeats's nations: gender, class, and Irishness* (Cambridge: Cambridge UP, 1996), pp 160–185.
The context of crisis, aesthetic and political, within which such sentiments emerged, how-
ever, is evaluated purely at an empirical level and, as a consequence, understood inadequate-
ly.   13 Foster, *Apprentice mage*, p. 209.   14 Ure, *Yeats the playwright*, p. 26.

gence of a more theatrically compelling play, observing in Yeats's revisions a writer who 'watches out for the worst archaisms in modes of address and speech, gradually eliminates the more self-conscious spots of local color and the weaker and more automatic lapses into Jacobean rhythms'.[15] These observations imply that *The Countess Cathleen* improved theatrically as it moved away from association with Irish political history, and as a sense of antiquity impinged less on its theatrical form. Indeed, Leonard Nathan implies that the identifiably historical nature of the original play was part of its theatrical failure, when he complains of the absence of an 'unorthodox vision of a cosmic struggle between natural and supernatural' controlling the play.[16]

Such critical positions arise from a misunderstanding of Yeats's dramatic project in relation to history. The autobiographical and idealist interpretations of the drama presume the play's indifference to general historical conditions on the basis of his enduring commitment to an anti-realist theatrical form, and his subscription to beliefs regarded as anachronistic to his age. Whether celebrated or criticized on this basis, Yeats's plays are not generally regarded as reflecting the historical realities of his age. In support of this assertion, it is worth considering the most self-consciously historical work of nineteenth century European intellectual activity, *Capital*, in relation to *The Countess Cathleen*. The choice is not arbitrary; Marx's comments on the advent of money as the normative measure of value in an historical moment where commodity production and exchange had become universal, bear directly on the play's concern for gold and exchange. Facile claims such as Nathan's that the play expresses 'the Christian war between divine and satanic wills' are wholly inadequate because no account is taken of the play's historiographic structure.[17] Marx's theory of money provides a means of addressing this shortcoming, not just in illustrating just how alert *The Countess Cathleen* is to those patterns of historical development that have shaped European society since the Reformation, but also in showing how such alertness is registered through a crisis of historical representation within the play.

Marx argues that, with the development of processes of exchange, the universal equivalent form 'crystallizes out into the money-form'.[18] He defines the universal equivalent form of a commodity as the aspect it takes when its value is considered in relation to all other commodities. Money, therefore, arises in the forms that we know today when the level of commodity exchange reaches universal proportions, that is, when the universal equivalent form of commodities becomes economically transparent. Its emergence in the modern form, therefore, particularly in the form of capital, presumes the decline of the feudal system of localized exchange of commodities, within Marx's account. Crucially, he iden-

---

15 Ibid., p. 28.   **16** Leonard F. Nathan, *The tragic drama of W.B. Yeats: figures in a dance* (New York: Columbia UP, 1965), p. 28.   **17** Ibid., p. 28.   **18** Karl Marx, *Capital*, vol. 1, trans. Ben Fowkes (London: Penguin, 1990), p. 183.

tifies as necessary the adaptation of precious metals, gold and silver, for the manifestation of money as the universal equivalent of each individual commodity:

> In the same proportion as exchange bursts its local bonds, and the value
> of commodities accordingly expands more and more into the material
> embodiment of human labour as such, in that proportion does the
> money-form become transferred to commodities which are by their
> nature fitted to perform the social function of a universal equivalent.
> Those commodities are the precious metals.[19]

Of immediate relevance here is Marx's claim that precious metals are 'by their
nature' suited to act as the universal equivalent that is money:

> Only a material whose every sample possesses the same uniform quality
> can be an adequate form of appearance of value, that is a material embod-
> iment of abstract and therefore equal human labour. On the other hand,
> since the difference between the magnitudes of value is purely quantita-
> tive, the money commodity must be capable of purely quantitative dif-
> ferentiation; it must therefore be divisible at will, and it must also be pos-
> sible to assemble it again from its component parts. Gold and silver possess
> these properties by nature.[20]

On the basis of this formulation, the precious metals are positioned at the center
of the system of exchange that extends to universal proportions; yet they remain
outside of this system in that they are fundamentally distinct from all other commodities in their role as the universal equivalent, the 'material embodiment of
abstract and therefore equal human labour'. The position of gold and silver, therefore, is dialectically riven in Marx's theory of value, a position on the threshold
of feudal and modern forms of economic organization:

> Without any initiative on their part, the commodities find their own
> value-configuration ready to hand, in the form of a physical commodi-
> ty existing outside but also alongside them. This physical object, gold and
> silver in its crude state, becomes, immediately on its emergence from the
> bowels of the earth, the direct incarnation of all human labour. Hence
> the magic of money.[21]

The final sentence is striking in its own right in the light of the dialectical-mate-
rialist form of analysis throughout the volumes of *Capital*, and it points to a

---

19 Ibid., p. 183. **20** Ibid., p. 184. **21** Ibid., p. 187. For a thorough analysis of the role of money
in Marx's theory of value, production and exchange see Karl Marx, *Grundrisse,* trans. Martin
Nicolaus (London: Penguin, 1973), pp 115–238.

source motivating the revised forms of Marxist analysis to be found in the work of thinkers such as Benjamin, Adorno and Sartre, and, more recently, Deleuze, Guattari and Derrida. For Benjamin, the category of magic is crucial to his understanding of the historical materialist critique.[22] Adorno's negative dialectical hypothesis is, to a significant degree, shaped by his belief that the Enlightenment drive to dominate Nature sublimated rather than superseded the shamanic strategies of magical ritual that preceded the rise of the scientific method in Europe.[23] More recently, Deleuze and Guattari have extended the critique of capitalism into the arena of Freud, by reconfiguring the materialist critique in psychoanalytical terms in the process, a strategy that involves the magico-technological mode of discourse they introduce in *Capitalism and Schizophrenia*; while Derrida offers us an exposé of the magical and thanatotic within Marx.[24]. My discussion of *The Countess Cathleen* here is informed by these revised accounts, if they could be called such; however, a more pressing relevance to the play is the manner in which Marx's comments above bring into question the conventional assumption that the play dramatizes the conflict between materialism and spirituality.

In the critical response that the play evoked on its first performance at the Antient Concert Rooms in May 1899, the opposition between souls and gold was universally presumed to be the opposition between spiritual and material values, between good and evil. George O'Neill summed up the negative criticism the performance received in his review of the play for the *New Ireland Review*:

> Let us hope that he [Yeats] will gradually come to agree more and more fully with his critics that it was not proper to represent Irish Christian peasants as a set of superstitious criminals, impatient of physical suffering, without trust in the Almighty, without respect for sacred things, without faith in a hereafter, prompt to sell the soul for the body, the spiritual for corporal, the eternal for the temporal. One is tired, and probably

22 Throughout Benjamin's writing, from *The origins of German tragic drama* to the notes of the *Arcades* project, a sense of the magical quality of the sign prevails, most succinctly expressed in 'On language as such and on the language of man,' *One-way street and other writings*, trans. Edmund Jephcott and Kingsley Shorter (London: Verso, 1985), pp 107–23. **23** Theodor Adorno & Max Horkheimer, 'The concept of Enlightenment,' *Dialectic of Enlightenment* (London: Allen Lane, 1973), pp 3–42. **24** 'As long as we are content to establish a perfect parallel between money, gold, capital, and the capitalist triangle on the one hand, and the libido, the anus, the phallus, and the family triangle on the other, we are engaging in an enjoyable pastime, but the mechanisms of money remain totally unaffected by the anal projections of those who manipulate money.' Gilles Deleuze and Felix Guattari, *Anti-Oedipus: capitalism and schizophrenia*, trans. Robert Hurley, Mark Seem and Helen R. Lane (London: Athlone, 1984), p. 28. See also Jacques Derrida, *Specters of Marx,* trans. Peggy Kamuf (London: Routledge, 1994).

tiresome, in returning to a point which has been successfully laboured by so many critics in so many styles – from the fervid rhetoric of Mr. Frank O'Donnell to the sober opining of the *Irish times*. Yet the wrong done was a grievous one, not to be too easily condoned.[25]

The criticism is quietly prescient of the rise of hostile tempers that would culminate in the riots that accompanied the opening performances of Synge's *The Playboy of the Western World* and O'Casey's *The Plough and the Stars* years later at the Abbey Theatre. Fundamental to the criticism of O'Neill, O'Donnell and others was the assumption that Yeats was presenting the 'exchange' between souls and gold as an exchange between the spiritual and the temporal. Certainly, the play does not bear this out, particularly when its 1890s versions are considered in relation to Yeats's occult activities. However, equally flawed is the opinion that negative criticism of the play in 1899 was misplaced because it arose from an interpretation of the play in terms of recent Irish history and that Yeats intended no reference to such history. Terence Brown writes that Yeats 'may have liked to believe that his play was set in an unspecified Irish past made merely poetic by the passage of time'.[26] Evidence of the play's development suggests that a historiographic form inimical to the crude didacticism of much criticism of the play is present within its dramatic structure. The presence of this element suggests that original criticisms of the play were flawed not in their literal historical response to a purely 'poetic' play but in the narrowness of their historical reference and their failure to identify the deeper historical pattern within the play's symbolist form.

It remains to consider aspects of the play in relation to the question of historical form and specifically in relation to the functions of gold and exchange. The setting for the opening scene in the 1892 version of the play, later to become act one in printed versions of the play from 1895 to 1908, sets the scene for the subsequent development of Irish drama in its peasant, rural and romantic aspects. At the Inn of Shemus Rua, 'a wood of oak, hazel and quicken trees is seen through the window, half hidden in vapor and twilight'.[27] It is interesting to note that this opening scene was originally set in a 'public' house, rather than a 'private' cottage (as in later versions), when considering the play in relation to the orthodoxies of 'kitchen sink' drama that evolved at the Abbey during the first half of the twentieth century. Yeats's decision to change the setting from an inn to a cottage, and to capitalize 'Catholic' in his opening reference to the shrine in 1895 and subsequent versions of the play, indicates his responsiveness to those Catholic nationalist sensitivities that would sharpen during the 1900s.[28]

25 W.A. Henderson Press Cuttings, National Library of Ireland, Pos7271, p. 249. **26** Terence Brown, *The life of W.B. Yeats: a critical biography* (Dublin: Gill & Macmillan, 1999), p. 127. **27** Alspach, *Variorum plays*, p. 6 **28** Ibid., p. 5.

The setting is misinterpreted, however, if it is seen simply as a stereotypical rural Irish location. The woods outside the window recall the woods of Ibsen's *Peer Gynt*, Old Ekdal's warning of the power of the forest in *The Wild Duck*, the symbolic allure of the apple trees for Jean in Strindberg's *Miss Julia*, while also anticipating the symbolic power of the trees in Chekhov's *The Cherry Orchard*. Indeed, Hamm's opening speech in Beckett's *Endgame* alludes implicitly to the Symbolist stage practice of depicting woods as emblems of the dreamworld of the unconscious, albeit in a tongue-in-cheek fashion: 'What dreams! Those forests!'[29] The note of satire here registers the extent of Beckett's alienation from the motifs of 1890s symbolist theatre, while acknowledging a line of influence; whereas *The Countess Cathleen* depicts a forest, *Waiting for Godot* has a simple tree. However, it is also the case that a characteristic feature of Yeats's revisions of *The Countess Cathleen* is a tendency towards a Spartan stage in which the forest comes to be depicted in a simple emblematic form, with pretensions to the misty atmospherics of the nineties discarded. It may be argued, in other words, that the line of development from the symbolist theatre of the 1890s to Beckett's avant-garde minimalism is actually pre-figured in the internal development of Yeatsian theatre.

Through the course of the play's many revisions, a consistent feature was a ritual pattern that inscribed Yeats's occult concerns within the play in a manner that carried strong Oedipal undertones. All versions subsequent to 1892 begin with a mother figure, Mary, alone on the stage as her son Teigue enters. Mary, the husband of Shemus, occupies an important role in the play; she is a pious woman who displays devotion to the Virgin Mary and, in spite of the impoverished condition of her household, she will resist the offer made by the demon merchants. She will also display empathy toward the countess that is not shared by her husband. Thus, she occupies an important role in the three main feminine roles within the play; her own, that of the virgin statue, and that of the countess. Her son Teigue plays a more minor role; he is of one voice with his father on the central question of whether the family should make a bargain with the merchants.

At the outset of the play, Mary worries for her husband as Teigue speaks of a land that is 'famine-struck' and of a herdsman who had 'met a man who had no mouth, nor eyes, nor ears; his face a wall of flesh'.[30] This image instigates a dialectic of material privation and imaginative license that develops through the course of the play. In its most basic sense, it is an image of sensory deprivation resulting from starvation, of a man who cannot speak, see nor hear. It may thus be linked simply and exclusively to the experience of famine in rural Ireland. However, it is difficult not to notice a hint of the general preoccupation with mummification and the automaton (the 'unhuman'), in plays such as Maeterlinck's *The Blind*,

29 *Samuel Beckett: the complete dramatic works* (London: Faber, 1986), p. 93. **30** Alspach, *Variorum plays*, p. 7.

Strindberg's *The Ghost Sonata* or the *Stationendramen* movement in German Expressionism, in which a failure to see or to speak becomes a pretext for a modernist dramatization of entrapment.[31] Certainly, the impossibility of communication that the image suggests anticipates the fact that, later in the play, the countess's mother, the aging Oona, senses that that 'it is time I was forgot'.[32] When the gardener and then the herdsman come to warn the countess of the destruction befalling her estate, Oona complains that she could not hear the words of either of these servants because 'they stood on my deaf side'.[33] This indicates the critical lack of a 'common currency' at the centre of this play, which is dramatically captured in 'The second coming': 'The falcon cannot hear the falconer.'

The dialogue between Mary and her son at the start of the play is interrupted when Shemus, her husband, enters from the forest outside, where he has been searching for food. His name, Shemus Rua, or 'Red Seamus', carries an echo of the rebel leader of Ulster, Red Hugh O'Donnell, who was defeated at the battle of Kinsale. He appears as a strong man who is nonetheless on the verge of despair because of the famine conditions in which the people find themselves. His symbolic role is important, in his gesture of stamping on the broken shrine in the opening act of the play, just before the merchants enter their household. He takes up a role opposite to Mary in the welcome he gives to the merchants and his willingness to bargain his soul for the gold they offer. His welcome of the merchants, both males, forms a mirror image to the empathy between Mary and Cathleen.

With the entry of Shemus onto the stage at the beginning of the play, an oedipal triangle is established within which the identities Shemus, Mary and Teigue are framed. This frame, however, constantly threatens to disintegrate in the face of those elements, libidinal and economic, standing outside it. The piety of Mary for example, is rooted in her identification with the Virgin Mary, an identification that raises the possibility of incest while simultaneously placing such a possibility under the interdiction of taboo. Under the guise of an appeal to the Virgin Mother, Mary expresses her desire for the enclosed circle of mother-father-son. The appeal to the Virgin displaces the subliminal eroticism of such a desire unto the external world of the forest. The threshold of the cottage, therefore, acquires a heightened symbolic resonance in the play, in the manner in which it marks off the space of incestuous familial enclosure yet simultaneously placing all erotic energy outside this space. It is highly significant, therefore, that when the merchants enter the cottage for the first time, the Virgin shrine falls to the floor. After the first performance of the play in 1899, great offence was taken at the image of Shemus kicking the broken shrine to pieces, on the grounds of blasphemy. Perhaps the real motive for such offence lay not

31 For a discussion of *Stationendramen* and *Schreidrama* in European expressionist theatre see Peter Nicholls, *Modernisms: a literary guide* (London: Macmillan, 1995), pp 136–64.   **32** Alspach, *Variorum plays*, p. 59.   **33** Ibid., pp 63, 67.

so much in theological blasphemy as in its 'threat to the family', its admission of erotic desire into the private circle of family life; with the smashing of the shrine, the taboo displacing the sexual energies of the family triangle is neutralized, by energies symbolized at one level in the presence of 'demons' on stage.

The second movement of the play centres on the countess's visit to the cottage. She is the central character of the play; her personality is portrayed as wistful and dreamlike, though she gives whatever practical help she can to assist this beleaguered community. Her diction is soft, and her presence on stage appears weighed with sorrow. In versions of the play subsequent to 1908, Cathleen's visit is preceded by Shemus cursing first the beggars and then the rich, while Mary pities the rich, making biblical reference to 'the needle's eye at the end of all'.[34] Shemus's double curse of rich and poor in post-1908 versions indicates Yeats's sharpening sense of 'double-vision' subsequent to the rows of the Irish National Theatre Society and the *Playboy* debacle of 1907, but it also points to a maturing sense of his age as an antithetical moment in history for which the ironic sensibility was most appropriate. Mary's expression of pity displays Yeats's need to defend his class and its values within circumstances that grew increasingly unsympathetic and recalls Standish O'Grady's appeal for a unity of peasant and landlord against the rising middle-classes in Britain and Ireland at the end of the nineteenth century.[35] The discrepancy between the aristocratic code and the material circumstances of the peasantry is highlighted in Shemus's disgruntled response to the elevated music coming from the forest that signals the arrival of the countess. In post-1908 versions, he asks: 'Who's passing there? And mocking us with music?'[36] This discrepancy is invested with a low-level dramatic intensity in the scene of encounter between the countess and the inhabitants of the cottage. Emphasis is laid here upon the threshold as border, as the point of contact and separation between the interior world of the cottage and that which lies beyond. Shemus welcomes the countess and Aleel in, commenting:

> This threshold worn away by many a foot
> Has been passed only by the snails and birds
> And by our own poor hunger-shaken feet.[37]

In conversation with the countess some lines later, he states:

> I fell but now, being weak with hunger and thirst,
> And lay upon the threshold like a log.[38]

These allusions to the threshold invite a variety of readings. First of all, they point to an increased privatization of human experience in which what lies beyond

---

34 Ibid., p. 65.   **35** Standish O'Grady, *Toryism and the Tory democracy* (London: Chapman & Hall, 1886).   **36** Alspach, *Variorum Plays*, p. 57.   **37** Ibid., p. 15.   **38** Ibid., p. 19.

the domestic dwelling appears increasingly inhospitable, thus making of that dwelling a more private space. Secondly, this privatization is implicitly linked to privation; symbolically, in his hunger, Shemus lies upon the threshold, the boundary marking a private space. The image will be used again in Yeats's play *The King's Threshold* where the poet Seanchan starves himself to death on the threshold of the king's court in protest at his dismissal from the court. Thirdly, the threshold suggests a limit experience, the point beyond which one can only travel at the risk of annihilation. Emphasis on the threshold, therefore, points to the close proximity of death and what is, in one sense, literally unspeakable; that is, a surrender to the 'demonic' in which all boundaries, material and emotional, disappear. Finally, underlying all these senses of threshold is the sense of epochal transition, in which the forms of a civilization have outlived their material content, while new forms are yet to emerge. The threshold, in other words, is both a rune of psychic containment and historical upheaval, an emblem of the transition from the feudal to the modern era in European history and the psychic disturbance consequent upon this, a disturbance heightened by the arrival of the merchants on the stage.

The first gesture of the countess is to empty her purse of whatever money remains and to promise Shemus twice the sum should he come to her house the following day. This contrasts with the money offered by the demons to Shemus in the scene to follow; the countess's gesture appears purely hospitable, whereas the merchants' offer of gold is framed within a system of exchange. However, upon further reflection, this contrast is not as simple as it appears initially. Certainly, Cathleen's concern for the predicament of a starving peasantry and the selfless nature of her gesture are Yeats's way of conveying his belief in the magnanimity of the aristocracy as the sign of the fitness for rule. With an almost bohemian flagrancy, Cathleen dispenses with her wealth, motivated by what was for Yeats one of the most refined and inexpressible of human emotions, the feeling of pity. However, from the position of Shemus and his family, her gesture is underwritten by a contradiction that makes the contrast between her and the merchants less straightforward. In dispensing with her wealth, Cathleen sets the values of human emotion above those of practical necessity. Shemus, however, has no choice but to accept her gift; he is driven by the basic human instinct of self-preservation. Nonetheless, in accepting Cathleen's money, he defers to a feudal aristocratic code in which values of sentiment are placed above pragmatic self-interest. The sentimental self-abandonment of Cathleen, therefore, rests on the foundation of the peasants' practical self-preservation. Consequently, an exchange does, in fact, take place when Cathleen offers her money to Shemus; in exchange for practical relief of him and his family, he must defer to an order of nobility and sentiment in which practical self-interest occupies a subordinate role. In view of this, it is over-simplistic to regard her as the heroic alternative to the mercenary demons.[39]

39 In one of his final essays 'A general introduction to my work', Yeats reveals that he thought

There is certainly a strong symbolist quality in Cathleen's dialogue with Mary at this point in the play in versions published between 1895 and 1908. The resonance of Villiers-de-l'Isle Adam's *Axël* is felt when Cathleen speaks of being the owner 'of a long empty castle in these woods'.[40] The same anodyne quality we find in 'The wanderings of Oisin' is evident here; Cathleen admits to wrapping herself round 'with music and sweet song' in an attempt to hide from 'the terror of the times'.[41] She reveals to Mary that she has 'lost [her] way'. At its most basic level, this indicates that the countess has not traveled through the wood for many years, indicating that she has been out of contact with the inhabitants of this and the neighboring cottages for a considerable time. If we regard the countess as an emblem of Anglo-Irish civility, her statement becomes evidence of the withdrawal of the landed gentry from intimate contact with their 'people' that Standish O'Grady bemoaned in *Toryism and the Tory Democracy.*

However appropriate this allusion might be, it does not obscure the broader sense of *unheimlich* that Cathleen's statement intimates, a sense carried in the obvious psychic symbolism of the forest and the subtle dialectic of memory and forgetfulness at play in the dialogue between Cathleen and Mary. There is a notable intimacy between the two women that suggests a sister solidarity contrary to the division in class: Cathleen apologizes to Mary for the music that plays while people are starving; while Mary tells Cathleen how to find the castle she seeks. Mary, therefore, directs the countess towards the element of continuity she seeks in the face of the crisis of famine; she outlines for Cathleen the trace of historical continuity, the 'green shadowed pathway' and 'a trodden way among the hazels'.[42] This mnemonic trace, however, is caught in a self-woven web of irony; it leads the countess through the delirium of the forest, the symptom of those forces of history, libidinal and economic, that has shattered the possibility of commemorative continuity. Thus, while an image of recollection, this pathway induces the same anodyne effect as the music, thereby serving opposing desires to recollect and forget. It is the element of form and continuity within the formless primitive chaos of the forest and also a means of forgetting, a way out of the nightmare of history surrounding the countess. Yet even in this evasion of the unpalatable present, this pathway is a sign of those forces of history Cathleen seeks to escape. It is a dormant trading path, anticipating new forces of commerce that render the feudal life of the court redundant – the castle to which it leads lies empty.

There follows the song of Aleel, revised in post-1908 versions as 'Were I but crazy for love's sake,' during which Cathleen and Oona depart, then followed

---

of the countess 'as medieval and thereby connected her with the general European movement,' *Essays and introductions,* p. 525. This indicates strongly that the play is located historically in the period of transition from feudal to early modern society and that its orbit is European rather than uniquely Irish in its dramatic context. **40** Alspach, *Variorum plays,* 21. **41** Ibid. **42** Ibid.

by Aleel. Their departure paves the way for the next movement in the play, wherein the demons, the merchants of the east, enter the cottage. Reflecting the contrast between Cathleen's empathy with Mary and Aleel's disdain of her husband Shemus, Shemus acts as the catalyst for the entrance of the demons while Mary resists. In the versions between 1895 and 1908, speaking of the Mother of God who 'cannot hear the poor', Shemus anticipates a communication breakdown between the Countess and her servants that becomes apparent later in the play. He speaks of Satan pouring 'famine from his bag' and has in mind to pray to him 'to cover all this table with red gold'.[43] The image of gold is, of course, central to the play and it carries specific occult connotations for Yeats. In the ritual of the wayfarer's entrance recorded in 'Notes for a Celtic Order of Mysteries' that Yeats formulated with Fiona MacLeod (William Sharp), Gonne and Annie Horniman, gold represents the sun on the Philosopher's stone, thereby connecting to the masculine principle of the solar hero. Red is the colour symbol on the western axis of the circular colour spectrum devised for the ritual entrance of the wayfarer in the third part of the proposed rite of initiation for the Celtic Order.[44] In conjunction with this alchemical aspect is the sense of a shift from Cathleen's idealism to the merchants' materialism. In the light of Marx's discussion of money in volume one of *Capital*, the advent of the merchants in the play can be viewed as a moment of historical transformation conveyed through the form of occult ritual pattern. Thus, it is not incredulous to suggest that the colors may allude to revolutionary (red) transformation of society with the advent of money (gold) as the universal equivalent form of commodities.[45]

The disturbance consequent upon a transgression of threshold limits is captured in Shemus's violent gesture – smashing the shrine – just before the merchants enter the cottage. The 'bond is crack't' and the idea that the new order of bourgeois mercantilism personified in the merchants involves dehumanization or even a Nietzschean post-humanism, is captured in Mary's fear-ridden assertion to the merchants; 'you are not human.' This sense of the unhuman is recurrent throughout the play in its many incarnations. In scene one of the 1892 version, Mary speaks to Shemus of her fear of the 'wood things'.[46] In versions between 1895 and 1908, she observes that the merchants pour out wine 'as the wood sidheogs do'.[47] Here Mary reveals her belief in the totem, which is indicated from the outset in the position occupied by the virgin shrine within the household. In *The Golden Bough*, James Frazier explained the totem in terms of a primitive belief

---

43 Ibid., p. 29. **44** National Library of Ireland ms. 13568, part 3. **45** Notwithstanding the specific esoteric context of the proposed rituals of the celtic order of mysteries, it is nonetheless significant that in the rite of the cauldron, the wayfarer takes an oath in which he promises to bow his head 'before no God nor Spirit except such as sacrifice daily to Eternal Man, for Man only is the eternal labourer,' National Library of Ireland ms. 13568, part 1. This runs close to the Marxist concept of the primacy of labour, perhaps suggesting the kabbalistic aspect to Marx's own work. **46** Alspach, *Variorum plays*, p. 22. **47** Ibid., p. 41.

in the possibility of externalizing of the soul. He offers this as an explanation for an aspect of the rite of passage common among tribes with a belief in totemism, in which a boy of puberty undergoes an initiatory rite involving the pretence of killing him and bringing him back to life. Frazier believed that this expressed a tribal belief in the transference of the boy's soul to his totem.[48] The relevance of this to *The Countess Cathleen* is that it links totemic belief to a process of exchange in which the spiritual entity takes on a material, even inanimate form. Mary's revelation of totemic belief is also, of course, invested with the kind of significance explored in Freud's *Totem and Taboo*, but it is, perhaps, more important to recognize that her belief is expressed in the context of a situation of exchange the centre of which is money.[49] Thus, identifying her attitude as straightforward primitivism is unsatisfactory – Mary's attitude is deeply, if opaquely, implicated in the crisis of modernity that runs through the play, which is most disturbingly captured in the suggestion that people are commodities, exchangeable things in the world.

Through Yeats's revisions of the play over many years, a distinctive occult pattern of initiation emerges and becomes more tautened in later versions. The aspect of dehumanization that connects the play to a modernist aesthetic is framed within this occult pattern. The play commences with the archetypal family triangle of mother, father and son. This triangular structure is then doubled (and disturbed) when the countess, Aleel and Oona enter the cottage. Following their departure and the destruction of the virgin shrine, the two merchants arrive at the cottage. Their twin features and parallel actions are employed by Yeats visually to create an unsettling atmosphere in order to suggest how, during the course of their initiation, the participants' forms of vision become unsettled. The audience sees this in the gender difference of responses to the merchants within the household: Sheamus and Teigue welcoming them as trading men, Mary warning them away as demons.

This difference is complicated by the fact that while the men cannot see beyond the illusion of the demons' initial appearance as material creatures interested solely in material activity (trade), Mary sees through the illusion of this material appearance to the 'reality' of the merchants' non-material natures, beings from a world beyond material perception. In later versions of the play, Mary not only attributes supernatural powers to the merchants but also believes that they are 'not of those who cast a shadow.'[50] This, of course, draws on folklore regarding spirit creatures that Yeats would have encountered in numerous sources. In this particular context, however, Mary's assertion acquires an additional significance consonant with the occult structure of correspondence shaping the play. The shadow becomes the insubstantial supplement to the materiality of those

48 James Frazer, *The golden bough* (London: Wordsworth Editions, 1993), p. 692.   **49** Sigmund Freud, *Totem and taboo*, trans. James Strachey (London: Norton, 1950). It is worth reminding ourselves in this context of the shortcomings of a-social oedipalization as illustrated by Deleuze and Guattari, *Anti-Oedipus*, pp 51–67.   **50** Alspach, *Variorum plays*, p. 41.

'real' figures in the play, the vaporous signifier of their solid substantiality. Consequently, the absence of the insubstantial shadow does not simply indicate the ghostly nature of the beings standing before Mary; it also highlights the irony that her own material solidity is signified by something as vaporous and insubstantial as a shadow, a supplement that, like the threshold, marks the border between material historical certainties and an invisible spirit world. Indeed, a parallel between the shadow, understood in this manner, and the threshold is evident in the First Merchant's rebuttal of Mary's invocation of God:

> Pray, you shall need Him.
> You shall eat grass, and dock, and dandelion,
> And fail till this low threshold there seems a wall[.][51]

The threshold and the shadow both admit contact between inner and outer worlds; the wall closes off such contact. Thus, Mary is imagined here as literally encaged in a purely material, animal existence. This brutish reduction to physical necessity is concentrated in the image of the wall that admits no redeeming contact with a realm beyond the 'despotism of fact,' a realm suggested in the ethereality of shadow. This, however, serves only to remind us that this wall is no more substantial than the merchants; like them, it ostensibly embodies the triumph of materialism, but only at the cost of admitting its own spectral, illusory nature. The wall in this instance is, unlike the threshold, an illusion.[52]

Yeats's strategies of doubling, therefore, are not evident simply in the overt twining of the merchants; they are also present in a more discreet process of *Darstellung*, in which the demons, as figures whose ghostly natures are revealed in their shadow-less aspect, 'mirror' the living characters, whose shadows mark their materiality. This web of oppositional correspondence grows more thickly with the realization that the merchants are embodiments of an ethos of materialistic self-interest destined to replace the elevated spirituality of the countess. These occult procedures of shadowing and doubling might be conceived in terms set out by Derrida in his critique of Lévi-Strauss, particularly given the congruence of the play's primitivist aspect and the objects of Lévi-Strauss's study in *The Elementary Structures of Kinship* and *The Savage Mind*. This would appear even more plausible when the historiographic implication of this dialectic of shadow is considered: namely, how it manifests a simultaneity of primitive and modern, apparently failing to provide conditions for a linear chronology in the process. Certainly, the interaction of structure and play, center and periphery, presence and absence,

---

51 Ibid., p. 49. **52** One might counter that Yeats appears to grant this image a more substantial reality in versions subsequent to 1908 when he replaces 'seem a wall' with 'becomes a wall.' Alspach, *Variorum plays*, p. 49. What this actually indicates, however, is Yeats's more forthright sense of Mary's imagined incapacity to distinguish reality from illusion; in pre-1908 versions, the word 'seems' points to her sense that what she sees may be an illusion, a sense that is absent in post-1908 versions.

within which Derrida's critique is framed, bears resemblance to the forms of parallel, inversion and, finally, exchange, within the play.[53] The remarkable (and overlooked) aspect to this play, however, is that its infinite play of material and insubstantial correspondences, with their undoubted sources in kabbalah, is so deeply shaped by conditions of material privation and historical disjunction.

In versions of the play prior to 1908, the first encounter between the merchants and the household of Mary, Shemus and Teigue is followed by three more acts. In subsequent versions, Yeats converted these acts to scenes, added a short penultimate scene and substantially revised the dialogue and settings. The overall effect was a greater stylistic tightness, with the symbolism of speech, gesture and image becoming more concentrated, creating a dramatic effect more consonant with intensity and artifice of the European experimentalist theatre. Throughout the revisions, a sense of ritual pattern remained. Act two remained concentrated around a dialogue between Cathleen, Aleel and Oona that formed a parallel to the opening triangular exchange between Mary, Shemus and Teigue. Through the intervention of their servants, the gardener and peasants, the disturbance following the arrival of the merchants is communicated to Cathleen. The attitudes of hostility and welcome, within the circle of Cathleen, Aleel and Oona, to what lay beyond the boundary of their court reflects the attitudes of Mary, Shemus and Teigue to the forest beyond their household in act one. Each intervention by a subordinate in act two deepens Cathleen's sense of anxiety in a manner akin to that experienced by Mary in act one. Act two is full of esoteric reference; the herdsman is a figure include in the plan for ritual initiation for the Celtic Order of Mysteries and recalls the herdsman referred to by Teigue in act one, who claimed to have seen a man whose face was a wall of flesh. The fruit to which the gardener refers in his conversation with the Countess carries occult significance; the exchange strongly prefigures the concerns of Chekhov's *The Cherry Orchard*, particularly the relationship between Ranyevskaya and Firs, her footman.[54] This prepares the audience for the merchants' first encounter with the Countess in act three, preparing the way for the climactic gesture of Cathleen's self-abandonment in the final act when the audience is returned to the cottage of Shemus and the body of the dead Mary.

In conclusion, while it is not possible here to provide a full analysis of the later acts in regard to the dialectical form of exchange in the play that this paper has attempted to highlight, it can be stated that Cathleen's sacrificial act is only

53 Jacques Derrida, 'Structure, sign, and play in the discourse of the human sciences,' *The languages of criticism and the sciences of man,* ed. Richard Macksey and Eugenio Donato (Baltimore: Johns Hopkins UP, 1970), pp 247–65.   **54** Firs has a deeply affectionate devotion to Ranyevskaya, but his struggle to communicate with his lady due to a deafness brought on by old age is also an oblique echo of Oona, whose deafness prevents her hearing the gardener's words to Cathleen. Like Oona, Firs is pre-occupied with the idea of being forgotten. Anton Chekhov, *The cherry orchard*, trans. Michael Frayn (London: Methuen, 1978), pp 8–9, 67.

comprehended fully in terms of that form. Hers is foremost an act of exchange, hardly immune from the ambivalences in the play surrounding gold; its esoteric alchemical significance and its centrality to a system of exchange that would appear to render such significance obsolete. Marjorie Howes is only partly correct in arguing that while the countess's sacrifice reveals the magnanimity of the aristocracy, it also reveals an assumption of their inherent superiority over the peasantry, one aristocratic soul being worth more than countless peasant souls.[55] This reading leaves in the background the nature of the exchange that takes place. If Cathleen's soul is as rare and priceless as gold, it comes to occupy a position at the centre of a system of exchange in which reproducibility and price have the effect of commodifying even rarity itself.[56] Cathleen's gesture, selling her soul to the devil in order to save the souls of the peasantry, is a Faustian conclusion to a feudal aristocratic ethos within which such Faustian spirit would flourish and is a noble surrender of nobility itself. For no matter how selfless her motivation, Cathleen gives her 'soul' to merchants; her spiritual self-sacrifice allows the advance of a new ethos of pecuniary atavism. Her rarefied act is the moment of flattening of value itself in a newly emergent system of interchangeability. Commenting on Marx's writing on money in *Grundrisse*, Antonio Negri observes:

> The more fundamental the representation of value in the figure of money, the more fundamental is the refutation of value, the radicality of its inversion. Communism is not the realization of the interchangeability of value, the being in force of money as a real measure. Communism is the negation of all measure, the affirmation of the most exasperated plurality – creativity.[57]

It might be objected that Cathleen's redemption at the play's conclusion, in which, upon her death, angels take her to Heaven, reinstates the notion of sacred value at the point in the play where it appears on the verge of collapsing. It may have been that Yeats was not prepared to envisage the full implication of what he imagined theatrically and that this awkward conclusion represented a pulling back from disconcerting consequences similar to the way he revised the conclusion of *The King's Threshold*. In any case, the vision of the angels only occurs after the countess has made her pact with the demons and has died. Whatever we make of it, the salvation of her soul does not dispel the catastrophe of all value equalized that her pact (and her death) involves. Whether it unconsciously alludes to the 'exasperated plurality' that Negri envisages beyond all measure is another matter.

55 Howes, *Yeats's nations*, p. 61. 56 For Marx's comments on rarity as a necessary quality of gold as money, see *Grundrisse*, p. 176. 57 Antonio Negri, *Marx beyond Marx: lessons on the Grundrisse* (London: Pluto, 1991), p. 33.

Eighteenth-century European scholarship and nineteenth-century Irish literature: Synge's *Tinker's Wedding* and the orientalizing of 'Irish gypsies'

MARY BURKE

An anthropologist of Irish Traveller life has written that Synge 'participated in the lives and activities of the people he observed [...].'[1] However, Synge's *Tinker's Wedding* is not a realistic nor unproblematically sympathetic portrayal of Travellers he encountered. Furthermore, his prose does not uncover an ostensible chasm between 'tinker' and island minorities and a homogenous majority, as sometimes claimed. According to the dramatist's nephew, *The Tinker's Wedding* was derived from 'country lore', rather than 'any direct association with the tinkers themselves.'[2] The phrase 'country lore' is too vague: Synge's imaginative engagement with the so-called 'Irish Gypsy' emanates from centuries-long exoticizations of peripheral groups by Irish commentators. The late nineteenth-century 'Irish tinker' fad among writers of the British Isles, from which the drama simultaneously emerges, was the late and localized flowering of an eighteenth-century European academic craze centred on the investigation of Gypsy origins. Since this fad was perpetuated by a number of Irish writers, Synge's drama may be said to be the Revival-era culmination of over one hundred years of Irish construction and negotiation of the European fantasy of 'the Gypsy'.

A German study of 1783 that purported to expose the Indian origins of European Gypsies, Heinrich Grellmann's *Dissertation on the Gipsies*,[3] consolidated the exemplar of the heathenish, wild, asocial Gypsy, whose appetites and customs were an inverse of, or in monstrous excess of, sedentary norms – a construct that Synge's text rarely subverts. Grellmann was not the first European scholar to publish a text devoted entirely to Gypsies, or to suggest that 'exotic' origin was discernible in the Gypsies' language. However, he wrote the earliest and best-known

---

1 George Gmelch (ed.), 'J.M. Synge: observer of Irish peasant life', in *In Wicklow, West Kerry and Connemara* (Dublin: O'Brien, 1980), pp 11–12. 2 Andrew Carpenter (ed), *My Uncle John: Edward Stephens's life of J.M. Synge*, (London: Oxford UP, 1974), p. 157. The play's source is found in J.M. Synge, 'At a Wicklow fair', in Robin Skelton (gen. ed.), *J.M. Synge: collected works* (London: Oxford UP, 1962–8), vol. 2, p. 228–9. 3 Heinrich Grellmann, *Dissertation on the Gipsies / Historischer versuch über die Zigeuner* (1783), trans. Matthew Raper (London: Printed for the editor by G. Biggs, 1787).

'standard work', the significance of which lies in its crystallization of disparate stereotypes gleaned from earlier commentaries.[4] Unsurprisingly, he was accused by certain contemporary reviewers of having had no personal contact with the subjects of his study.[5] The *Dissertation* set the parameters of the subject, and studies in subsequent centuries often unashamedly paraphrased it. Grellmann was an ethnographer and historian based for most of his career at Göttingen University, the German enlightenment powerhouse, and he was academically active in an era in which the discipline of history was being institutionalized. He invented the category of 'Gypsy' as has been understood since then; his work brought various itinerant groups 'moving through different countries together under a single name, […] and provided them with a collective history'.[6]

Grellmann refined the previously obscure oriental origin theory by suggesting that language proved that Gypsies were descendants of an Indian pariah group, with all the negative associations the analogy implied: Gypsies were filthy eaters, addictive, vulgar in dress, animalistic, lacking in willpower, instinctive, lazy, lustful (especially the women) and dishonest. According to the German scholar, since the 'hideous trait' of cannibalism was an Indian custom, Gypsies might still practise it. He ascribed their tendency to cling to barbaric habits, unless encouraged to reform, to their unenlightened oriental origins. Most interestingly, in light of the discursive derivation of Synge's 'tinkers', Gypsies hypocritically professed the religion of whatever region they happened to be in and married merely to emulate their social betters. 'There is not, perhaps', Grellmann wrote, 'any other people, among whom marriages are contracted with so little consideration, or solemnized with so little ceremony, as among these Gypsies.' The marriages often being irregular, 'one of their people act the priest.'[7] The traces of such Europe-wide beliefs about peripatetic peoples are detectable in folklore collected in Ireland over one hundred years later. One informant explains to Synge that tinker men casually swapped wives,[8] and Lady Gregory is told that tinkers 'never go to Mass; and, […] it's […] likely they have no marriage at all'.[9] Mary, the tinker matriarch of Synge's play, derides her son's common-law wife for wishing to regularize the union, and Michael himself finds Sarah's desire to marry 'a mad thing'. (Similarly, in Yeats's near-contemporaneous *Where There Is Nothing* (1902), in which a tinker weds a country gentleman, the ostensibly slapdash and outlandish nature of tinker marriage ritual is noted.)

The Irish orientalist, William Marsden,[10] proposed a 'Hindostanic' link to the Gypsy language in a letter read before the Society of Antiquaries of London in

---

4 Wim Willems and Leo Lucassen, 'The church of knowledge: representation of Gypsies in Dutch encyclopedias and their sources (1724–1984)', in Matt T. Salo (ed.), *100 years of Gypsy studies* (Cheverly, MD: Gypsy Lore Society, 1990), p. 42. **5** Willems, *In search of the true Gypsy*, trans. Don Bloch (London: Cass, 1997), pp 70–83. **6** Willems, *True Gypsy*, p. 17. **7** Grellmann, *Dissertation*, p. 45–6. **8** Synge, 'The vagrants of Wicklow', in *CW*, vol. 2, p. 204. **9** Lady Gregory, 'The wandering tribe', in *Poets and dreamers* (1903), (New York: Oxford UP, 1974), p. 94. **10** William Marsden

February 1785, two years after Grellmann's German-language publication, but two years before the English-language translation of the *Dissertation* appeared. Marsden makes no reference to Grellmann and stresses that he made his discovery 'in the latter end of the year 1783'; Grellmann's preface is dated 4 September 1783, and the first review appeared that December. Grellmann cites Marsden in the list of sources of his second German edition and his 1787 English-language translation. A clue as to one reason that both Marsden and Grellmann arrived at the same conclusion may lie in the fact that the Irishman and Grellmann's English-language translator both acknowledge the help of Royal Society president, Sir Joseph Banks. Marsden's claim that 'the resemblance to the Hindostanic is the predominant feature in the Gypsy dialect' was a theory 'perfectly new to the world',[11] was swiftly disputed by the Mosaic ethnologist, Jacob Bryant, in a paper read before the Society two months later. Bryant implies that Marsden, a reputable scholar, disingenuously stole the thunder of earlier authorities, and the ethnologist claims for himself and William Coxe[12] the honour of having noted 'the affinity' of the Gypsies' vocabulary to 'the languages of ancient and distant nations' several years previously. Embarrassingly, Bryant's refutation was published immediately after Marsden's paper in volume seven of *Archaeologia*. The cachet of the supposed link of the 'Gypsy' language to oriental cultures led to an unseemly scholastic scramble for the credit of the 'discovery'.

The feeding frenzy for Gypsies impacted outside self-regarding scholarly circles: the *Belfast News-Letter* published a piece entitled 'The Gypsies' in its issue of 6–9 December 1785. The poem was not attributed to its author, William Cowper, and is an excerpt from *The Task*, a fact also unexplicated. *The Task* was written from late 1783–4, the period when Grellmann's study was making waves, and the excerpt given is permeated by common assumptions about the Gypsy lifestyle: Gypsies are a 'vagabond and useless tribe' of 'tawny skin' who eat 'flesh obscene' and demonstrate 'great skill' in palmistry, begging and stealing. Cowper's poem expresses bewilderment, characteristic of the enlightenment, that

> a creature rational and cast
> in human mould shou'd brutalize by choice
> His nature!

Though the contents of the poem are entirely consistent with its date of composition, its location in a provincial four-page establishment publication concerned with trade, agriculture and politics is unexpected, and indicates how

(1754–1836), orientalist, linguist and numismatist. Born 16 Nov. 1754 at Verval, Co. Wicklow. Elected FRS 1783; original member RIA, 1785.   **11** Marsden, 'Observations on the language of the people commonly called Gypsies', *Archaeologia*, 7 (1785), p. 384.   **12** Willima Coxe was a traveller who had obtained 'specimens of [Gyspy] language' in Hungary. Jacob Bryant, 'Collections on the Zingara, or Gypsey language', *Archaeologia*, 7 (1785), p. 387.

widely and quickly the discourse of the Gypsy percolated from the major European centres of scholarship. However, it is difficult to argue that the poem implies a contemporary perception of a local 'Gypsy' presence, given that it is one of a number of poems and songs emanating from the metropolitan literary scene to be published in the *News-letter* throughout 1785. The excerpt does, however, indicate that the European craze for Gypsies did not escape notice in Belfast's editorial circles.

As indicated by Bryant's reference to Coxe, eighteenth-century ethnography's reliance on travel writers ensured that they were credited with 'uncovering' the links of exotic minorities abroad to the Gypsies of home: [13] unflattering travel accounts of the Indian pariah caste quoted by Grellmann approximated with his pre-existent image of the Gypsy. [14] To this day, historians of the Gypsy refer to two travel writers with Irish connections as seminal commentators on 'the tribe'. The Irish bishop, Richard Pococke, [15] suggested in an account of a tour of Egypt, Ethiopia and the Middle East from the 1740s, that the Chingani of Syria, a nomadic people who 'pass for Mahometans', were 'relations' of the 'gypsies in England'. [16] The *Travels through Portugal and Spain, in 1772 and 1773* (1775) of Richard Twiss (1747–1821), the wealthy elder son of an Anglo-Dutch merchant family descended from 'the family of Twiss resident about 1660 at Killintierna, Co. Kerry', [17] contains one of the earliest discussions of Spanish Gypsies in English-language travel writing. Commercially and critically successful on publication, it provided Grellmann with information on *Gitanos*, and set the template for the 'description of Gypsies' scene common to later travel works on Spain. [18] Twiss refutes the claim by a French authority [19] that the Spanish Gypsy men 'are all thieves, and the women libertines', as being 'too general; I have lodged many times in their houses, and never missed the most trifling thing'. [20] The textual method by which the 'Gypsy' archetype is transmitted is

---

13 Willems, *True Gypsy*, p. 39.   14 Willems and Lucassen, 'The church of knowledge', p. 33.
15 Bishop Richard Pococke (1704–1765), extensive traveller. Appointed archdeacon of Dublin in 1745. Translated to the bishopric of Meath in 1765.   16 Pococke, *A description of the East* (2 vols) (London: Printed for the author by W. Bowyer, 1743–5), vol. 2, p. 207.   17 *Burke's landed gentry*, quoted in the *Dictionary of national biography* (1899) entry for Richard's brother, Francis Twiss (1760–1827).   18 George Borrow's semi-autobiographical writings on Gypsies in the nineteenth century consolidated Spain as a significant setting for fantasies of the Gypsy. Both Walter Starkie, author of studies of Spanish Gypsies and Abbey Board member, and Frank Carney, the Abbey dramatist whose *The righteous are bold* (1946) utilizes a 'Gypsy' song from Borrow, might be said to continue the Irish exploration of the *Gitano* construct initiated by Twiss.   19 Abbé Delaporte, *Le voyager françois, ou La connaissance de l'ancien et du nouveau monde* (26 vols) (Paris: Cellot, 1768–95).   20 Richard Twiss, *Travels through Portugal and Spain, in 1772 and 1773* (London: Printed for the author, 1775), pp 179–80. Such apparent subversion of stereotypes must be contextualized within the utilization of Spain as a site for 'contention between England and France' by French or English-language commentators playing to home audiences. (Joan K Stemmler, 'An Anglo-Irish view of Spain', *Dieciocho*, 23:2 (2000), pp 271, 274.) Twiss was not necessarily even-handed: his somewhat disparaging *Tour in Ireland in 1775*

observable when Grellmann cites this stereotype of female Gypsy behaviour paraphrased in Twiss's text as being Twiss's *own* opinion.[21]

Significantly, neither Twiss nor Pococke referred to Gypsies in their accounts of Ireland, though Twiss alluded to beggars.[22] Edward Clarke gave an account of Russian Gypsies in 1800, and seemed versed in the Indian-origin theory.[23] His account of Dublin makes no note of Gypsies but only, again, of undifferentiated beggars.[24] Neither Grellmann, Marsden, nor any of the eighteenth-century commentators mentioned refer to *Irish* 'Gypsies' *per se*. According to Sharon Gmelch, the *ethnic* category of 'tinker', as subsequently recognized in Ireland, emerged textually through government monitoring of marginalized social groups: The Commission on the Condition of the Poorer Classes (a body created in response to anxiety about widespread indigence and which reported in 1835), was informed that, in contrast to other itinerants, 'wives and families accompany the tinker while he strolls about in search of work, and always beg. They intermarry with one another, and form a distinct class.'[25] Unlike European and British Gypsies, Irish tinkers were generally understood to be indigenous.

It was left to late-nineteenth-century commentators to 'discover' that an element of the exotic 'Gypsy' was present all along in Irish tinkers. Post-Grellmann, a wave of English-language writings obsessed over the definition, record, reform and 'character' of British Gypsies, who were represented either as an undesirable itinerant group or as a Romany race in possession of a rich, mysterious culture intrinsically opposed to sedentary norms.[26] The literary fad for romanticized Gypsies exploded with George Borrow's mid-century picaresque writings. Borrow, later somewhat undeservedly considered an expert in the Romani language, whetted his linguistic appetite by learning Gaelic when he lived in Ireland as a child. Synge was obviously familiar with the author's work: in *People and Places* the dramatist refers to Borrow in his discussion of the superiority of the wandering lifestyle.[27] Yet another 'Gypsyologist' with Irish connections, Henry Thomas Crofton,[28] consolidated Romani as a subject of scholarly interest with *Dialect of the English Gypsies* (1875),[29] a principal branch on the 'genealogical tree of ideas'

(1776) was scorned by Irish readers. **21** Grellmann, *Dissertation*, p. 33. **22** Pococke, *Tour in Ireland in 1752*, George Stokes (ed.), (Dublin: Hodges & Figgis; London: Simpkin, Marshall er al., 1891); Twiss, *A tour in Ireland in 1775* (London: Printed for the author, 1776), p. 73. **23** See Dr Edward Daniel Clarke, *Travels in Russia, Tartary and Turkey* (1810) (Edinburgh: Chambers, 1839). **24** Clarke, *A tour through the south of England, Wales, and part of Ireland* (London: Minerva, 1793), p. 312. **25** *Report of the commissioners on the condition of the poorer classes in Ireland* (London, 1835), vol. 32, part 1, p. 495, quoted in Sharon Gmelch, *Tinkers and Travellers* (Dublin: O'Brien, 1975), p. 10. **26** David Mayall, *Gypsy-Travellers in nineteenth-century society* (Cambridge UP, 1988), pp 71–2. **27** Synge, 'People and places', in *CW*, vol. 2, p. 196. **28** Henry Thomas Crofton, born in 1848 at Preston. Gypsylorist, author of seminal papers on Shelta, and a member of an extensive Irish family descended from Queen Elizabeth's escheator-general of Ireland. **29** Crofton and Bath Charles Smart, *The dialect of the English Gypsies* (2nd ed.) (London: Ascher, 1875). (The first edition was privately circulated.)

of English-language Gypsy studies.[30] Throughout the nineteenth century, itinerant subcultures in the British Isles became increasingly subject to a process of orientalization: one commentator found the 'strange Oriental chaunt' of the Irish *bacach* (tramp) similar to 'the chaunting of a Fakeer',[31] and Synge noted that West Kerry beggars prayed with 'almost Oriental volubility.'[32] Contemporary race theory underpinned the obsession of the late nineteenth-century *Journal of the Gypsy Lore Society* (1888–) with cataloguing the 'disappearing' culture of 'pure-blooded' British Romanies of Indian origin. Although usually noting that Irish tinkers were of indigenous origin and occasionally constructing them as inferior to 'pure' Romanies, the journal nevertheless pseudo-anthropologically orientalized tinkers with accounts of sexually outlandish 'Gypsy' behaviour, such as wife-swapping and irregular weddings, similar to those Gregory later collected.[33]

The *Journal of the Gypsy Lore Society* informed readers that tinkers 'intermarry among themselves, often with but slight regard for the rites of the Church.'[34] *The Tinker's Wedding*'s much-lauded subversiveness, which supposedly inheres in the 'pagan' tinker clan's general indifference to the social pressure to formalize sexual relationships, is hardly convincing when it is considered that their amorality mirrors centuries-old stereotypes of Gypsy heathenism. To Jeanne Flood, Synge's 'lusty, hard-drinking, and violent' tinkers:

> live at ease in nature, neither having nor needing a shelter. The drunken, genial Mary Byrne, in the fullness of her experience, embodies the rich humanity of such a life.[…] Placed against Mary is the Priest, the guardian and representative of the religious and social order, thus of the forces of culture which separate man from nature […].[35]

The 'pagan' amorality of Mary, as much a socio-historical construct as the Christianity the play dismisses as the antithesis of the 'natural', contradicts the purported moral objectivity of the drama. Synge's preface situates the play within a putatively neutral and disinterested pseudo-anthropological framework: 'The drama, like the symphony, does not teach or prove anything.'[36] Mary describes prayer as 'queer noise', and in what amounts to incantation, is called a 'heathen' five times in Act 1 alone. Flood wilfully ignores the unorthodox behaviour of the drunkard priest in presenting him as the antithesis of the 'natural' tinkers who want to kill him: 'The Tinkers, perfectly integrated into the natural world,

30 Willems and Lucassen, 'The church of knowledge', p. 31. **31** William Hackett, 'The Irish bacach, or professional beggar, viewed archaeologically', *Ulster Journal of Archeology*, 9 (1861–2), p. 261. **32** Synge, 'In West Kerry', in *CW*, vol. 2, p. 265. **33** David MacRitchie, 'Irish tinkers and their language', *Journal of the Gypsy Lore Society*, 1:6 (1889), pp 351–2. **34** John Sampson, 'Tinkers and their talk', *Journal of the Gypsy Lore Society*, 2:4 (1891), p. 204. **35** Jeanne A. Flood, 'Thematic variation in Synge's early peasant plays', *Éire-Ireland*, 7:3 (1972), p. 75. **36** *The Tinker's Wedding* (Dublin: Maunsel, 1907), preface.

are thus appropriately presented in anarchic and violent act.' Man is 'an animal', Flood continues, and the 'wild Tinkers' are 'more humane' than the 'domesticated variety'.[37] Another critic represents the dramatist's depiction of a 'natural' tinker aversion to marriage as social realism.[38] Such liberal humanist endorsements of stereotypes of the tinker as anarchic, wild, 'natural', animalistic and intrinsically opposed to organised religion have been somewhat common in critical discussions of the play.

The Tinker's Wedding presents itself as transcending the romanticized or idealized tinker that, for instance, James Stephens' near-contemporaneous novel, *The Demi-Gods* (1914), might be accused of perpetuating. In his preface, Synge implies that the product of the 'neutral' dramatist is a force of 'nature', seeming to issue through, rather than from him: '[T]he best plays of Ben Jonson and Molière can no more go out of fashion than the blackberries on the hedges.' Lady Gregory commented that country people 'speak of a visit of the tinkers as of frost in spring or blight in harvest.'[39] Gregory's image of natural disaster to describe an unwelcome visit by tinkers is echoed in the play's preface, which constructs the tinker as a force of nature to whom the application of socially constructed moral values is irrelevant.

In *The Aran Islands*, Synge logocentrically privileges speech over doctrine: the religious beliefs of the islanders are ostensibly Catholic, but the authentic 'voice' of the people is 'pagan'.[40] Among the country people, tinkers had a reputation for 'unnatural powers,[41] and Aran is a realm of witchcraft potent enough to create storms.[42] The Catholic reform movement supposedly amended 'Patterns', the raucous celebration of feast days typical of pre-Famine cottier practice mentioned as occurring on Aran.[43] Synge's allusion to the practice is an attempt to reinscribe the islanders' Catholicism with the irregularity of an earlier era. He is a counter-missionary to the efforts of his uncle, the Revd Alexander Synge, who came to Aran in the previous generation to reform the islanders' religion. Galway was the location of the family estate that allowed Mrs Synge £400 a year[44] and Aran the site of Alexander's generally unsuccessful proselytizing. By stripping the prosaic Galway and Aran of his childhood and family history of its colonial, Protestant and familial associations, Synge refigures it as the pristine pre-Norman monoculture of Revival-era imagination.

Synge's nephew implied that the dialect utilized in Synge's drama was an appropriation of the language of Travellers: Hutchie wrote that 'it was the annual

37 Flood, 'Thematic variation', 76.   **38** Through Sarah's 'superficial aspiration to marriage, Synge explores the folly and frustration of trying to fit one's experience into a social or intellectual frame unnatural to it.' Weldon Thornton, *J.M. Synge and the western mind* (Gerrards Cross: Colin Smythe, 1979), p. 157.   **39** Gregory, 'The wandering tribe', p. 94.   **40** Synge, *The Aran Islands*, in *CW*, vol. 2, p. 75.   **41** Synge, 'The vagrants of Wicklow', in *CW*, vol. 2, p. 203. **42** Synge, *The Aran Islands*, in *CW*, vol. 2, p. 88.   **43** See Donal A. Kerr, *A nation of beggars* (Oxford: Clarendon, 1994).   **44** *My Uncle John*, p. 22.

gathering of tinkers to the Wicklow [town] regatta at the beginning of August in 1902 which brought to Synge ... a form of English in which he could really express himself'.[45] Synge was responding to a passing fashion for the tinkers' language in the 1880s and 1890s, which must be situated within the context of post-Grellmann Gypsy studies. Prior to the rise of the Indian origin theory, the language of the itinerant classes of the British Isles was dismissed as a 'cant' of no scholarly interest: as late as 1728, the 'Gypsy' entry in *Chambers' Cyclopaedia* dismissed their 'unknown' canting tongue.[46] Indicating that the paradigm of the Gypsy language as furtive thieves' cant was shifting to the new model of 'Gypsy' as fascinating proof of exotic, ancient origin, Marsden expresses wonder:

> that tribes wandering through the mountains of *Nubia*, or the plains of *Romania*, have been conversant for centuries in a dialect precisely familiar to that spoken at this day by the obscure, despised, and wretched people in England, whose language has been considered a fabricated gibberish and confounded with a cant in use amongst thieves and beggars, and whose persons have been (till within the period of a year) an object of the persecution, instead of the protection of our laws.[47]

Most itinerant groups were subject to harsh if unevenly enforced statutes against mendicancy and nomadism from the medieval period until the end of the eighteenth century, and Marsden's comments indicate that the relaxing of laws against Gypsies (the 'counterfeit Egyptians' cited in Elizabethan statutes) coincided with the new Indian origin theory; a group previously criminalized was now ethnicized, and delinquency became explicable in terms of oriental/pariah origin with its concomitant (and potentially fascinating) innate moral laxity. Despite late-eighteenth-century claims of the 'Gypsy' language's connection to Sanskrit, its speakers evolved as the negative image of the 'Aryans', who, in reductive nineteenth-century race discourse, arrived in Europe from India armed with a Protestant work ethic. By the nineteenth century, outlandish claims about Gypsy behaviour could be circuitously 'proved' by analogy with bizarre Indian custom.[48]

In an 1880 article entitled 'Shelta, the tinkers' talk', Charles Godfrey Leland claimed to have 'discovered' the language whilst conversing with a beggar, and the American writer may be considered the catalyst for the subsequent flood of material on the subject in the late nineteenth century.[49] Shelta was soon drawn into institutionalized orientalism: in 1886, Leland read a paper before the Orientalist congress in Vienna on the 'The original Gypsies and their language',

45 Quoted in W.J. McCormack, *Fool of the family: a life of J.M. Synge* (London: Weidenfeld & Nicolson, 2000), p. 320. **46** Angus Fraser, *Gypsies* (1992) (Oxford: Blackwell, 1995), p. 188. **47** Marsden, 'Observations', p. 385. **48** See Walter Simson, *A history of the Gipsies* (London: Samson, Low and Marston; Edinburgh: Menzies, 1865), pp 268–69. **49** Charles Godfrey Leland, 'Shelta, the tinkers' talk', *New Quarterly Magazine*, 3 (1880), pp 136–41.

in which he returned to the subject of 'pre-historic' Shelta. The German scholar of Irish, Kuno Meyer, became interested in Shelta in the 1890s on the basis
of its 'antiquity' and link to 'old Irish',[50] and the language became, to an extent,
a cultural treasure to be wrestled from its unappreciative possessors.[51] Due to the
rash of articles on the language that appeared in the exoticizing *Journal of the
Gypsy Lore Society* following Leland's 'discovery', Shelta was briefly fashionable
enough to be included in the 1893 edition of *Chambers' Encyclopedia* as 'a secret
jargon of great antiquity spoken by Irish tinkers [...] descendants of the [...]
bards' – an ironic contrast to the pre-'discovery' opprobrium heaped upon 'canting language' in the 1728 edition.

   This exoticization readily mapped onto an obscure pre-existent Irish tradition that tinkers were extrinsic to a putatively homogenous 'Gaelic' population:
Gregory was told that 'the tinkers are not the same as the rest of us; [...] they originated in themselves'.[52] In an era when the terms 'Gael', 'Celt' and 'Irish' were
increasingly conflated, Synge's tinkers and islanders are inflected by the Irish
mytho-historic and antiquarian tradition that exotic pre-Gaelic peoples from 'the
East' were a long-lasting presence in Ireland.[53] Pseudo-histories, such as the canonical twelfth-century *Book of Invasions* (*Leabhar Gabhála Éireann*), detail a series of
settlers entering ancient Ireland. The arrival of the Milesians (Gaels) from Scythia,
via Egypt and Spain, was constructed as the culmination of the ancient plantations by *soi-disant* 'Milesian' annalists. In *Phases of Irish History* (1919), a study pred-
icated upon the scaffold of mytho-history, Eoin MacNeill focuses on the Fir-bolg,
a population group represented by annalists as former slaves whose dominion was
overthrown by arrivals such as the Tuatha Dé Danaan and Milesians. MacNeill
employs the diction of orientalism in suggesting evidence of 'something like the
Hindu caste system' in the hierarchical organization of occupations 'among the
descendants of the Pre-Celtic' peoples, and suggests that 'tinker clans of recent
times in Ireland and Scotland may well be survivals of [...] ancient industrial communities [...] [who] remained in every part of Ireland after their conquest by the
Gaels.'[54] In saying so, MacNeill frames within academic discourse the exoticizing
folk tradition that Travellers were a 'remnant of the Firbolgs or degenerated Tuatha
De Danaan' to be 'differentiate[d] [...] from the Irish people'.[55]

   Synge's orientalization of literally and politically marginal population groups
partakes of such pseudo-historic and antiquarian theorising on the pre-Celtic

50 Kuno Meyer, 'On the Irish origin and the age of Shelta', *Journal of the Gypsy Lore Society*,
2:5 (1891), p. 260.   **51** See Mary Burke, '"Hidden like a religious arcanum": Irish writing
and Shelta's secret history', in John Kirk and Dónall Ó Baoill (eds), *Travellers and their language*
(Queen's University, Belfast: Institute of Irish Studies, forthcoming).   **52** Gregory, 'The wandering tribe', p. 95.   **53** Burke, 'Phoenicianism and the construction of Irish Traveller origins', in *New voices in Irish criticism*, ed. Karen Vandevelde (Dublin: Four Courts, 2002), pp 9–16.
54 Eoin MacNeill, *Phases of Irish history* (Dublin: Gill, 1919), p. 82.   **55** William Bulfin, *Rambles
in Eirinn* (1907) (London: Sphere, 1981), vol. 2, p. 205.

peoples. The tradition fascinated him, judging by his *Speaker* reviews of Geoffrey Keating, the seventeenth-century Hiberno-Norman who straddled antiquarianism and mytho-history. Synge attempted a verse play on the first inhabitants of Ireland based on a few lines in Keating's *History of Ireland*,[56] a work that, significantly, the dramatist first read while on Aran. Synge also read the more academically orthodox George Petrie and Whitley Stokes,[57] and the blind Gaelic tutor who had known Petrie, whom he encounters on his first embarkation, is a living link to that world. The dramatist's reference to the presence on the island of Firbolg implies that the islanders are descended from that mytho-historic people, thus allying them with tinkers as a people apart from the majority of mainlanders. Folkloric belief suggested that, once vanquished by the Tuatha Dé Danann, the Fir-bolg fled to the Aran Islands. Later, having been defeated by the Gaels, the Tuatha Dé Danann descended underground and became those afterwards referred to as fairies.[58] Having established that the island stones had been 'touched by the Fir-bolgs',[59] Synge subtly points to the association of pre-Celtic peoples with fairies in his account of a dream he later has on the islands in which he is made frenzied by mysterious music against his will, an incident that he suggests is a result of 'a psychic memory' attached to the neighbourhood.[60] This is an allusion to the tradition that 'the little people' enticed humans by their beautiful playing, or could be charmed by skilled human musicians, the latter being the basic plot of Douglas Hyde's *The Tinker and the Fairy* (1910). Aran is temporally mytho-historic: the description of 'the first invasion of Ireland before the Flood' in Keating's mytho-historic *History of Ireland* 'harmonize[d] fantastically with [Synge's] experiences of Aran' and his mother's early Old Testament lessons.[61] To rephrase Corkery's description of the Synges, the Aran islanders are *in* contemporary Europe, but not *of* contemporary Europe, an assumption accepted by certain Synge critics.[62] The south islanders 'represent some old type found on these few acres at the extreme border of Europe'.[63] Passing a tinker's camp, Synge muses that the 'precious' tinker children 'console us, one moment at least, for the manifold and beautiful life we have all missed who have been born in modern Europe ...'[64]

The islander is patently framed within orientalist discourse: 'The red dresses of the women who cluster round the fire on their stools give a glow of almost Eastern richness'.[65] A pair of girls Synge meets 'spoke with a delicate exotic intonation' and told Synge 'with a sort of chant' of how they guided visitors.[66] Backbreaking toil is seen through the rose-tint of Eastern picturesqueness: 'In

56 *Luasnad, Capa and Laine*, in *CW*, vol. 3, pp 194–205. **57** *My Uncle John*, p. 48. **58** Proinsias MacCana, *Celtic mythology* (London: Hamlyn, 1970), pp 63–5. **59** Synge, *The Aran Islands*, in *CW*, vol. 2, p. 69. **60** Ibid., pp 99–100. **61** *My uncle John*, p. 137. **62** '[...] Celtic culture is characterized by attitudes not typical of the Western mind [...] Irish culture [...] has retained many features from [...] pre-history.' Thornton, *J.M. Synge and the western mind*, pp 50–1. **63** Synge, *The Aran Islands*, in *CW*, vol. 2, p. 140. **64** Synge, 'People and places', in *CW*, vol. 2, p. 199. **65** Synge, *The Aran Islands*, in *CW*, vol. 2, p. 58. **66** Ibid., p. 52.

Aran even manufacture is of interest. The low flame-edged kiln, sending out dense clouds of creamy smoke, with a band of red and grey clothed workers moving in the haze [...] forms a [...] picture from the East.'[67] The 'eastern' nature of the *sean-nós* singing style of an islander is implied by its comparison with a 'chant' Synge 'once heard from a party of Orientals' he was travelling with 'in a third-class carriage from Paris to Dieppe'.[68]

The occasionally-voiced belief that contemporary Travellers 'are the descendants of Phoenician tinsmiths'[69] and other supposed pre-Celtic peoples also imbricates the pre-Indo-European interlingual hypothesis (formulated in seventeenth-century France by Samuel Bochart) that suggested Phoenician was the mother tongue of all non-Romance languages of western Europe.[70] This orientalization of Gaelic intrigued patriots, who wished to privilege the Celto-Phoenician linguistic paradigm over the competing claim that English culture derived from Graeco-Roman civilization.[71] The French theory influenced Sir James Ware, and Ware's amanuensis, Duald MacFirbis, versed as the latter was in Gaelic mytho-history, would have considered it a mere reiteration of established scholarship.[72] General Charles Vallancey, remembered for his attempts to aggrandize his adopted country by linking the prehistoric Irish to an alarmingly vast range of 'eastern' peoples, imaginatively fused Bochartian theory and mytho-history; the General suggested that invader Phoenicians, who also settled Spain, gave their letters to the Gaels and were one of the pre-Milesian races recorded by MacFirbis and Keating.[73]

Vallancey's explicit response to Grellmann, 'On the Origin and Language of the Gypsies' (1804), hibernicizes Grellmann's theory of the oriental origin of the Gypsies by grafting their putative journey from the Orient onto his previously conceived theories of the 'eastern' genesis of the pre-Celtic settlers of Ireland. Vallancey does not refer to Marsden's theory,[74] though he approvingly paraphrases Pococke's hypothesis. The General suggests that the Gypsies are from the ancient Black Sea district of Colchis and asserts that from there a 'body of Scythians', a population he suggests peopled Ireland in earlier writings, invaded India. Therefore, he argues in a dismissal of the Indian-origin hypothesis, 'what few Hindoostanee words [Gypsies] have, are derived from our [...] Indo-Sythæ, who returned to [...] Colchis, after their emigration to India'.[75] The General grafts his previously-cited Phoenician-Irish hypothesis onto Grellmann's theory by arguing that a splinter of the group who originally left Colchis, and continued wandering 'under the

---

67 Ibid., p. 77.   **68** Ibid., p. 141.   **69** 'An Irish tinker on the road', *Sphere*, 15 Dec. 1956, p. 462. **70** Joseph Leerssen, 'On the edge of Europe: Ireland in search of Oriental roots, 1650–1850', *Comparative criticism*, 8 (1986), p. 95.   **71** Ibid.   **72** See Nollaig Ó Muraíle, *The celebrated antiquary: Dubhaltach Mac Fhirbhisigh (c.1600–1671)* (Maynooth: An Sagart, 1996).   **73** Vallancey, 'An essay on the antiquity of the Irish language' (Dublin: Powell, 1772), p. 2.   **74** This, despite the fact that Marsden's paper was published alongside one of Vallancey's own in volume seven of *Archaeologia*.   **75** Vallancey, 'On the origin and language of the Gypsies', *Collectanea de Rebus Hibernicis* (1770–1804), vi (1804), p. 86.

name of *Phoinice*', eventually arrived in Ireland.'[76] Vallancey agrees with a contributor to the seventh volume of *Asiatic Researches* that 'many of Grellman's (*sic*)
words of the Hindoostanee are very incorrect', a view with which certain reputable linguists actually concurred.[77] Sir William Jones, founder, in 1784, of the
Asiatic Society, which published the *Asiatic Researches* journal at Calcutta, wrote
that the 'many Sanscrit words' contained in Grellmann's vocabulary list proved the
Indian origin of the Gypsies.[78] Vallancey's references within his article to the Asiatic
Society's journal and to Gilchrist's Hindustani dictionary[79] indicate that he eagerly ingested any British orientalist productions that seemed to be of service to the
vindication of Ireland's neglected glory;[80] the Gypsy becomes a mere prop in the
Vallancey theatre of Irish antiquity. Thus, echoes of centuries of Irish mytho-historic and antiquarian discourse resonate in Synge's belief that 'tinkers' were a 'semi-
gipsy' class with 'curiously Mongolian features'.[81]

However, for many other commentators on Gypsy origins, the medieval scholarly belief that 'the tribe' originated in Egypt was decidedly superseded by the
rise of the Indian origin hypothesis in the late eighteenth century. This paradigm
shift was entwined with the coalescence of British political and cultural interest
in India in the wake of the conquest of Bengal in 1757, and the resultant dissemination of 'scientific' knowledge about India by orientalists, missionaries and administrators working within or funded by institutional structures such as the Asiatic
Society and the East India Company.[82] By the 1780s, explorations of the relationship of Indian culture and language to that of Europe were laying the foundations of the nineteenth-century Indo-European interlingual paradigm.

Many of the commentators on Gypsy culture discussed were directly involved
in administrating the empire or the crown in India and Ireland; Marsden, later
a fellow of the Asiatic Society of Calcutta, joined the East India Company in
Sumatra in 1771, and co-founded an East India agency business; Gilchrist's first
medical post was with the East India Company in 1783; Vallancey was posted to
Ireland as a military engineer, and the English-born Pococke held various high
ecclesiastical offices in Ireland. Among nineteenth-century commentators on
Gypsy culture, the families of Synge and Crofton had long traditions of service
to crown and church. Far from being an unmediated portrayal of a 'colourful'
Irish minority, the multi-layered construct known as *The Tinker's Wedding* emerges
from centuries of Irish, British and European dominant-class scholarship and
lore about marginal or 'vanquished' population groups.

76 Ibid., pp 64–5. **77** Willems, *True Gypsy*, pp 78–9. **78** *The works of Sir William Jones* (1807),
vol. 3, pp 170–1, quoted in Thomas R. Trautmann, *Aryans and British India* (University of
California, 1997), p. 49. **79** J.B. Gilchrist (1759–1841), British orientalist. Posted to India as
a physician by the East India Company in 1783. Produced dictionaries and studies of
Hindustani from the 1880s onwards. **80** Trautmann, p. 95. **81** Synge, 'People and places', in
CW, vol. 2, p. 198. **82** For a thorough discussion of the context of late-eighteenth-century
British orientalism, see Trautmann.

'The sneering, lofty conception of what they call culture': O'Casey, popular culture and the Literary Revival

PATRICK LONERGAN

In *Strange Country*, Seamus Deane writes that one of the difficulties faced by writers of the Revival was that they maintained 'the position that a traditional culture had been destroyed while still making the integrity of that culture the basis of a claim for political independence'. This difficulty was overcome, Deane states, by 'the remarkable feat of ignoring the famine and rerouting the claim for cultural exceptionalism through legend rather than through history'[1].

Deane's statement illustrates the ways in which Sean O'Casey differs from many other writers of the Revival. Famously anti-heroic, O'Casey's plays ignore legend; most of them are set in the immediate environment of the Abbey Theatre itself, and they are for the most part comprised of a language and subjects taken directly from O'Casey's own experience of life in Dublin. Moreover, rather than making a case for cultural exceptionalism, O'Casey was careful to present the literary revival as only one part of a much richer Irish cultural environment, which included not only the work of Synge and Yeats, but also such varied elements as Shakespearean drama, the Bible, popular theatre and music, and cinema.

The purpose of this essay is to present a reappraisal of the Revival in two senses. I want to articulate some of O'Casey's reservations about the Revival, on the basis that they had an important effect on the development of his work, and are also worth considering in their own right. I also want to reappraise the Revival myself, by suggesting that, although he is widely regarded as one of the canonical figures of the movement, O'Casey might better be understood as one of the revival's earliest critics.

Shortly before *Juno and the Paycock* premiered at the Abbey, Lennox Robinson provoked controversy in Ireland by asserting that most Dubliners did not consider the Abbey to be worth attending. Questioned at a meeting of the Oxford Union, Robinson was, according to a report in the *Irish Statesman*, 'compelled to give the lamentable answer that the patrons of the theatre consisted almost entirely of visitors to the city.'[2]

---

1 Seamus Deane, *Strange country: modernity and nationhood in Irish writing since 1790* (Oxford: Oxford UP, 1997), p. 51. 2 'Mr Lennox Robinson in Oxford' in *Irish Statesman*, 1 Mar. 1924, p.106, cited in Robert Hogan and Richard Burnham, *The years of O'Casey* (Cranbury: Associated University Presses, 1992), p. 188.

This difficulty in attracting Dubliners to the Abbey may seem surprising: in the early years of the twentieth century, drama was so popular a source of entertainment in the city that one commentator claims that working class Dublin was 'addicted to the theatre'[3]. Melodrama was the most popular form of entertainment on the Dublin stage in the decades before the production of *Juno and the Paycock*. As Chris Morash points out: 'The vibrancy of Irish melodrama in the decade and a half after 1910 was only partly due to the over-heated political climate of the time; it was equally the first fruits of a Faustian pact with the cinema.'[4] Pantomimes and adaptations of popular novels such as *The Prisoner of Zenda* and *The Three Musketeers* were also common, and Shakespeare was very popular too, as we know from *Ulysses*. As is the case today, star-actors guaranteed to draw an audience were cast in plays like *King Lear*, which were often the main feature in triple bills that could run for up to five hours, starting at seven and ending at midnight.[5] This explains O'Casey's inclusion in *The Shadow of a Gunman* of an exchange between Davoren and Seamus that audiences today find surprising. When Davoren quotes, 'The village cock hath thrice done salutation to the morn', Seamus is able to identify the source of that quote instantly: 'Shakespeare, *Richard III*, Act Five, Scene III. It was Ratcliffe said that to Richard just before the battle of Bosworth.'[6]

Throughout the first decades of the twentieth century, people in Ireland engaged with many forms of culture that existed beyond the confines of the revival. These included many different forms of popular entertainment, but also included recognizably Irish literary work. For example, writing about Emily Lawless's 1904 biography of Maria Edgeworth, Colin Graham points out that:

> Through Lawless as an Irish woman author writing about another Irish woman Author … Through the shamrocks and harps which decorate the covers of Blackburne, and through Edgeworth's novels (kitschly) republished by Dent in 1893, it is clear that Irish literature had, between 1890 and 1910, a definable and marketable existence beyond and at a remove from the Revival's rhetoric.[7]

Lennox Robinson made his comment at a time when the Dublin theatre was thriving and when the Irish public showed themselves to have an enthusiasm for many different forms of recognizably Irish culture. The Abbey's difficulty in attracting an audience is therefore not easy to understand. One expla-

3 C. Desmond Greaves, *Sean O'Casey: politics and art* (London: Laurence and Wishart, 1979), p. 27. **4** Chris Morash, *A history of Irish theatre, 1601–2000* (Cambridge: Cambridge UP, 2002), p. 154. **5** This is treated in detail in Stephen Watt, *Joyce, O'Casey and the Irish popular theatre* (New York: Syracuse UP, 1991). **6** Sean O'Casey, *The Shadow of the Gunman* in *Plays 2* (London: Faber and Faber, 1998), p. 38. **7** Colin Graham, *Deconstructing Ireland* (Edinburgh: University of Edinburgh, 2001), p. 36.

nation for it may be that, after the turn of the century, cultural life in Ireland became increasingly stratified according to social class. Lance Pettitt illustrates this with his discussion of early Irish cinema:

> Within a short time of its introduction into Ireland, watching films quick-
> ly became a popular activity. By 1916, there were some 150 cinemas and
> halls showing films, about 30 each in Belfast and Dublin. This produced
> socio-political tensions that were as much about class differences as nation-
> alist politics. While cinemas in the USA and Britain were consciously
> gentrified by owner-managers to make them more acceptable to middle-
> classes, in Ireland the reverse happened. Apart from certain select audi-
> ences, like the Metropole in Dublin, cinemas developed large working
> class audiences, which were viewed with suspicion by an emergent Irish
> middle class.[8]

The existence of social class as a determinant of access to culture may partially explain the Abbey's difficulty in attracting a Dublin audience. It certainly had an impact on O'Casey's dealings with the theatre. He states in his autobiogra-phy *Inishfallen, Fare Thee Well* that he was uncomfortable with what he perceived to be an elitist ethos at the theatre. He was criticized for not having read such writers as Andreiev, Giacosa, Maeterlinck, or Pirandello. Instead, he:

> Whispered the names of Shaw and Strindberg, which [the staff at the
> Abbey] didn't seem to catch, though he instinctively kept firm silence
> about Dion Boucicault, whose works he knew as well as Shakespeare's;
> afterwards provoking an agonised *My Gawd!* from Mr [Lennox] Robinson
> when he stammered the names of Webster, Ford and Massinger.[9]

From a very early stage in his association with the Abbey, O'Casey felt that many people at the theatre had a very narrow view of what was culturally valuable. By the time he came to write *Juno and the Paycock*, O'Casey was also becoming uncomfortable with what he saw as a tendency among certain writers of the Revival to dismiss some forms of culture as inferior. Although at that time he still had a high level of respect for Yeats and Gregory, and thought well of James Stephens and some others, he tells us that he saw in many of the writers of the Revival a: 'Sneering, lofty conception of what they called culture … The mighty semblance of self-assurance in the most of them was but a vain conceit in them-selves which they used for their own encouragement in the pitiable welter of a small achievement.'[10]

8 Lance Pettitt, *Screening Ireland* (Manchester: Manchester UP, 2000), p. 32   9 *Inishfallen, Fare Thee Well* in *Autobiographies 2* (London: Macmillan, 1963), p. 105.   10 Ibid., p. 157.

Whereas it is common for the autobiographical statements of such writers as Yeats to be taken as accurate, there is a tendency to assume that O'Casey's writings about the Revival reveal far more about the resentment and bitterness of the writer living in self-imposed exile in 1949, than they do about his experience of the early 1920s. Nevertheless, there is evidence in his early work that the dominance of this 'sneering lofty conception' of Irish cultural life presented a number of difficulties to O'Casey. This is particularly apparent in the determination with which he includes popular culture in that work.

As Captain Boyle in *Juno and the Paycock* puts it, people in Dublin knew 'more about Charlie Chaplin an' Tommy Mix than they do about SS. Peter and Paul',[11] and the same could have been said about their knowledge of popular theatre and music. O'Casey therefore could not have excluded popular culture from his work, even if he did feel too ashamed to admit his knowledge of it to Robinson and others. However, his use of melodrama, music and cinema was not entirely for the purposes of verisimilitude, but may be seen as an attempt to come to terms with that 'sneering, lofty conception of culture'. To illustrate how this affected O'Casey's work, I want to examine briefly his use of music and melodrama in *Juno and the Paycock*.

O'Casey uses music of the kind found on the stage of the popular Dublin theatre throughout *Juno*, not only as a device to authenticate the play's action, but also to serve many important dramatic functions. Firstly, music acts as a means of revealing character. It's not a coincidence that Captain Boyle, who spends the play's first act trying to deceive his wife, will at that act's conclusion choose to sing 'Oh Me Darlin' Juno, I Will Be True to Thee'[12] – a song intended to emphasize his honesty, which therefore reveals his duplicitous and hypocritical nature. Another example of this is Mrs. Madigan's choice of the song 'If I Were a Blackbird' to sing in the play's second act:

> If I were a blackbird I'd whistle and sing;
> I'd follow the ship that my true love was in;
> An' on the top riggin', I'd there build me a nest,
> An' at night I would sleep on me Whillie's white breast![13]

This seems quite an innocent choice, but given that her audience includes Captain Boyle – a former sailor who is supposed to have inherited a large amount of money – her choice of a love song with a maritime setting reveals a great deal about her motives.

Most importantly, O'Casey uses music to facilitate the movement of his action from comedy to tragedy. The play's turning point occurs when we hear Juno

---

11 Sean O'Casey, *Juno and the Paycock* in *Plays 1* (London: Faber and Faber, 1998), pp 43–4. 12 Ibid., p. 35. 13 Ibid., p. 50.

and Mary singing 'Home to Our Mountains' from Verdi's *Il Travotore*. O'Casey does not transcribe the words of this piece; he does not change them to reflect the accent or social status of the singers, but states that they must sing the song well.[14] By showing that the two characters can express themselves perfectly well in this art form, O'Casey hints that they are capable of transcending their circumstances—and indeed makes the case that they must do so.

Music and song appear on twelve occasions in the play, thereby making it seem to its audience like a typical melodrama. O'Casey's use of music was therefore part of a wider attempt to manipulate that audience's familiarity with melodrama for dramatic purposes. It is quite difficult to appreciate now the extent to which the first audiences at *Juno* felt that they were on familiar territory in the play's first two acts. With the possible exception of Johnny, all of the characters in the play are recognizable melodramatic stereotypes. We have Juno, the put-upon mother who is well intentioned, if bad-tempered. We have Mary, the innocent but intelligent young woman, who is prey to the seducer, Bentham (whose name, in melodramatic fashion, reveals his character: 'bent' referring to his dishonesty, and 'ham' to his sycophantic insincerity). We have Boyle and Joxer, the two likeable rogues who always deny that they have been drinking. The audience would therefore have complacently assumed a great deal about the play's conclusion: that the Boyles would eventually receive their inheritance, that Mary would marry Jerry Devine, that Bentham would be exposed as a fraud, and that the loveable Boyle and Joxer would end the play humbled but essentially unchanged. In fact, the play's first two acts are an almost perfect imitation of Boucicault, whose plays were:

> Drama as a mixed or impure form, a combination of comedy and melodrama, farce and sentiment, song and burlesque, sensational and gothic elements … His hero is a wise fool, the master of the mischievous revels who is the inevitable occasion of hilarity in others as well as natural humour in himself. To be sure he is a blithering rogue, a cheerful liar with a powerful thirst.'[15]

O'Casey's characters were therefore so stereotypical and predictable to a Dublin audience that the tragedy of the play's ending came as a complete surprise to them,[16] thereby making its impact very powerful. O'Casey emphasizes to his audience that they have been fooled into accepting tragedy as melodrama by having Joxer refer drunkenly to *The Colleen Bawn* in the play's final shocking moments.

14 This part of the play is the subject of further analysis in: David Krause (ed.), *O'Casey annual number 4* (London: Macmillan, 1984). **15** David Krause, *The Dolmen Boucicault* (Oxford: Oxford UP, 1964), pp 9–13. **16** As documented in Robert Hogan and Richard Burnham, *The years of O'Casey* (Cranbury: Associated University Presses, 1992), pp 190–200.

By drawing attention in this way to his manipulation of his audiences' familiarity with melodrama, O'Casey is showing them that the play should be understood as an attempt to blend the literature of the Revival with the popular forms
of culture with which he himself was so familiar. This synthesis of high and low
art was, however, an imperfect one, since both elements are quite clearly distin-
guishable from each other in *Juno* – and indeed the play succeeds on that basis.
The impact of the tragedy of the final act is entirely dependent on the audiences' acceptance of the action that preceded it as melodrama. Furthermore, as
Tony Roche points out, although *Juno and the Paycock* saved the Abbey from
financial ruin, its politics meant that it had little impact on its artistic policy:

> The potent theatrical fusion of music-hall and politics in O'Casey's plays
> of the 1920s did not succeed in taking over from or displacing the kitchen
> comedies which had become the Abbey's stock-in-trade. The mixture of
> high and low art which the socialist playwrights O'Casey and Behan
> favour along with Beckett has always offended equally the caretakers of
> high culture, the bourgeois middle-class audience, and the cultural nation-
> alists, whose view of an Irish theatre always insists that it come embla-
> zoned with certain insignia.[17]

Nevertheless, it seems fair to state that O'Casey intentionally wrote in a way
that was different to what he perceived to be the literature of the Revival. Can
it therefore be said that his work represents any form of criticism of the Revival?

It would appear from O'Casey's later work that we might regard these features of his early works as part of an attempt to critically evaluate the Revival.
In order to illustrate this, I want to consider O'Casey's 1940 play *Purple Dust*,
which presents one of his most important critiques of the Revival.

Written in 1937–8, *Purple Dust* presents Stoke and Poges, two Englishmen
who, accompanied by their Irish mistresses Souhan and Avril, have arrived in a
remote part of rural Ireland to renovate a Tudor mansion – and to avoid the
Second World War. Described by O'Casey as a wayward comedy, the play is best
understood as a mock pastoral and as a 'full-length cartoon in which caricatured
Englishmen are gulled by their witty Irish rivals'.[18]

One of the most interesting aspects of the play is its use of a number of literary sources to illustrate O'Casey's themes and to develop his characters. The
play closely resembles Shaw's *John Bull's Other Island*, and it borrows from the
work of Somerville and Ross, Jonathan Swift, George Moore and Joyce – and
from Wordsworth, Andrew Marvell, Shakespeare, Thomas Gray and many other
writers. The purpose of literary quotation and allusion in the play is principal-

17 Anthony Roche, *Contemporary Irish drama: from Beckett to McGuinness* (Dublin: Gill and
Macmillan, 1994), p. 108.   18 John O'Riordan, *A guide to O'Casey's plays* (London: Macmillan,
1984), p. 205.

ly to reveal O'Casey ideological concerns. An interesting example of this occurs in the exchange between Souhan and O'Killigain, a workman recently returned from fighting in Spain, and (arguably) the play's hero. Souhan asks O'Killigain his familiar name, 'the name your girl would call you by'. When told that his name is Jack, she responds rapturously: '[Lingering over it] Jack. What a dear name, Jack! What a dear name – [she suddenly stands on tiptoes and kisses him] Jack!'[19] This is a reversal of the famous exchange between Gwendolen and Jack in Wilde's *The Importance of Being Ernest*, in which Gwendolen explains that her 'ideal has always been to love someone of the name of Ernest': 'There is something in the name that inspires absolute confidence. The moment Algernon told me that he had a friend called Ernest, I knew I was destined to love you.' When asked if she wouldn't prefer a man named 'Jack', Gwendolen replies with conviction: 'No, there is very little music in the name Jack, if any at all, indeed. It does not thrill. It produces absolutely no vibrations. I have known several Jacks, and they all without exception, were more than usually plain.'[20] O'Casey reverses Gwendolen's desire for a man named 'Ernest' by having his own character respond in a similar way to the name 'Jack'. There is a suggestion here that characters such as Stoke and Poges – and Gwendolen and Ernest – must give way to people like Jack O'Killigain, a workman who is prepared to fight for his (and O'Casey's) beliefs.

Another example of this is his choice of the names Poges and Stoke for his two English characters. Stoke Poges is of course the setting for Gray's 'Elegy Written in a Country Churchyard'. By relating his English characters to that poem's lament for the passing of a way of life, O'Casey makes explicit his thesis that the British empire – as represented by the two characters – is in decline[21] or that 'in a generation or so the English Empire will be half-remembered only as a half-forgotten nursery rhyme'.[22]

Literary quotation is also used as a means of revealing character. The workmen in the play draw their cultural references from popular works, such as Moore's ballads, Greek and Irish mythology, and the Bible; whereas the English characters attempt to reinforce their sense of superiority over the Irish by using their knowledge of what they consider to be high culture. Stoke declares himself worthy of being listened to because he has 'read every word written by Hume, Spinoza, Aristotle, Locke, Bacon, Plato, Socrates, and Kant, among others'.[23] Despite this declaration, O'Casey makes clear throughout the play that Stoke is incapable of any form of original or rational thought – and indeed, we must be skeptical about anyone who claims to have read 'every word written'

19 Sean O'Casey, *Purple Dust* in *Plays 2* (London, Faber and Faber, 1998), p. 344. **20** Oscar Wilde, *Complete works* (Glasgow, Harper Collins 1994), p. 366. **21** Indeed, the characters' futile attempts at the beginning of the play's second act to light a fire could be seen as a direct allusion to Gray's 'For them no more the blazing hearth shall burn'. **22** *Purple Dust*, p. 343. **23** Ibid., p. 298.

by Socrates, since, as O'Casey must have been aware, that philosopher never wrote anything.

In similar fashion, Poges deploys a number of half-remembered quotations from romantic poets. He incorrectly quotes Wordsworth to O'Killigain: 'Life is too much with us, O'Killigain; late and soon, getting and spending, we lay waste our powers. But you've never read good old Wordsworth, I suppose?'[24] This mis-quotation[25] is intended to expose the pomposity of Poges, while also showing the superiority of O'Killigain, who refrains from correcting him, and from point-ing out that the next line of the poem – 'Little we see in Nature that is ours' – applies very clearly to Poges. Poges repeatedly patronizes the Irish characters by quoting from literature – yet he does not once do so correctly. Hence, Wordsworth's 'Peter Bell' and Poe's 'To Helen' are both misquoted before being attributed to Shakespeare, and Browning's 'Home-Thoughts, from Abroad' takes place not in April, but in winter. For the purposes of the present discussion, the most important literary references in *Purple Dust* are to works of the revival, specifically to those of Synge and Yeats.

O'Dempsey, the second workman, seems to be modeled on Synge's tramp from *The Shadow of the Glen*. Attempting to convince Souhan to leave Poges, O'Dempsey tells her that: 'Your shinin' eyes can always say you are; an' soon you'll tire o' nestin' in a dusty nook with the hills outside for walkin'. Souhan skeptically asks, 'I will, will I?' to which O'Dempsey replies:

> Ay will you, an' dance away from a smoky bragger who thinks th' world spins round on the rim of a coin; you'll hurry away from him, I'm sayin', an' it's a glad heart'll lighten the journey to a one'll find a place for your little hand in the white clouds, an' a place for your saucy head in th' blue sky.[26]

This is very similar to the speech made by the tramp to Nora at the end of Synge's play, in which he asks her to leave Dan and come away with him:

> Come along with me now, lady of the house, and it's not my blather you'll be hearing only, but you'll be haring the herons crying out over the black lakes … And it's not from the like of them you'll be hearing a tale of get-ting old like Peggy Cavanagh, and losing the hair off you, and the light of your eyes, but it's fine songs you'll be hearing when the sun goes up, and there'll be no fellow wheezing the like of a sick sheep close to your ear.[27]

24 Ibid., p. 293.   **25** It could be argued that Friel was referring to this part of *Purple Dust* when in *Translations* he presents an exchange between Yolland and Hugh in which Hugh asks regarding Wordsworth: 'Did he speak to you of me?' before saying patronisingly that, 'We're not familiar with your literature, Lieutenant'. Brian Friel, *Translations* in *Selected plays* (London: Faber and Faber, 1984), p. 417.   **26** *Purple Dust*, p. 362.   **27** JM Synge, *The Playboy of the Western*

Interestingly, whereas Synge presents his tramp in a positive fashion, O'Casey seems very uncomfortable with his character. O'Dempsey's romanticism is consistently balanced out by the pragmatism of O'Killigain, so that, as Christopher Murray puts it, we 'are given, as it were, two tramps for the price of one.'[28] O'Casey explains that: 'It is true that while O'Killigain is a realist, O'Dempsey is a romanticist, but as the play shows, O'Killigain can understand, and further, the romanticism of his friend, and O'Dempsey can understand, and aid, the realism of O'Killigain.'[29] O'Casey is by no means negative about O'Dempsey, but he makes it clear that his character cannot exist anywhere other than on the stage, by stating throughout the play that the Irish are generally neither eloquent nor poetic. When Avril asks if there is 'an Irishman goin' who hasn't a dint o' wondher in his talkin'?'[30] O'Killigain rather curtly replies that if such people exist, he has not met many of them. Similarly, the first workman praises a chicken because it does not 'set about the business o' layin' [an egg] like a member o' Doyle Eireann makin' his maiden speech'.[31] Perhaps the best example of O'Casey's opinion of Irish eloquence is a speech made by Poges's Irish servant Barney, who warns his companion Cloyne that: 'We'll be worse than we were before we're as bad as we are now, an' in a week's time we'll be lookin' back with a sigh to a time, bad as it could be then, that was betther than the worst that was on top of us now.'[32] This statement certainly cannot be regarded as an example of eloquence. In fact, romanticized Irish eloquence is shown to be a form of rhetoric that may be used by anyone. Poges attempts to ingratiate himself to O'Dempsey by imitating his manner of speaking: 'Looka that, now. Arra, whisht, an' amn't I told it's strange stories you do be tellin' of the noble things done by your fathers in their days, and in the old time before them.'[33] Stage-Irish speech is shown by Poges to be a mode of communication between two people who are attempting to exploit each other. The romanticized eloquence of Synge's tramp is thereby shown to be a fabrication, a theatrical device that may be exploited by people like Poges. This implies that, if O'Dempsey is a rendition of Synge's tramp, he also owes something to Shaw's Matthew Haffigan.[34]

This critique is also developed in O'Casey's references to Yeats. Poges's attempts to restore a ruin are of course very similar to those made by the Yeats of *The*

World and other plays (Oxford: Oxford UP, 1995), p. 25. **28** Christopher Murray, *Twentieth century Irish drama: mirror up to nation* (Manchester: Manchester UP, 1997), p. 108. **29** Sean O'Casey, 'Purple dust in their eyes' in *Under a colored cap* (London: Macmillan, 1963), p. 265. **30** *Purple Dust*, pp 286–7. **31** Ibid., p. 303. **32** Ibid. p. 322. **33** Ibid., p. 337. **34** Cf. G.B. Shaw, *John Bull's Other Island*. (London: Penguin, 1984), p. 78. 'Don't you know that all this top-o-the-morning and broth-of-a-boy and more power to your elbow stuff is got up in England to fool you? No Irishman ever talks like that in Ireland, or ever did, or ever will. But when a thoroughly worthless Irishman comes to England and finds the place full of romantic duffers like you, who will let him loaf and drink and sponge and brag as long as he flatters your sense of moral superiority by playing the fool and degrading himself and his country, he soon learns the antics that take you in.'

Winding Stair and *The Tower* to restore Thoor Ballylee. This connection between Poges and Yeats is made clear in many ways. As Richard Ellman tells us, Yeats 'is said to have declared to George Russell that if he had his rights he would be Duke of Ormonde'[35] and O'Casey would have been aware of this from his reading of Yeats's poem 'Demon and Beast'.[36] It is therefore surely no coincidence that Yeats's belief is shared by O'Casey's character Souhan, whose supposed relationship to the Ormondes is used by Stoke and Poges to justify their aristocratic pretensions. There are many other similarities between Poges and Yeats. Directed to 'lean on a stick as if it were a sword' Poges sorrowfully asks:

'Where are the kings and queens and warriors now? Gone with all their glory! The present day and present men? Paltry, mean, tight, and tedious. [disgustedly] Bah!'[37] This is a wonderful send-up of Yeats, resembling very closely 'The Song of the Happy Shepherd' in particular:

> Where are now the warring kings,
> Word be-mockers? – by the Rood.
> Where are now the warring kings?
> An idle word is all their glory.[38]

Similarly, when Poges criticizes the impact of priests on Ireland, he declares that:

> If the misguided people would only go back to the veneration of the old Celtic gods, what a stir we'd have here! To the delightful, if legendary, loveliness of – er – er – er – what's his name, what's her name, what's their name? ... The chief god of the ancient Celts?

> SOUHAN: Was it Gog or Magog, dear?

> POGES [with fierce scorn]: Can't you remember that Gog and Magog were two Philistinian giants killed by David or Jonathan or Joshua or Joan or Samson or someone? It's the old Celtic god I have in mind, the one – what was his name?

> SOUHAN: Gulliver?

> POGES: Oh no, not Gulliver

> SOUHAN: Well, I don't know who the hell it was

> POGES [slapping his thigh exultingly]: Brobdingnag! That was the fellow.[39]

---

35 Richard Ellman, *Yeats: the man and the masks* (London: Penguin, 1979), p. 180. **36** 'The glittering eyes in an death's head/ Of old Luke Wadding's portrait said/ Welcome, and the Ormondes all/ Nodded upon the Wall'. W.B. Yeats, 'Demon and beast' in *Michael Robartes and the dancer*, in Daniel Albright (ed.), *The poems* (London: Everyman, 1992), p. 234. **37** *Purple Dust*, p. 332. **38** W.B. Yeats, 'The song of the happy shepherd', *Crossways* in *The poems*, p. 34. **39** *Purple Dust*, p. 311.

Again, this passage shows that Poges uses his half-remembered readings – in this case of Swift, of whom Yeats wrote so much in *The Winding Stair* – to reinforce his sense of superiority over his Irish companions.

The manner in which the Irish characters are irritated by this talk of ancient Celtic Gods is very similar to a passage O'Casey later wrote about Yeats in *Inishfallen, Fare Thee Well.* When, in the early 1920s, O'Casey visits Yeats to discuss his work, the detective guarding Yeats's house warns O'Casey that Yeats's company can be tedious:

> I don't envy yeh, Sean, for I wouldn't like to be around him long. His oul' mind's full of th' notion of oul' kings and queens the half of us never heard of; an' when he's talkin', a fella has to look wise, pretendin' he's well acquainted with them dead an' gone ghosts.'[40]

Both Poges and Yeats use Irish legend to portray themselves as aristocrats but in doing so, only alienate themselves from the Irish people around them, who are generally more interested in the present than in a fabricated past. Furthermore, the use of high culture by Poges to aid him in his attempt to present himself as being noble does not make him superior to the Irish characters but makes him incapable of adapting to change. O'Casey explains that, unlike Poges and Stoke: 'The Irish peasants of the play, less comic, less picturesque, less lovable maybe … survive the winds and the rising flood because they are more adaptable, and so of the two contraries, the fitter to survive: life – not O'Casey – chooses these and destroys the others.'[41]

Purple Dust expresses very clearly O'Casey's discomfort with his perception that the Revival tended to ignore the lived reality of Irish people, while valuing antiquity for its own sake. This is futile, since, as the play makes clear:

> The winds of change come, and no one feels them till they become strong enough to sweep things away, carrying men and women … bearing off their old customs, manners and morals with them … There are those who clutch at things departing, and try to hold them back. So do Stoke and Poges, digging up old bones, and trying to glue them together again. They try to shelter from the winds of change but Time wears away the roof, and Time's river eventually sweeps the purple dust away.[42]

O'Casey is therefore not attacking Synge but is suggesting that a romanticism rooted in legend must not be used as a distraction from the present. The militaristic past of Irish history and legend constantly referred to in *Purple Dust* need not be forgotten, but O'Casey points out that this past does not, for example, excuse Irish neutrality and isolation in the face of approaching war.

40 *Inishfallen, Fare Thee Well*, p. 160.   **41** *Under a colored cap*, p. 265.   **42** Ibid., p. 262.

The play also attempts to blend the literature of the Revival with popular culture. Accordingly, O'Casey mixes the pseudo-Yeatsian pomposity of Poges with high farce. As David Krause states: 'He used the stage as if it were a combination music hall and circus ring, whirling through a profusion of burlesque turns and clowning acts, and bringing the whole performance to a spectacular conclusion with a supernatural extravaganza.'[43] While we listen to poor imitations of Yeats, we are also watching a circus. It is possible therefore for the audience of *Purple Dust* to admire O'Casey's artistry in his use of literary quotation, while also being entertained by the slapstick farce taking place on stage. As Jack Lindsay puts it, O'Casey 'achieves the very things Yeats long wanted to do—to vivify the mythic images [of the Revival] by linking them effectively with modern life and its issues'.[44] *Purple Dust*, therefore, represents the synthesis of high and low art forms that O'Casey first attempted with *Juno and the Paycock*, a synthesis achieved by his putting under close scrutiny those aspects of the revival he found most troubling.

Many of O'Casey's criticisms of the Revival were explicit in his later work, but they also appear in his earliest plays. His love of Shakespeare as a writer of and for the people is an important theme of *Red Roses for Me* (1942), but it also appears in *The Shadow of a Gunman* (1923). His love of the language of the bible and of the Irish tradition of protestant oratory is evident in his autobiographical *Rose and Crown* (1952) – yet it may also be found in *The Plough and the Stars* (1926) and *The Silver Tassie* (1928). Similarly, many of the criticisms of the Revival evident in *Purple Dust* are discernible in more subtle form in O'Casey's earlier work. His primary difficulty with the Revival seems to have been that it ignored a great deal of Irish culture, but he also appeared troubled by the fact that its celebration of legend could be used as a means of ignoring the needs and duties of people in the present. *Juno and the Paycock* and O'Casey's other Abbey plays ought therefore to be seen as early attempts to come to terms with issues that O'Casey would not fully resolve until *Purple Dust*.

This shows that there is a great deal more in common between O'Casey's early and later work than is often recognized, and also that the factors that led to the collapse of O'Casey's relationship with the Abbey were discernible even in *The Shadow of a Gunman*. I would conclude therefore that we ought to consider in more detail the extent to which O'Casey's later works may help us to understand the canonical work of the Revival and the society in which the Revival took place. I would also suggest that the status of plays like *Juno and the Paycock* as canonical works of the Revival ought to be re-considered, and that instead we should consider the work of O'Casey as being in its entirety one of the earliest examples of a post-Revival literature.

43 David Krause, *Sean O'Casey: the man and his work* (London: Macgibbon and Kee, 1960), p. 187.   **44** Jack Lindsay, 'Sean O'Casey as a socialist artist', in: Ronald Ayling (ed.), *Sean O'Casey: modern judgements* (London: Macmillan, 1969), p. 201.

Index